The Israeli–Palestinian Conflict

The conflict between Israelis and Palestinians is one of the most enduring and complex in the modern world. But, why did the conflict break out? Who is demanding what, and why is peace so difficult to achieve?

The Israeli–Palestinian Conflict tackles the subject and analyses the conflict from its historical roots in the late nineteenth century to the present attempts at conflict resolution in the twenty-first century.

Framing the debate and analysis around issues such as Zionism, Palestinian nationalism, international peace efforts, the refugees, state-building, democracy and religious opposition, and highlighted by first-hand quotes and sources of the conflict from its major participants, Beverley Milton-Edwards explores the deep impact of the conflict on regional politics in the Middle East and why the enmity between Palestinians and Israelis has become a number one global issue drawing in the world's most important global actors.

An essential insight into the complexities of one of the world's most enduring conflicts, this textbook is designed to make a complex subject accessible to all. Key features include:

- Chronology of events
- Annotated further reading at the end of each chapter

The Israeli–Palestinian Conflict is an ideal and authoritative introduction to aspects of politics in Israel and among the Palestinians – a vitally important issue for those studying the politics of the Middle East.

Beverley Milton-Edwards is Professor in the School of Politics, International Studies and Philosophy at Queens University Belfast. She is the author of *Islamic Fundamentalism Since 1945* (Routledge 2004) and *Contemporary Politics in the Middle East* (2006).

The Israeli–Palestinian Conflict

A people's war

Beverley Milton-Edwards

Routledge
Taylor & Francis Group

LONDON AND NEW YORK

First published 2009
by Routledge
2 Park Square, Milton Park, Abingdon, Oxon OX14 4RN

Simultaneously published in the USA and Canada
by Routledge
270 Madison Ave, New York, NY 10016

Routledge is an imprint of the Taylor & Francis Group, an informa business

© 2009 Beverley Milton-Edwards

Typeset in Baskerville by
Book Now Ltd, London
Printed and bound in Great Britain by
MPG Books Ltd, Bodmin

British Library Cataloguing in Publication Data
A catalogue record for this book is available from the British Library

Library of Congress Cataloging in Publication Data
Milton-Edwards, Beverley.
The Israeli-Palestinian conflict: a people's war / Beverley Milton-Edwards.
  p. cm.
Includes bibliographical references and index.
1. Arab–Israeli conflict. I. Title.
DS119.7.M497 2008
956.04—dc22   2008001509

ISBN10: 0–415–41044–4 (hbk)
ISBN10: 0–415–41043–6 (pbk)
ISBN10: 0–203–89426–X (ebk)

ISBN13: 978–0–415–41044–1 (hbk)
ISBN13: 978–0–415–41043–4 (pbk)
ISBN13: 978–0–203–89426–2 (ebk)

To Cara daughter of Bethlehem and light of our lives

Contents

List of Illustrations   x
Acknowledgements   xi

Introduction   1

1   Roots of conflict   9
Ottoman idyll? 10
Zionism 13
The Palestinian nationalist 'awakening' 17
The First World War and its consequences 21
Balfour bombshell 23
Parallel points 27
Further reading 29

2   Between the wars   32
The gloves are off: determining the future of Palestine 33
The mandate 35
Ascendance 39
Prelude to revolt 40
Sheikh, rattle and revolt 41
The Palestinian revolt 43
Resistance 45
The Peel Commission: partition of Palestine 47
The revolt and the Zionists 48
End of an era 49
World war and rethinking the mandate 51
Further reading 52

3   Palestine after the Holocaust   54
War clouds 55
After the dust has settled 57

The UN Partition Plan of 1947 59
The future decided 63
British blight? 66
What came next 68
Whose history? The events of 1947–48 70
Legacy 72
Further reading 73

4   Israel reborn   **76**
Divine model or democracy by expediency 78
Political parties and the Israeli–Palestinian conflict 82
Labour Zionism 83
Revisionist Zionism 85
The religious Zionists 87
Between a rock and a hard place: the Israeli Arabs 90
Israel's democratic future 94
Further reading 96

5   The dispossessed   **98**
Becoming refugees: origins of an issue 99
We who are refugees 101
Refugees: the key to peace? 108
Compensation 111
Talking about refugees 113
Further reading 117

6   The occupation generation   **119**
The Six-Day War 119
Spoils of war 121
A framework for control 123
Facts on the ground: Israel's settlements 125
Resistance under occupation 131
Liberating Palestine through an organization 132
Occupation and employment 136
The pressure cooker 137
Further reading 139

7   The war of the stones and guns   **141**
Insurrection 143
Palestinian political goals 145
An Arab 'shaking off'? 147
Israel responds 148
The strategy for change 150

Consolidation and political progress 152
Actions speak louder than words: getting to the second Intifada 153
The al-Aqsa armed Intifada 154
Operation Defensive Shield: unequivocal victory? 157
Further reading 160

8 A global concern   **161**

Date with destiny: America and the conflict 165
A regional concern 172
The international arena 176
A European approach 178
A concert of actors? 179
Further reading 180

9 Moving from zero   **182**

The broken path to peace: resolving or managing the conflict 187
Making it to Madrid 188
Oslo and all that 190
Opposition to Oslo 193
Camp David and the second Intifada 195
The second Intifada and death of peace 197
Disengaging for peace? 200
The rocky road to peace 202
Annapolis or bust 202
Further reading 204

Chronology   206
Bibliography   210
Index   223

Illustrations

Figure

6.1 Image of subversion: Handala, the small Palestinian boy penned
by cartoonist Naji al-Ali   138

Tables

8.1 Important United Nations resolutions   177
9.1 Israeli–Palestinian peace process 1993–2006   198

Acknowledgements

I would like to thank Joe Whiting at Routledge for persuading me to tackle this most difficult and complex of current day political conflicts. I hope the book will offer some alternative perspectives to the Israeli–Palestinian conflict and the ways in which it can be understood. I'd like to extend my especial gratitude to Ray Dolphin and Stephen Farrell, both of whom helped me with the thinking and writing of the book.

During my time as a visiting scholar at the Kenyon Institute in Jerusalem I was fortunate enough to access some rare books and other sources that have allowed me to add real colour and depth to this project. I am thus deeply indebted to all the staff there, including Yuri Stoyanov, Tim Moore and chief librarian, Hussein Gheith, for their assistance and help. The lively lectures and debates to which many Israelis and Palestinians attended also allowed me the opportunity to explore many ideas associated with the conflict and responses to them.

To the many Israelis and Palestinians who have helped with this book I would like to offer my sincere thanks for their insights over the years. I also truly benefited from the help of Rema Hammami, Bassima, Mustafa, Sanabel, Ghassan and Mohammed Qawasmi, Ra'ad Malki, Khalil and Saha Malouf, Hassan Bazarlit, Khalid Ifrangi, Nancy, Edin and Liel Zeitlin, Colin Smith, Michael Pearson, Nabil Feidy, Barbara Surk, Mouin Rabbani, Alex Pollock, Nuha Awadallah Muslih, Fares Akram, Abu Bilal, Ashraf al-Masri, Abu Mahmoud, Ilan and Galia Katsir, Dina Masri and Nadim Shehadi for some unique insights into the daily dynamics of conflict and coexistence between Palestinians and Israelis.

My final thanks, as ever, to Graham, Cara and Joshua for their continuing support.

Beverley Milton-Edwards
December 2007

Introduction

What the colonial in common with Prospero lacks, is awareness of the world of Others, a world in which Others have to be.

(Frantz Fanon, 1969: 107)

Turn right moments after you pass the Israeli and then Palestinian military check-points that control the West Bank town of Jericho and you enter the tightly guarded compound of Palestine's only casino and hotel complex with its darkened windows and glitzy OASIS signage glinting amidst the desert dust.

Deathly quiet, the Oasis building echoes to the gambling ghosts of the past who came in their thousands from Israel to try their luck at the gaming tables and the slot machines under a star-studded ceiling. The $50 million Oasis Casino was but one part of a venture to turn 'peace into tourism' benefiting both Israelis and Palestinians alike. On the opposite side of the road the Palestinian refugee camp of Aqabat Jaber, however, remains full of life and its residents remain in eternal hope of a peace settlement that means a return to their homes. Today the Oasis Casino is closed, the gamblers have gone home and the peace deal that heralded it in 1993 feels like a hopeless mirage.

In its heyday the Oasis Casino was a surreal epitome of a peace process that had been inaugurated by Israeli Prime Minister Yitzhak Rabin and the Chairman of the Palestine Liberation Organization, Yasser Arafat, when they signed the Oslo Accords on the lawn of the White House in September 1993.

This iconoclastic institution represented the trashy transient reality of a peace process that failed to resolve the conflict between Israelis and Palestinians.

A thousand news photographs rendered into one archetype the handshake between Rabin and Arafat that September day in 1993. 'A Peace of the Braves' was declared as first Rabin and then Arafat spoke of 'war, blood, tears, and battles' and how they would transform them into 'peace, co-existence, and dignity'. But the archetype belied the true face of a deal that so many more declared stillborn. Within less than a decade the peace process would be in tatters, Rabin would be dead and Yasser Arafat in his last throes holed up in his presidential compound in the West Bank city of Ramallah. Violence and bitter enmity would stalk Israeli and Palestinian towns and a sense of empathy would be lost.

While it is true that the Oslo Accords represented a turning point in the

Israeli–Palestinian conflict, it was not the peace deal that so many deluded themselves into believing it was. True some condemned the deal as a 'Palestinian
Versailles' or a heresy against the Jewish covenant with God in the Holy Land.
Others truly believed that peace was possible and that the international environment typified by the New World Order would make the task of healing between
the Israelis and Palestinians viable. If international statesmen like President
Clinton could bring peace to Northern Ireland and the Israelis and Palestinians
then maybe the USA deserved its global pre-eminence after all.

Explaining why and how it went wrong is one of the tasks that will be undertaken in this book.

The conflict between Israelis and Palestinians is one of the most enduring and
intractable to beset the contemporary world order. Today the 'battle' between the
citizens of the state of Israel and the stateless Palestinian people is part of a charred
and twisted landscape of increasingly envenomed enmity. The relationship
between Israelis and Palestinians is deeply complex and thus lacks a simple explanation or solution. This absence of a single or simple explanation has made the
conflict hard for other people to understand. Too many questions and not enough
answers commonly dog anyone that starts to consider the conflict. This book is an
attempt to identify and analyse the most important features of the conflict. The
book takes both the historical and contemporary dimension into consideration
when outlining the ways in which relations between Jews and Arabs have been
altered and affected by the context of Palestine.

The conflict over national ideals, colonialism, religion, class, economy, land,
self-determination and sovereignty is also a motif for the wider debates and issues
that have characterized the international system. The historical ebbs and flows of
the Israeli–Palestinian conflict thus also reflect the dynamics of larger political
themes that have animated the study of the international political system
throughout the twentieth and early twenty-first century. Issues such as reconciling
the demands of nationalism not merely as a concept but as a set of demands for
statehood and territoriality in the world order are epitomized by the Israeli–
Palestinian conflict as two nations establish themselves and a sense of distinct identity. The dynamic of defining statehood and nation is thus reflected as a case study
when examining, as we do in this book, the development of identity as a means to
acquire power and independence. In many ways the Israeli–Palestinian conflict
has also been shaped by the ways in which developments in the international
arena, such as the superpower rivalry between the USA and the former USSR,
the declining power of European colonial powers such as Britain, the rise of a
hegemonic global power such as the USA, have enveloped the Middle East. In the
twenty-first century it is not uncommon for major external powers to cite the resolution of the Israeli–Palestinian conflict as a major, if not the major, foreign policy
objective of their state and yet the conflict appears to be getting harder, not easier,
to resolve.

The resolution of the conflict is perceived as the key to securing better prosperity, security and stability in the wider Middle East region and thus within the
international system and international economy. As the former Palestinian

National Security Advisor, Jibril Rajoub, contends, 'building peace is to want peace and to want to pay the price of peace . . . in this way we will find security, peace and prosperity for Israel and the Palestinians' (Rajoub, 2007). This in part explains why this conflict matters so much to the rest of the globe. In some respects the course of the Israeli–Palestinian conflict has altered and affected the politics of neighbouring states such as Syria, Egypt, Jordan and Lebanon, as well as regional issues such as Arab unity, Muslim identity and the growing notion that the Middle East has come to represent a cradle of modern violence and terrorism. Moreover, throughout the history of the conflict a variety of regional and international actors including independent sovereign states such the USA or Britain, regional organizations such as the European Union and the Arab League, as well as international actors such as the United Nations or the World Bank have all been drawn into this conflict.

But it is the people – Israeli and Palestinian – constituted as distinct nations and with competing aspirations for statehood over the same territory that truly explain why this conflict came about. This is why the conflict may be considered to be a people's war and a war of people's increasingly irreconcilable perspectives and ambitions. In this conflict there have been episodes of war when the army of Israel has faced the armies of Syria, Egypt and Jordan (and others) on the battlefield. But the historical and contemporary norm has seen the mobilization of two competing nations: Israeli versus Palestinian in a conflict with each other that is military, economic, political, cultural, and religious in expression at one time or another. As one Western journalist acerbically noted, 'this is not about them [Israelis and Palestinians] not being on the same page but they are not even sharing the same book when they talk about the conflict and the way they see it'.

Some nine themes will be dealt with in the analysis that follows in this book. Each chapter will explore one theme in order that some aspects of the subject can be broken down and made more comprehensible. The first theme as outlined in Chapter 1 is that this conflict has an important historical background. The book then will begin with an examination of late nineteenth-century Palestine – a Muslim Ottoman province and largely rural society. Palestine, as a province of the Ottoman Empire, with its centre of power in Constantinople (Istanbul), caught the attention of Western Europeans. The European interest in the land was motivated by a number of factors: spiritual, cultural, colonial, economic and political/strategic. Some factors – such as the spiritual attachment and renaissance in romantic Christian associations with Zion and the Jewish people – led to a growing sympathy for the Zionist cause of Jewish nationalism.

It is from these sorts of historic roots that the British supported the growth of Jewish settlement and the Zionist movement in establishing a homeland there. In turn, when Britain ended up in control of the country it led them to view with sympathy Zionist aspirations to settle the territory under their control. Such developments inevitably encouraged the development of parallel points of identity issues and politics between Jews and Arabs and their nascent nationalist ideologies – including Zionism and Palestinian nationalism. But this led to growing tensions between the Jews and Arabs associated with Jewish land settlement and growing

Palestinian frustration and revolt at British intervention and interference in the incipient conflict.

This means that the roots of contestable conflict are outlined. The conflict resulted from the growing consciousness of both Jews and Palestinian Arabs of a new political identity forged in the ideologies of nationalism and self-determination. The context in which this was occurring was also coloured by the incipient national interest of Britain (in competition with France) to enhance its role in the Middle East (and by extension India). Western rivalry in the region during the First World War and its effects on Palestine were thus deeply significant. In 1917, for example, the British had issued a declaration to the leadership of the Jewish national movement: the Zionists, outlining their support for the establishment of a Jewish homeland in Palestine. But they had already agreed, in secret promises to both the French and the Arabs, a different future for Palestine. The advent of British interference and rule changed the course of history with respect to the desire for statehood and independence as expressed in the nationalist ideologies of both the Jews and the Palestinian Arabs at the time.

In 1918 at the end of the First World War Britain and France persuaded the new League of Nations, in which they were the dominant powers, to give them authority over the Ottoman territories that had fallen into their hands during the war. The whims of the British mandatory power – rather than the principle of the mandate system – would determine the future of Palestine and in Chapter 2 I will critically examine its impact. These new British and French regimes were known as mandates and protectorates. Britain obtained the Mandate for Palestine in 1920–23, plus the newly established states of Transjordan and Iraq. Britain then tried to persuade the Arabs to embrace the idea of a Jewish homeland in Palestine as underscored in the written terms of the mandate for British rule in Palestine when it was formally issued in 1923. The incompatible promises made as wartime expediency to the Arabs and the Zionists began to cause problems for the British in terms of fulfilling their mandate in Palestine.

The rise of Nazism in Hitler's Germany, new waves of Jewish immigration, plus restive nationalism leading to the outbreak of the 1936–39 Uprising and general strike by Palestinians will also be analysed in Chapter 2. British responses – including the somewhat pointless commissioning of one government committee of investigation after another, repression, and attempt to play the old colonial card of divide and rule – demonstrated the inability of the British authorities to do justice to the Palestinian Arabs or respond sensitively to the growing force of Zionism made manifest in Jewish immigration and settlement activity. Re-thinking the mandate and the rising conflict in Palestine resulted in a proposal for the partition of territory.

In Chapter 3 the process of British withdrawal from Palestine as it sought an exit strategy from the unfolding conflict will be examined within the framework of the wider international environment after the Second World War and the perpetration of the Holocaust and decimation of the Jewish population of Europe. The focus, therefore, will be on issues of immigration, political development of opposing elements, the incipient military campaign waged by the Zionists against the British and the concurrent developments within the Zionist movement with respect to the aspiration for Jewish statehood. The UN Partition Plan will be examined along with the Zionist acceptance and Arab rejection debate. The prelude to war – including the controversial Zionist violence and the massacres of 1947–48 – will be debated within the framework of contemporary analysis of ethnic cleansing, population transfer and other dimensions of ethnic and national politics. The issue of international intervention also needs to be explained in terms of the Second World War, the Holocaust and Western guilt and reparation issues to the Jewish people. The British decision to withdraw from Palestine and relinquish its mandate will be explored in terms of both domestic and foreign factors.

The events of 1947–48 and their consequences in terms of the following decade for the new state of Israel and its evolving polity will be explored in Chapter 4. The chapter will then analyse the institutions of the Jewish state, state- and nation-building and the growing issue of enmity with Israel's Arab neighbours. This evaluation of the new state will delineate the nature of Israeli society including its secular and religious dimensions as well as the emergence of the Israeli political party system. This evolving political system also reflected Israeli concerns and responses as a state to the Palestinian people, their demands and the threats that Israel perceived them as posing. This threat has led the Israeli state to develop as a highly militarized democratic system on near-permanent war footing and often compelled to concern itself with strategic issues as they relate to the military balance in the wider Middle East region, demographic warfare through encouraging Jewish immigration, and territorial expansion.

According to the United Nations, 'by far the most protracted and largest of all refugee problems in the world today is that of the Palestine refugees' (UNHCR, 2006). Estimating refugee numbers is a highly 'political debate' but it is estimated that today there are over 7 million Palestinian refugees and their descendents. Moreover, the entire nation of the Palestinian people has been stateless since 1948. Dispossession and statelessness have thus increasingly defined the Palestinian experience. Chapter 5 examines the establishment of the refugee phenomenon in 1948 and 1967 as well as responses to it by a variety of actors. The chapter will outline the effective dismemberment of Palestine between Israel, Jordan and Egypt after the first Arab–Israeli war of 1948. Post-1948 it will look at the impact in terms of the regional nature of the conflict, and the political disempowerment of the Palestinians as a result of their refugee status. The chapter will also examine the emergence of the Palestine Liberation Organization (PLO), founded in 1964 with Egyptian help, including its structure in relation to refugees in the Arab states of Jordan, Lebanon and Syria, armed activities, and the burgeoning culture of nationhood without a state. The chapter will focus on themes such as human rights, citizenship and the 'right of return' and examine the response of the international community.

It was not only the events of the June 1967 Six-Day War that changed the dynamic of the Israeli–Palestinian conflict but the consequent process of Israeli occupation, Israeli settlement, Arab crisis, Palestinian dispossession again and the emergence of a Palestinian resistance force and the state-like entity of the PLO.

Hence Chapter 6 addresses themes such as occupation, settlement policies, terrorism, and the continuing internationalization of the conflict – either through peace settlement (between Israel and Egypt in 1978) or Israeli military adventure (in Lebanon in 1978 and again in 1982) and the subsequent expulsion of the PLO and its factionalism. By looking at, for example, settlement policy and the establishment of 'facts on the ground' the economic and geographic dimensions of the conflict will also be revealed.

Human rights debates will be examined through the growing intimacy between these enemies that became constructed around the institutions and mechanisms of occupation. In this way the chapter will demonstrate the effects that occupation had on the dynamics of both Israeli and Palestinian society.

In Chapter 7 of the book the outbreak of the Palestinian uprising in December 1987, known as the Intifada, both challenged and changed perceptions of the Israeli–Palestinian conflict. The future viability of the Israeli occupation was called into question and the prospects for a peaceful resolution to the enmity between Israel and the PLO were seen to increase.

The political strategies adopted and pursued by the Palestinians and the Israelis during this period had an effect on their internal polities and created new pressures and a demand for responses that centred on the principle of conflict resolution through negotiation. Palestinian political strategies during this period included the pursuit of mass-based civil disobedience as a means of resisting the occupation and demanding statehood and independence. Palestinians were perceived differently as a result of the media focus on Israel's action and, perhaps for the first time in their history, the Western perception of them was as victims rather than terrorists. This led to a political momentum that some argue culminated in the 1991 Madrid peace talks and the 1993 Oslo Accords otherwise known as the Declaration of Principles. Aspects of the conflict also changed. On both sides of the divide the voice of the religious right, the fundamentalists and conservatives emerged amidst the cacophony of chaos that the Intifada induced. In both cases the conservative and religious elements acted as spoilers on the attempts coming from both sides to build peace and seek a 'land for peace' deal.

Throughout the early 1990s the movement for peace, on both sides of the divide, appeared to gain momentum and culminated in a series of events that concluded in the Oslo Accords being signed in 1993. This process and those who both supported and rejected it will also be examined in this chapter. The return of PLO Chairman, Yasser Arafat, first to Gaza and then the West Bank and the establishment of the Palestinian Authority (PA) in the West Bank and Gaza Strip were greeted with immense optimism. But because Oslo was not a peace deal but the framework for final status negotiation on issues such as settlements, borders, refugees and Jerusalem things began to unravel throughout the middle to late 1990s.

The advent of proto-state politics, institutions and structures with the Palestinian Legislative Council (PLC) and the elections of 1996 will be addressed in this chapter, particularly in respect of wider debates about state-building, sovereignty, civil society, corruption and authoritarianism. Spoilers and rejectionists and their impact on the peace process will be analysed in the context of categories such as the religious elements, etc. Israeli withdrawal and Palestinian autonomy will be reviewed. The Hebron massacre and the killing of Yitzhak Rabin will be presented in terms of the difficulties associated with moving societies from militarization and violence to normalization and peace. The settlements factor, the politics of precariousness, stalemate and suicide bombings will also be considered. The beginning of the dissolution of the Oslo process – Netanyahu, Wye, Camp David, Taba – the resumption of the armed struggle and the outbreak of the armed or 'Al-Aqsa' Intifada of 2000 and its impact on the conflict will be examined at the end of this chapter.

One unique dimension of the Israeli–Palestinian conflict has been its 'international character'. Chapter 8 focuses on a series of debates and discussions about the role of regional and other international actors in the conflict and the various effects this has had in both exacerbating and contributing to the resolution of the conflict. Various 'circles of interaction' will be revealed with respect to such regional actors as Arab states, including the Arab League, plus radical versus conservative regimes and their role in the conflict. It will examine the 'Muslim dimension' of the conflict as well as the response and symbolism of the conflict for the worldwide Jewish Diaspora and Christianity. This is important because these vital constituencies of support in turn have lobbied, supported and played a part in shaping the conflict. Additionally international actors such the USA, the former Soviet Union, and Britain will be scrutinized for their involvement and foreign policy motivations. Finally the role of international and regional organizations such as the United Nations (UN), the Organization of Islamic Conference (OIC), and the European Union (EU) will be debated with respect to historical turns in the international order as well as with respect to the specific issues that determine the nature and character of this conflict.

The last chapter of this book will introduce the idea of peacemaking and conflict resolution and its impact on the Israeli–Palestinian conflict. It will examine the ways in which the later events of 1987 and the outbreak of the Palestinian uprising changed the perceptions internally and externally of the conflict. This includes looking at or examining issues of conflict settlement or peace-building such as civil disobedience, mass protest, the role of civil society, victims versus terrorists, and popular resistance. I will examine dimensions of conflict resolution and transition from conflict that have been proposed, attempted, succeeded at and failed in the context of the Israeli–Palestinian dynamic. Hence the themes examined will include: transfer, annexations, one-state versus two-state solutions, and how to end conflict. Issues of state recognition, legitimacy, strategies for negotiation, asymmetry, and reciprocity will be debated. Ceasefires, 'periods of calm', and military and civilian evacuations for territory will be assessed for their contribution in creating or maintaining the 'resolution momentum'. In this chapter the economic (particularly in terms of wider discourses of global capital and international and regional competitiveness) will be examined in the context of both societies as well as future integration ambitions. The chapter ends by examining the prospects for peace in the wake of the collapse of the Oslo process following the outbreak of the second Intifada in 2000, the Road Map issued by the international community in 2002, the election of the Hamas government by the Palestinians in January 2006, and the regular changes of government in Israel. It reflects on the decline of people-to-people peace-building efforts, the growing internal political infighting that gripped both the Israeli and Palestinian domestic arena and the huge obstacles that now seem to block the path to peace through the formula of a two-state solution for Israel and the Palestinian people.

1 Roots of conflict

Chapter outline

- Ottoman idyll?   10
- Zionism   13
- The Palestinian nationalist 'awakening'   17
- The First World War and its consequences   21
- Balfour bombshell   23
- Parallel points   27
- Further reading   29

The Israeli–Palestinian conflict is one of the most enduring of the modern era and it continues to entangle and engage the international community to the present day. The ongoing battle between the Israelis and Palestinians is rooted in a struggle between the two peoples over land, national identity, political power and the politics of self-determination. The initial context of the conflict lies in the decline of Ottoman Muslim power and the opposition from within this society from a new breed of nationalist. European territorial ambitions and the emergence of new notions of territorial nationalism that would come to bind both the Palestinian and Jewish people to ambitions for independence and statehood in the same territory are also clearly significant factors shaping the period that can be considered as epitomizing the roots of the conflict.

By the late nineteenth century the leaders of the Ottoman Empire, who were based in Constantinople (Istanbul) in Turkey, had ruled over much of the Arab world for centuries. Palestine and its principal city of Jerusalem had been characterized by Ottoman rule for some 500 years. The subject inhabitants of the territories known as Palestine included native Muslims, Christians and Jews. While the Muslims constituted the majority this religiously mixed population had lived in relative harmony for hundreds of years but this situation was soon to change.

This chapter, then, will outline the historical background to the conflict. It will begin with an examination of late-nineteenth-century Palestine – an Ottoman province and largely rural society. It will then outline emerging discourses on

Jewish nationalism and the ascendance of Palestinian national identity. It will trace the events of the late nineteenth and early twentieth century in respect of rising European interest in Palestine and the outbreak of the First World War in 1914 and its impact in the arena of the Middle East. This is because the region became subject to the competing strategic and other ambitions of European powers, of Britain and France in particular. Moreover, the dominant Ottoman Turkish authorities sided with Germany during the war, leading to a series of battles and revolts in its empire territories of the Middle East between and on behalf of the warring parties.

The writing will draw out parallel points of identity issues and politics between Jews and Arabs and their nascent nationalist ideologies – including Zionism and Palestinian nationalism. The chapter will address growing tensions between the Jews and Arabs associated with Jewish land settlement and growing Palestinian frustration and revolt at British mediation of the incipient conflict. This means that the roots of the conflict are outlined. It will detail Western rivalry in the region during the First World War and its effects on Palestine. This will thus include examination of French–British machinations, including the Sykes–Picot Agreement of 1916, in addition to an explanation of the Balfour Declaration of 1917 as well as the earlier Hussein–McMahon Correspondence of 1915. This gives a dimension of much needed political analysis in terms of theories of state, nation and colonial ambition as well as attitudes towards the region.

Ottoman idyll?

The story of the Israeli–Palestinian conflict is rooted in the last decades of Ottoman Turkish rule over Palestine. The Ottomans ruled over Palestinian territory for hundreds of years but in the last decades of the nineteenth century and the early decades of the twentieth events conspired to bring change instead of Ottoman continuity. Although ethnic difference may have divided the Ottoman Turkish rulers from their Arab subordinates the common faith of Islam had largely united the Middle East. Jews and Christians, minority subjects, also enjoyed a close relationship with the Ottoman authorities, where the usual strictures about non-Muslim subjects were often overlooked (Levy, 2002).

This common unity of Muslim faith between Turk and Arab was, however, challenged by growing foreign infiltration and involvement in Palestine, leading to a variety of European rivalries and contests, which often cost the local population dearly. In this respect matters in Palestine were a mirror of events elsewhere in the Ottoman Empire as its grip on power declined in the face of growing European penetration. Economic as well as political and religious imperatives largely explain the changes that would beset the area. Such changes would impact on a local population that was mostly rural, Muslim, and had largely contented itself with a way of life that they had enjoyed as a result of centuries of relatively stable Ottoman rule.

The population of Palestine, as previously noted, was mostly Muslim, but did include other religious minorities, such as Christians and Jews, in major cities and towns such as Jerusalem, Bethlehem, Jaffa and Hebron. By the 1870s this minor cosmopolitan mix was described as a patchwork quilt of different cultures, religions and ways of life:

> spawned by the endless waves of invasion [which] had produced a network of anarchic *bonhomie* where Maghribi mystics, Armenian craftsmen, Talmudic scholars, British mercenaries, Turkish gendarmerie and Greek orthodox traders lived side by side with the merchants, landowners and religious elite who made up the upper echelon of Sunni Muslim society.
>
> (Smith, 1984: 8)

By the 1870s–80s Ottoman-ruled Palestine also included a highly stratified societal structure presided over by the rulers from Istanbul and their local agents, sometimes referred to as the Effendi class. They oversaw a series of reforms called the *tanzimaat* (1839–76) that were meant to modernize education, the status of minorities, the bureaucracy of state, political and religious institutions and law and order (Abu Manneh, 1990). The initial intent behind such reforms was also to reassert the hegemony of Ottoman power in its Palestinian province at a time when rebellion, banditry, lawlessness and general insecurity were said to characterize the area.

European travellers at the time often described at length the extent to which lawlessness prevailed in the Holy Land. In the 1880s William Thomson remarks in his lengthy account of travels in 'The Land and the Book' that journeys in and around the environs of Jerusalem had improved considerably as a result of Ottoman reforms after 'Ibrahim Pasha had broken up the nest of robbers'. For before such changes, 'no-one could reside outside the walls of Jerusalem for fear of those lawless robbers, nor were the city gates kept open after sunset' (Thomson, 1883: 61). Thomson was just one of a succession of Europeans who by the 1880s were having an impact on Palestinian society and the way it was represented back in Europe. The establishment of myriad competing European missions and religious societies, pilgrims, tourists, artists, writers, poets, foreign trade, and the settlement of new communities in Palestine increasingly led to contact and impact on the local landed and notable families. Inevitably the politics and the economy of Palestine began to alter. New class alliances and interests emerged to challenge and ultimately diminish the influence of traditional elements such as the tribal chiefs and heads of clans. Urbanization and modernization gave rise to new elements within society – Muslim, Christian, Jewish – who prospered through trade and commerce and educated their children in modern and/or European style schools, missions and other institutions.

Meanwhile the vast majority of the population – the peasants (*fellahin*) from the many hundreds of villages and hamlets that typified the area – were part of a social and economic system of clan and tribe and loyalty to local lords (Muslih, 1988: 17). Local networks of power and patronage were further challenged by the impact of Ottoman reforms, which created new structures of power and challenged the hegemony of village sheikhs or *mukhtars*. There is some disagreement on the extent to which the Ottomans were successful in altering power relations within the village but there can be no doubting the impacts on village life in general that the last decades of the Ottoman Empire had (Gerber, 1986: 30).

By 1900 immigration to Palestine by Jews also led to the establishment of about 20 new exclusive communities or colonies where some 5,000 Jewish immigrants lived (Smith 1984: 15). In the wake of the anti-Jewish Russian pogroms of 1881–84 and 1903–06 thousands of Jews chose to escape to Palestine. These waves of immigration were known in Hebrew as *aliyah* (ascent). This concept of *aliyah*, of an 'ascent' to the Holy Land by Jews through immigration, became one of the fundamental tenets of modern Zionism and was later enshrined in the 'Law of Return' by the state of Israel. The first waves of immigration to Palestine during this period were made for ideological, pragmatic and spiritual reasons. The first *aliyah* dates from the period of 1882–1903. Jews came to Palestine to settle the land. During this time the majority of these Zionist immigrants came from Eastern Europe or Russia and they established new communities (*moshav*) mostly in the countryside. They did, however, also found new towns such as Rishon LeZion and Zikhron Ya'akov.

The second *aliyah* (1904–14) was much more ideologically motivated by socialist Zionist ideals and it was from this group of immigrants that the first socialist utopian community known as kibbutz (gathering) was founded. These collective communities would come to form a cornerstone of the state of Israel as well as modern Zionism. The kibbutz communities were interpreted as a symbol of redemption Zionism where the modern Jew could fully reach his or her potential free of the shackles of anti-Semitism and oppression that had dogged their experiences as a minority and Diaspora community in Europe and Russia. In this way, as will be explained in Chapter 3, the differences between Labour Zionism with its socialist ideals and epitomized by David Ben Gurion, right-wing revisionist Zionism led by Ze'ev Jabotinsky and the religious Zionist community also became apparent (Segev, 2001: 209–10).

The kibbutzim are often described as one of the largest and most successful examples of collective community. This is where the realization of the ideal of socialism and Zionism in Palestine had been successfully achieved. The kibbutz implied a form of communal living, which in the early years of state independence gave rise to a generation of political, military and other leaders. The settler founders of the kibbutz movement also saw the land that they settled as the means to the foundation of a Jewish nation and state based on the principles of freedom and equality. The kibbutzniks, as they became known, were considered to be 'pioneers', farming and growing on Palestine's 'empty lands' and 'making the desert bloom'. With a desire for the establishment of a self-sufficient utopian enterprise centred on the Jew it was little surprise that contacts with the indigenous Arab population would be tenuous at best. And although the number of kibbutzniks was relatively small they were considered to be the 'guardians of Zionist land, and their patterns of settlement would to a great extent determine the country's borders . . . the kibbutzim also had a powerful effect on the Zionist self-image' (Segev, 2001: 249). One critic, however, opines that such projections 'leave out the facts that . . . Arabs were never admitted as members, that cheap (Arab or Oriental Jew) labor is essential to kibbutz functioning, that "socialist" kibbutzim were and are established on land confiscated from Arabs' (Said, 1980: 21). The same was true of later developments within Labour Zionism such as the formation of the Jewish Labour Federation (the Histadrut) in 1920; 'its objectives were considered synonymous with those of the Zionist movement' (Segev, 2001: 209). Hence the rights of Arab labour were basically excluded. The fact is that these early waves of settlement, on lands that had been owned or dwelled on by Palestinians for generations, contributed to a nascent tension and hostility between these Zionist settlers and the indigenous Palestinian population. Critics consider this to be a form of colonization by an alien group of settlers seeking economic output from the enterprise. This emphasis on the nationalist, Zionist and religious sentiments behind early Jewish settlement overlooks the pressing need to escape persecution in the European continent.

Zionism

The history of the Jewish people, like Christianity and Islam, is intimately tied to the Holy Land or Palestine. The spiritual and historical chronicles of Judaism are rooted in experiences that took place in and around the lands of Palestine. The ancient kingdoms of the Jewish kings were located in cities such as Jerusalem. For those that are seeking it, Palestine is a repository of Jewish history, spirituality, hopes, dreams and aspirations for the reunification of a people tied to each other through the profession of faith made modern as a form of ethnic and distinct identity. Persecution of the Jewish Diaspora communities of Europe and Russia, typified by the Dreyfus Affair in France in the 1880s and the Russian pogroms of 1881 and 1903, clearly stirred some to think anew about the promise of unification of the Jewish people. These events served to underscore the pervasive anti-Semitic prejudices at large in many European societies and the belief that integration or assimilation would never truly materialize. The Jews would always be considered the 'other' or the 'outsider' or a threat to notions of overarching loyalty in the newly emergent state system of late eighteenth and early nineteenth-century Europe.

The recognition of European anti-Semitism by a range of Jewish thinkers and ideologues led to proposals and solutions that most powerfully included ones proposed by people like Theodor Herzl and Moses Hess of the establishment of a Jewish national state. The ambition to establish a national state for the Jewish people would need support not only from those within the Jewish Diaspora but others outside it as well. The anti-assimilation argument was outlined in what would become Herzl's famous treatise entitled *Der Judenstaat* [The Jewish state] published in 1896. Determined to promote his plan, Herzl convened the first Zionist Congress in the Swiss town of Basle in August 1897. Nearly 200 delegates from over 15 countries attended the congress to discuss the Zionism platform as expressed in the aspiration for a Jewish national state and the practical steps that could be taken to realize the project. The success of the congress spurred Herzl in his quest for Jewish nationalism and nation state. He declared:

was I to sum up the Basle Congress in one word which I shall guard against pronouncing publicly, it would be this: At Basle I founded the Jewish State. Perhaps in five years but certainly in 50 everyone will know it.

(O'Brien, 1986: 54)

For Herzl the actual location of the new Jewish state was not initially as important as it was to others. He would have settled on a state outside of Palestine and had been amenable, for example, to one proposal for the Jewish state to be established in Uganda.

The roots of Jewish nationalism and the gathering of intellectuals around this project created a fusion of nationalist thinking and ambition that was often both religious and fervently secular. Zionism in these early years came to symbolize many things to many people. Some religious intellectuals and leaders coalesced around the project for nationalism as a Jewish expression. The famous Kabbalist Rabbi, Abraham Kook, committed himself to the new project by immigrating to Palestine in 1904 and becoming, in 1921, its chief rabbi. Kook advocated the fusion of faith and Zionism where religion and nationalism could be achieved.

The intimate connection between faith and practice through the physical establishment of Zion in Palestine was urged by Kook as a means by which Jews could achieve complete redemption within their faith.

Secularists, such as Asher Hersh Ginsberg, whose pen name was Ahad Ha'Am, sought to track a different course for the Zionist project. For him the Jewish state should be the embodiment of modern secular Jewish Enlightenment thinking. He no longer believed that Jews could be successfully assimilated in Eastern European society so the only alternative appeared to be devoting the Jewish people to a plan for independence. These aspirations are summed up by Ginsberg in the following:

This Jewish settlement, which will be a gradual growth, will become in course of time the centre of the nation, wherein its spirit will find pure expression and develop in all its aspects to the highest degree of perfection of which it is capable. Then, from this centre the spirit of Judaism will radiate to the great circumference, to all the communities of the Diaspora, to inspire them with new life and to preserve the over-all unity of our people. When our national culture in Palestine has attained that level, we may be confident that it will produce men in the Land of itself who will be able, at a favourable moment, to establish a State there – one which will be not merely a State of Jews but really a Jewish State.

(Ginsberg, 1897)

The form of nationalism that Ginsberg personified can be termed as emancipation-nationalism, for not only was the project he proposed about the establishment of a separate state for the Jewish people but that the task of creating this state and its ultimate realization would promote an empowered and modern emancipated Jew who had thrown off the shackles of the ghetto and the hatreds behind centuries of anti-Semitism. Ginsberg envisioned the redundancy of the perception of impotent and disempowered Jews of Europe's ghettoes and in their place would stand the modern Hebrews forging a new nation and state with exclusive identities and ambitions.

In this secular vision of modern statehood faith would form part of the private realm of expression rather than the core of a state binding the Jewish people together. In this way Jewishness acquired an ascribed ethnic dimension that built on primordial bonds in a much more instrumental fashion (Kimmerling, 1982). Such early visions, of course, were purist ambitions that would, over time, become tainted by the realities of fusing the religious with the secular in the modern state of Israel. For these early Zionists, though, the impulse lay in persuading those within their own communities as well as those outside it to support their cause. By projecting an image of 'native' born Jews (sabra), who would redeem the land and Jewish society through their manual effort to build the Jewish state, the Jews would find a sense of collective belonging and nation. The sabra were, in some respects, part of the cultural myths important to the founding of the Jewish state; they 'startled the midwives who saw them being born with a monkey wrench and pistol in hand' (Wasserstein, 2003: 33).

The cause was hindered from within. Some Jews simply rejected Zionism because they felt that it undermined assimilation and gave further cause for anti-Semites to pursue policies of exclusion and marginalization of Jewish communities. They feared that the realization of the ambition of a Jewish state for the Jewish people would lead to their expulsion from countries and communities that had been their homes for generations. Jewish leaders in the Reform movement, for example, contended that Zionism contradicted the universal dimensions of Judaism. In the USA the Reform movement in the nineteenth century also oriented their followers away from notions of exile and messianic fulfilment through settlement in the ancient lands of Zionism. Their sights were set on establishing a home for Jews among the pioneers of the USA. Others rejected Zionism because of its dominant secular intellectualism, Enlightenment foundations and betrayal of the Jewish religious belief that the restoration of the Jewish people to Zion could in fact only take place after the return of the Messiah. To pre-empt events by building a Jewish nation state in Zion would be an anathema to such people.

Herzl's successor to the mantle of Zionism was a Russian chemist called Chaim Weizmann (1874–1952). Weizmann, as a young man, had developed an interest in the ideas of Zionism. Weizmann became a key link between the Zionists and the British government – or more particularly Arthur Balfour who served both as Prime Minister and Foreign Secretary. Balfour was sympathetic to the Zionist cause. At this early stage of Zionism, however, its proponents sought support from all, and often competing, quarters. This was because, as stated earlier, they were often contending with as much opposition to their project from within Judaism as they were from outside it. Many religious leaders were antagonistic to Zionism because the dominant secularists within the movement were interpreted as seeking to establish a modern nation state of the Jewish people where faith (rabbinic rule) would be absent from its centre. This new nationalism of the Jewish people appeared to ignore the key element that bound such people together in terms of their primary religious identity and survival after hundreds of years of persecution. Some orthodox Rabbis were concerned that Zionist domination would sever the link between the spiritual and Israel. Others within the family of Judaism were also implacably opposed to the Zionist project, fearing that such a plan would lead to divided loyalties between state and faith, nation and belonging, and identity as modern or ancient. Many in the Jewish community in the USA, for example, resisted the construction of Zionism as a nationalist project where a people bound by ties of faith were reconstituted as a nation aligned to the political project of state construction in Palestine. Jewish citizens of the USA had already emigrated from their European and Russian homes and were successfully integrating into a society that constructed important myths around the notion of a 'national melting pot' where all faiths and creeds were united under one flag.

Within Zionism itself the lines of unity quickly broke down and early fissures between the pragmatists and idealists, secularists and religious, revisionist and socialist wings of the movement emerged. These differences within Zionism also coincided with the second and third waves of *aliyah* (1904–23) following further tumult in Europe and Russia, as well as rising anti-Semitism and pogroms. In 1901 the Jewish National Fund (JNF) had been founded and this organization, along with others such as the Palestine Land Development Company, started buying land in Palestine as a means of territorializing the ambition for Zionist settlement (Newman, 2002). Slowly but surely these land purchases (often from absentee landlords) contributed to the encouragement of Jewish immigration. The new Jewish settlements and communities founded by the immigrants from Europe were known collectively as the new Yishuv. The 'old Yishuv' referred to Palestine's pre-existing Jewish community.

For these early Zionists the issue of the pre-existing native or indigenous population was acknowledged and sometimes even debated. Some Zionists were oblivious to the native presence, others chose simply to ignore the presence of an indigenous population, while a few saw them as an impediment to Zionist ambition. For the founding fathers of Zionism the logic of Palestine as a Promised Land for the Jewish people implied that the indigenous non-Jewish population should in some way be absent. An oft-repeated mantra was that Palestine was 'a land without a people for a people without a land'. Israel Zangwill, the author who coined the slogan, was an early supporter of Herzl's Zionist vision but split and formed his own group, the Jewish Territorialist Organization, with the objective of establishing a Jewish state in locations as diverse as Australia and Urganda. Chaim Weizmann then became the chief banner-man of the 'land without a people for a people without a land' vision.

Returning back to Jewish settlement in Palestine, 'the idea,' therefore, 'that the Palestinian Arabs must find a place for themselves elsewhere' formed part of the early ruminations of the Zionist leadership (Masalha, 1992: 8). Nur Masalha contends that such ruminations were tantamount to proposals for transfer – 'an euphemism denoting the organized removal of the indigenous population of Palestine' and that such ideas would form the basis of Zionist thinking and objectives' (Masalha, 1992: 1). It becomes apparent that interpretation of early Zionist ambition leads certain authors and scholars to conclude that behind the aspiration to settle a 'land without a people' was a desire that would later transform into a specific objective, to get rid of the existing indigenous population. Such an interpretation is countered with the argument that there is little by way of evidence to prove such a hypothesis. The evidence on the ground did, however, demonstrate that Zionist Jews and their supporters were willing to expedite their vision through the organization of land settlement and territorialization according to nationalist goals in Palestine. If the notion of an empty land for a repressed and exiled people helped, then there was little by way of political resistance locally to stop its perpetuation.

The Palestinian nationalist 'awakening'

It is true that the Zionists and their supporters needed to construct a series of myths in order for their project to gain a foothold in the consciousness of those who would help them realize their dreams. Myths are almost essential to any nation- and state-building project (Hutchinson, 2004). Founding myths forge much needed unity – often where none was previously present. Such myths bind people together in a 'collective' experience and allow the often unpalatable truths behind modern state construction to be ignored until a time when a nation feels secure enough in its stability and identity within the borders of a state to revisit such events. 'A land without a people for a people without a land' was one such founding myth associated with the Zionist project in Palestine. Of course the Zionists knew there was an existing indigenous and mostly Arab population in Palestine. In 1895, the issue of Palestine's existing population clearly engaged Theodor Herzl. In his diary he proposed that:

> We shall have to spirit the penniless population across the border by procuring employment for it in the transit countries while denying it employment in our own country. Both the process of expropriation and the removal of the poor must be carried out discreetly and circumspectly.
>
> (Patai 1960: 88)

The presence of this population was clearly an obstacle, but one that could be overcome by the Zionists and their supporters. There emerged a number of strategies for dealing with this issue. First, in terms of the project to actualize Zionism in Palestine through the establishment of the early communities of yishuv and kibbutzim, the Arabs were to be excluded. If Jewish national identity allied to the goal of establishing a state for the Jewish people were to stand a chance of succeeding then it was obvious that an alternative national, ethnic or religious presence would undermine such a goal. In this context the Zionists sought to rearticulate religious identity and status as the essential construct for nation and ethnic bonding. Jews, with their distinct faith and common ties to the land of Israel, would be constituted anew as a nation (Goldschneider, 1995). This modernization of Jewish identity required the negation of alternative national identities in relation to the state-building project.

Second, as Edward Said contends, the Zionists sought to represent the Arabs to outsiders (and principally at that time the British) as an inferior backward set of natives who could be conveniently overlooked. Such representation was not uncommon in the discourse of European imperialism and colonialism at its apogee in the late nineteenth century. The Arab population was perceived and represented negatively through an 'orientalist' lens (Said, 1980). By extension, Zionism as a form of European discourse about the nation and settlement could get away with embracing a similar discourse as an echo of the colonial project as fulfilment of a plan to establish European settlement in Palestine. If imitation was the sincerest form of flattery then the Zionists were astute in terms of representing Palestine to its potential European supporters as an opportunity to 'civilize' the population of a territory that was different from other European colonial territories in only one respect. This one difference lay with the status of Palestine as *terra sancta* (Holy Land) to those of Judaism as well as Christianity (the sacred status of the land to Islam was simply deliberately overlooked). By the late nineteenth century the European 'rediscovery' of the Holy Land was already well-established among elite classes across Europe. But local Palestinian Muslim and Christian society was largely depicted as populated by 'natives' who were nothing short of barbarian. As Macalister states:

> The native civilization, such as it is, is a painful illustration of the evils of what may be called unredeemed practicality . . . In such a community, the interests that to a western [person] seem almost essential to the happiness of life are scarcely thought of. Literature is neglected; historical monuments are allowed to fall into ruin . . . as for art . . . there is practically none.
>
> (Macalister 1912: 123–24)

This was contrasted with the 'Jewish agricultural colonies', which 'appeared to be successful enough', and the 'officers of the various legitimate mission agencies . . . doing a noble work, ministering to the spiritual and bodily needs of the dwellers in the land' (Macalister 1912: 125).

To a certain extent this 'conspiracy of representation' allowed European support for Zionism to garner momentum unhindered by the voice of the local Palestinian Arab community. The continuity and presence of an Arab population was denied. This quote from two renowned British academics written in the late nineteenth century encapsulates this point: 'during the interval of [the last] five hundred years Jerusalem has been without a history. Nothing has happened but an occasional act of brutality on the part of her masters towards the Christians' (Besant and Palmer 1899: 520). What seems remarkable about such a quote today is that its authors, clearly uninhibited by any form of political correctness, can simply deny history has taken place because it is Muslim and not Christian or Jewish. Zionist leaders were similarly as open in their dismissal of the local population and their place in their grand schemes for the creation of modern Zion in

Palestine. Chaim Weizmann, leader of Zionism and Israel's first president, wrote to a British official that the local inhabitants consisted of the following: 'the fellah [who] is at least four centuries behind the times, and the effendi [who] is dishonest, uneducated, greedy, and as unpatriotic as he is inefficient' (Ingrams 1973: 32). As previously noted, however, it was not only the Zionists that denied the obvious by pretending that the Arabs of Palestine simply did not exist. This attitude was also obvious in official British correspondence and documents. Parliamentary Under-Secretary for the Colonies, one Honourable William Ormsby-Gore MP, had denied that the population west of Jordan (i.e. in Palestine) were Arab though he admitted that they were 'Arabic speaking' (Ingrams, 1973: 33).

If one is frank it is not difficult to understand why the penetration of such views – when they filtered into the homes and meeting places of Palestinian elite society – sometimes roused feelings of antipathy towards the Europeans. By the late nineteenth and early twentieth century, then, the first stirrings of Palestinian national identity and opposition to foreign interference and the threats posed by Zionism in particular were discernible. Nationalist consciousness among Palestinians was developing. Palestinian Arab nationalist consciousness was a product of the rising intellectual and region-wide trend of Arab nationalism in opposition to Ottoman rule, as well as a response to the specific manifestation of European attachment to Zionism in Palestine.

It should be understood, however, that irrespective of an indigenous and continuous occupation of a territory for centuries by the Palestinians they were not conceived of as a nation either by the Zionists nor the British authorities. Their identity was contested and disputed by Jewish opponents to a Palestinian Arab presence in the land that they refer to as *Eretz Israel*. Nevertheless the indigenous Palestinian Arab population did begin to organize and resist Zionist and British plans to determine their future. First, the elite of Palestinian society as I have already noted were influenced by wider intellectual trends that gripped the region with respect to ideas and ideologies associated with nationalism, identity, autonomy and independence (Porath 1974). In this respect they were like many other elite groups that emerged throughout many of Europe's colonies in the Middle East at the time. The well-educated (and often Western-educated) elite engaged with ideas and a form of consciousness-raising that made them chafe under the yoke of foreign rule and yearn for freedom and independence. A sense of nation was moulded by the elite through a variety of forms – including arts, culture, writings, myths, history, language, religion and race, and of course economic, social and political activities (Khalidi, 1998).

A sense of national identity and national consciousness also progressed as a reactive ideology in the face of Jewish settlers who were determined that their experiment in nation- and state-building would be exclusive rather than inclusive. This was experienced in a very real way during the early years of Zionist settlement when a policy known as *avodah ivrit* (Jewish labour) prohibited the employment of Arabs in the new colonies and settlements that the Zionists were establishing. This policy was exacerbated by the formation of the Jewish labour movement (Histadrut), which privileged Jewish over Arab labour in sectors of the developing economy. The effects of such policies were primarily felt among Palestine's peasant classes and made them hostile to Zionism. Thus even from its earliest days the Palestinian nationalist movement comprised elements from all quarters of contemporary society.

Fences were not making good neighbours between the Zionist settlers and Palestinian Arabs. Stirrings of discontent grew as the Ottoman authorities permitted land sales and thus undermined aspects of the traditional rural land-holding system. The Zionists were perceived as posing a very real threat to the indigenous population and its way of life. Early clashes took place between the Palestinians and Zionists in the late 1880s and centred, somewhat inevitably, on issues that related to land rights and land use. The Palestinian peasantry was experiencing first hand the impact of Zionist settlement on lands that they believed they had traditional and historical entitlement to. In some respects then – whether in the countryside, town or city – the Zionist threat was first interpreted by Palestinian Arabs as having an economic dimension as well.

From 1900–10 Palestinian nationalist antipathies against the Zionists grew and locally produced newspapers, pamphlets and other literature outlined the ways in which the Zionist project in Palestine was undermining Palestinian Arab rights and livelihoods. The local elite was obviously threatened by the external support that the Zionists seemed to be garnering from important actors such as the Europeans, Russians and Ottoman powers, as well as the internal impact they were having on the fabric of traditional society. Their nationalism was defensive and strived to resist Zionism and preserve power at the same time. Their self-interest sometimes led them into local internal rivalries with other members of the elite as they sought to meet the challenges presented by the great upheavals that were besetting their society. By and large, however, their energies were absorbed in meeting the challenges presented by the changes at the centre of Ottoman society – where the revolution in 1908 of the 'Young Turks' had heralded nationalist change and secular reform – as well the growing impact of Zionist-inspired immigration to Palestine. The political organization of Palestinian Arab society would start at the highest levels but quickly filter down and generate relevance and resonance among the majority peasant population. As Muslih notes, 'Palestinian peasants, urban notables and merchants . . . knew of Zionism and began to express their opposition to it as early as 1882 [but] . . . it did not develop into fully-fledged anti-Zionism before 1908' (Muslih, 1988: 86). From 1908, however, the seed of Palestinian patriotism quickly grew in the context of wider regional events into a flower of nationalism that would blossom in fully fledged opposition to the Zionists and their British sponsors in Palestine. Resistance would take many forms and seek to disrupt both Zionist and British colonial ambition for Palestine.

The nascent Palestinian Arab identity would be forged in a variety of ways as an expression of a nation with legitimate rights to self-determination and independence in its own land. While it was true that in the late nineteenth century Palestine's inhabitants had many layers of identity, by the early twentieth century the pronounced identity of being Palestinian was apparent. Khalidi contends that it was not only among the elite that this sense of being Palestinian occurred but that it was apparent too among the peasant classes losing their lands and livelihoods as a result of the process of colonization (Khalidi, 1998). Khalidi also argues that to perceive Palestinian nationalism as solely reactive to Zionism overlooks the intimate and diverse development of Palestinian national identity as opposed to other emergent Arab identities in the Middle East region.

As we shall see, such rights would be thwarted in the face of the dual obstacle of Zionism and British colonial policy. Moreover, the Zionist project for Palestine was also seized upon by prominent Arab intellectuals elsewhere in the Arab world. Muslih highlights the fact that one leading Egyptian-based Islamic thinker, Rashid al-Rida, addressed the Palestine issue as early as 1898:

> Think about this question [Zionism], and make it the subject of your discussion to determine whether it is just or unjust . . . If you find out that you have failed to defend the rights of your homeland and the service of your nation, study and examine.
>
> (Muslih, 1988: 75)

Other secular Arab thinkers also took up an early defence of Palestine against Zionism in their writings and debates.

The First World War and its consequences

The outbreak of the First World War and the events in the Middle East that took place throughout its duration would have profound consequences for Palestine as well as the rest of the region. The so-called exigencies of war led to open as well as secret alliances and accords between and among the allied European powers, to agreements between European actors and Arab leaders, and to declarations from European actors in support of the Zionists – all of which would lead to confusion and conflict at the end of the war. The imprint of this war would be catastrophic for the fortunes of Palestine's Arabs setting off, as it did, a chain of events that would lead to dispossession.

In Palestine itself the most immediate effect of the war was evident in the public displays of Palestinian support for the Ottoman powers linked to Germany against the European Allied powers. There were some, however, among the younger generation of the notable classes, who turned their back on their Ottoman overlords and supported Arab nationalism and revolt. Academics though have differed with each other on the extent to which this made for a proper Palestinian contribution to Arab nationalism or not. It is fair to say that by and large pro-Zionist scholars seek to debunk any claim to a Palestinian nationalist trend in the late nineteenth and early twentieth century. Pro-Palestinian scholars assert that there is evidence of such a trend and its influence vis-à-vis wider debates on Arab nationalism, pan-Arabism and pan-Islamism at this time.

A number of deals and agreements were reached during this period and they would impact directly on the future status of Palestine. The first deal that impacted on Palestine transpired as early as 1915 when the leader of the Arab independence movement, Sharif Hussein of Mecca, and the British High Commissioner of Egypt, Sir Henry McMahon, exchanged a series of letters – the Hussein–McMahon Correspondence – in which in return for Arab support against the Turks the British promised independence to the Arabs. 'Great Britain is prepared to recognize the independence of the Arabs in all the regions within the limits demanded by the Sharif of Mecca', declared Sir Henry McMahon in his famous epistle signed on 24 October 1915 (Smith, 2004: 61). In return the Arabs, led by Sharif Hussein's sons, delivered victory against the Turks and 'liberated' Arab territories from their rule. The Allies, however, would repay the Arabs by deposing their leaders and carving up their territories to create new states and kingdoms that would bedevil the region.

The second agreement affecting Palestine occurred between unlikely European allies: Britain and France. Although until the First World War Britain and France had often found themselves locked in sometimes bitter rivalry in the Middle East, aspects of this relationship were put aside as they allied themselves against the Axis powers of Germany and Turkey in the region. This alliance had led the British and the French into a secret agreement in early 1916 to share control over large swathes of Arab territory in the region between them and grant independence to the Arabs only in the present-day territories of Saudi Arabia and Yemen.

The Sykes–Picot Agreement defined the spheres of power that Britain and France would enjoy post-war. Modern-day Syria and Iraq, for example, enjoy a common border that was determined under the terms of the Sykes–Picot Agreement. It was agreed that Palestine would probably be subject to some form of international administration referred to as an 'allied condominium' but that further consultations with other international powers such as Russia would have to take place first. The cities of Haifa and Acre, however, fell into the 'bubble' of a British-ruled zone. The agreement could be perceived as a contradiction of the terms laid out in the Hussein–McMahon Correspondence. In 1917, following the Russian Revolution, Lenin exposed the Sykes–Picot Agreement and this led to tensions with the Arabs. It appeared that the French–British agreement reneged on the promises of independence that the Arabs thought they had secured from the British.

British and French control included the territories of Palestine. Secrecy was the order of the day because of fears that news of the agreement would turn nascent Arab support for the allies against them. The Allied powers needed the Arab promise of a revolt against the Turks as part of the wider war strategy but they were determined that any form of 'Arab independence' would take place at their convenience, would not prejudice British and French interests in the region (most of it) or hinder any other agreements (secret or otherwise) that they might determine for the region. Thus by 1917 there were two contradictory promises made by the British government regarding the disposal of Turkish-held territory (including Palestine) after the war. By November 1917 the British were offering up the promise of Palestine to a third interested party: this time to the Zionists.

By that time Palestine became subject once again to the forces of foreign occupation. This time the forces were the British who were at war with Germany and its Turkish allies in the region. Yet even before the British general, General Allenby, and his forces had captured Jerusalem, the government in London – persuaded by the grist of the argument of the Zionists and choosing to ignore the contradiction inherent in its previous agreements with the Arabs and even perhaps the French – issued a statement that became known as the Balfour Declaration.

Balfour bombshell

> Probably no other scrap of paper in history has had the effect of this brief letter, the cause of conflict [that] still shows no sign of settlement.
>
> (Ingrams, 1973:)

There can be little doubt that the British occupation of Palestine as part of its military campaigns in the Middle East accelerated Zionist ambitions for the land and played a large part in determining its future. Without British patronage the dreams of Jewish statehood in Palestine may well have withered on the vine. The Zionists had the dreams and the ambitions and British support resulted in the practical wherewithal and control of the territory they sought to make their own. Balfour was an early convert to the Zionist cause but in Britain support was also lent by figures such as Lloyd George and Herbert Samuel. The British, however, would not give the Zionists their homeland free of impediment. The British would 'facilitate' the process by keeping this procedure of Jewish state creation under their control. It was hoped that under British rule:

> facilities would be given to Jewish organizations to purchase land, to found colonies, to establish educational and religious institutions . . . that Jewish immigration . . . would be given preference so that in course of time the Jewish people, grown into a majority and settled on the land, may be conceded such degree of self-government that the conditions of that day may justify.
>
> (Bowle, 1957: 175)

The statement, issued on 2 November 1917, outlined in a letter from the British foreign minister of the time, Arthur Balfour, to the British Zionist, Lord Rothschild, gave the following commitment:

> His Majesty's government view with favour the establishment in Palestine of a National Home for the Jewish people, and will use their best endeavours to facilitate the achievement of this object, it being clearly understood that nothing shall be done which may prejudice the civil and religious rights of existing non-Jewish communities in Palestine or the rights and political status enjoyed by Jews in any other country.
>
> (Anglo-American Committee of Inquiry [AAIC], 1946: 1)

The Balfour Declaration has been interpreted in a number of ways. First its author appears to have understood the paradox in British policy that the statement would appear to cause. There is evidence of this in a memo that he wrote a couple of years later:

> The contradiction between the letter of the Covenant is even more flagrant in the case of the independent nation of Palestine . . . For in Palestine we do not propose even to go through the form of consulting the wishes of the present inhabitants of the country . . . The four great powers are committed to Zionism and Zionism, is rooted in age-long tradition, in present needs, in future hopes. In my opinion that is.
>
> (Sykes, 1973: 5)

There is evidence then in Balfour's thinking that Britain could flex its muscle in deciding the fate of other nations and people. There had been a clear decision to ignore the facts and paradox presented by the presence of a pre-existing population of Arabs in Palestine in order to pursue an alternate policy of not only allowing the territory to be populated by another people but to assist and support these people in their ambitions for statehood at the expense of others. It is also certain that a number of issues motivated Balfour and the British government in making this offer to the Zionist movement. Among these issues were sympathy and support for the ideals of Zionism and the predicament of the persecuted Jewish communities of Europe. Strategic sentiment no doubt played its part in supporting the offer to the Zionist movement to play its part in securing a British supported foothold in Palestine. Colonial sentiment also accounted for Britain's decision to ignore the political aspirations and rights of the native population of Palestinian Arabs. For in this respect the Palestinians were a non-people, a non-nation and devoid of meaning to those engaged with the high politics of imperial governance.

The Balfour Declaration became significant to the people of Palestine because it appeared to ignore their nascent political rights to self-determination and independence. While it was true that their civil and religious rights appeared to be recognized, their aspirations for self-rule and power were simply not reflected in the commitment outlined by Arthur Balfour on behalf of the British government. To this day the Palestinian people mark the issuing of the Balfour Declaration in 1917 as a day of national commiseration and mourning. During the first Palestinian Intifada (1987–93) the anniversary of the Balfour Declaration was marked each year by orders from the United National Leadership of the Uprising (UNLU) and Hamas for a general strike that would shut all Palestinian institutions such as schools, factories, universities, shops and businesses. In 2004 Hamas leaders argued that US government 'assurances' to the government of Israel amounted to 'a new Balfour Declaration'. 'The Balfour Declaration gave Palestine to Jews as a national homeland at our expense. Now Bush is telling Sharon he can keep the loots. This is another Balfour Declaration', said Mohamed Nazzal, a Hamas spokesman (Amayreh, 2004). The declaration is viewed as an act that fundamentally changed the course of history for the Palestinian people, leaving them vulnerable to a chain of events dictated by others that would leave them dispossessed and stateless.

For the Zionist movement the declaration was the first tentative step towards achieving the support of a powerful foreign government in support for the goal of establishing a state for the Jewish people in Palestine. Other Zionist potential allies, such as the Germans, were out-manoeuvred by the British declaration of support (Kimche, 1968: 21). Moreover the Declaration was approved by the US President, as well as other important European powers active in the region of the Middle East such as the French and the Italians. From a Zionist perspective, writes Gerner, 'That Palestine had an existing population, with its own history and aspirations, was no more relevant . . . than was Kenyan history to the British or Algerian society to the French' (Gerner, 1994: 15). Balfour himself was frank in his opinion of the Zionist project, 'Zionism, be it right or wrong, good or bad, is of far profounder import than the desires and prejudices of the 700,000 Arabs who now inhabit that ancient land' (Segev, 2000: 45). The issuing of the Declaration was certainly a victory but many within the movement knew and understood that this meant that they could not rest on their laurels. They knew that a 'homeland' was not the same as an independent state but they also understood that the British promise was an important development for them.

The Balfour Declaration assumed new meaning when the British occupied Palestine in late December 1917. General Edmund Allenby's proclamation to the population of Palestine in December 1917, however, gave no hint of the political machinations that would take place once the British fully controlled Palestine post-war:

> Since your city is regarded with affection by the adherents of three of the great religions of mankind, and its soil has been consecrated by the prayers and pilgrimages of devout people of these three religions for many centuries, therefore do I make known to you that every sacred building, monument, holy spot, shrine, traditional site, endowment, pious bequest or customary place of prayer . . . will be maintained and protected according to the existing customs and beliefs of those to whom [these] faiths they are sacred.
>
> (AACI, 1946: 15)

Despite being aware of the inconsistency of its policy vis-à-vis its promises to the Arabs and its declarations of support to the Zionists, the British government doggedly pursued this approach when it came to the post-war conferences that would determine the future of the Middle East. Hence the British delight at the award of a Mandate for Palestine made to them by the League of Nations and as a consequence of the long hours of negotiations that had culminated in the Treaty of Versailles. The award of this mandate was supported by the government of the USA with negotiations prolonged until its formal operation on 29 September 1923. The text of the mandate merely reinforced the status quo and communicated with clarity and certainty the maintenance of British support for the Zionist project in Palestine:

> Whereas recognition has thereby been given to the historical connexion of the Jewish people with Palestine and to the grounds for reconstituting their national home in that country; and . . .
>
> Whereas His Britannic Majesty has accepted the mandate in respect of Palestine and undertaken to exercise it on behalf of the League of Nations . . .
>
> The Mandatory shall have full powers of legislation and of administration . . . shall be responsible for placing the country under such political, administrative and economic conditions as will secure the establishment of the Jewish national home.
>
> (AACI, 1946: 4–11)

Little mention was made of provision – political, economic or otherwise – for the Palestinian population that had been enduring British military occupation of their land since 1917. It would be a mistake to assume that the Palestinian Arabs of Palestine would quietly agree to the lack of rights, rule by a foreign colonial power and the active support of this power in the immigration and establishment of a homeland for the Jewish people. As one Palestinian Arab writer of the time declared:

> A nation which has long been in the depths of sleep only awakes if it is rudely shaken by events, and only arises little by little . . . This was the situation of Palestine, which for many centuries had been in the deepest sleep, until it was shaken by the great war, shocked by the Zionist movement, and violated by the illegal policy [British], and it awoke, little by little.
>
> (Quoted in Khalidi, 1998: 158)

British colonialism and Zionist settlement in Palestine were actively resisted by all elements of Palestinian society. British high-handedness and bias was greeted with discontent, demonstration, uncooperativeness and violence in Arab ranks. As early as 1920 and 1921 when the details of the Balfour Declaration were first made public in Palestine riots broke out with antipathies directed at Jewish targets. Palestinian leaders refused to be a party to British plans. By 1922 a delegation of their leaders had travelled to London to argue their case with the British government. According to official documents the delegation 'declared their refusal to cooperate in any form of government other than a government responsible to the Palestinian people' (AACI, 1946: 19). They also demanded a constitution for Palestine that would accord its people equality of rights including those of minorities and foreigners. Most of all they demanded independence and thus were categorically rejecting British rule and its plans for Zionist immigration and a homeland for the Jewish people in Palestine. The stage was set for contest and conflict.

Parallel points

One aspect of Western society in the twenty-first century is the extent to which our identity appears to matter to us. The politics of identity – who belongs and who does not, who we are and who we are not – shapes our sense of community and nation. We are obsessed with what we look like and this in turn has established degrees of uniformity and difference. Do we look the same as the next person or are we different? Do we want to fit in or do we dare to be different? Identity has come to form a core of nation and culture and established a sense of belonging in national units that today we refer to as nation states. Identity, of course, really starts to matter when it is challenged or altered by someone else. Some nationalist elements that have arisen throughout contemporary history have sought to deny and even exterminate the national identity of others. In the modern Middle East the national identity of the Kurds has, during the manic episodic rule of Saddam Hussein in Iraq, been subject to denial and extermination. In Palestine the politics of identity has played out in a bitter conflict that was established between Zionist settlers and Palestinian Arabs. The problem in Palestine, as many have previously opined, is that 'both Israel's Jews and Palestinians have legitimate and inalienable rights. These rights are rooted in the historical experience of each people' (Tessler, 1994: xi). The parallel points that characterize the issue at this historical juncture were: nationalism, national identity, the state, the impact of external powers and the colonial project in the Middle East.

The idea of nation – a community bound together by common identity – is obviously central to the story of Zionism and Palestinian nationalism in the period that we have just been examining. In a series of more or less congruent steps Jewish intellectuals in Europe and Arab intellectuals in Palestine and elsewhere established modern notions of nation – the Jewish people or the Palestinian Arabs – and to that idea tied territoriality and statehood. The role of the intelligentsia in such a task is acknowledged in respect of their 'vanguard' function as literates in the cultural norms of Western liberal thinking at the time (Anderson, 1991: 116). In undertaking these tasks of 'imagining' the nation, varieties of interpretation quickly arose within each movement (Anderson, 1991: 5–7). Within Zionism, for example, much of the early secularist writing addressed their goal as the creation of an advanced Jewish nation in Palestine where progressive modern Jews could promote principles of socialism and new community. The Zionists actively worked to establish the notion of a modern nation of Jews bound together by a common language (modern Hebrew), a common faith (Judaism), a common history (Jewish), common culture (Jewish) and common territoriality (Palestine). Herzl encouraged Zionism to define the Jews as a nation (a separate ethnic group) and for others to see the Jews as a nation. The Jewish national home in Palestine was also envisaged by religious Zionists as offering Judaism (faith) a central and defining role in determining the establishment of a Jewish state (Israel) in Palestine. In other words, for the religious Zionists, Judaism would define the state and serve as its core. This perspective was and remains a difficult one for secular Jews to absorb. Secular Zionists see their goal as uniting the Jewish people in the right to self-determination in a modern nation state that would leave them free from perse-cution, pogrom and genocide. For them Zionism was a modern movement of European Jews linked to emancipation theories.

Europe had failed to deliver equality to the Jews and instead discriminated against them. Zionism was the alternative; it advocated the revival of national identity and defence of the nation through a return to Zion where they could achieve their independence. This notion of national identity and territory became key: 'The heart of the Zionist revolution was the reform of the Jew as a person . . . The founders believed that national revolution necessitated an absolute social and emotional break with exile' (Sternhell, 1998: 36).

Defining the nation and its state has absorbed Jews from one end of a political and religious spectrum to the other but, with the exception of a minority of reli-gious Jews, they were united from the start around the idea of territoriality in Palestine.

The congruency of Palestinian nationalism and Zionism may be denied. Critics of this approach do not see it as a parallel point but argue that the Palestinian nation did not exist in late Ottoman Palestine and that the Palestinian people – as such – simply do not exist. Debating the evolution of Palestinian nationalism then becomes highly contentious and part of the writing and analysis of the conflict which in itself also perpetuates positions of conflict! Other writers offer evidence of an early and evolving notion of the Palestinian people as a nation and a parallel development of nationalist ambition and sentiment. As noted above, Palestinian nationalism evolved within the wider emerging narratives of Arab nationalism, pan-Islamism and anti-colonialism. Rashid Khalidi highlights the various polit-ical, intellectual, cultural, economic and social factors that during the late Ottoman period in Palestine led to the articulation of a discrete Palestinian iden-tity, which then quickly found itself in contest with Zionist identity and British colonial ambitions for their country. Khalidi, however, reminds us that Palestinian national identity is not merely a foil to Zionism. Articulations of national consciousness among the Palestinians predate Zionist immigration (Khalidi, 1997).

The presence of the Palestinian Arab indigenous population was also an issue in terms of the colonial ambitions of the major European powers in the late nine-teenth and early twentieth centuries. In one form or another then a parallel point between the Zionists and the Palestinian Arabs was colonialism. For the Palestinian Arab population of Palestine the penetration of their territory by Europeans heralded an era of change that would lead by the end of the First World War to direct rule through the British Mandate authorities. Palestine and its Christian shrines was a prize that more than one European power coveted and sought to underscore through the establishment of religious legations, seminaries, schools, hospitals, restored churches, rediscovered sites and shrines, diplomatic and trade missions. This idealized ambition was also allied to the strategic mission of the governments of states such as Britain and France to secure their already-established interests in neighbouring territories of the region. In terms of the Zionists and the Palestinian Arabs one party benefited more than the other. Once again, however, there is academic dispute over the extent to which the Zionists acted as a European settler colonial movement aided and abetted by the British or merely benefited from British support. The first view – that Israel is the embodiment of a colonial state – has long been advocated by Marxist and leftist analysts. The second view is apparent in the more recent work of what is referred to as the 'new Israeli historians'. Tom Segev's account of the British Mandate period, for example, posits the argument that the British were pro-Zionist at the expense of the Palestinian Arab population. In this respect Segev is contending that to a certain extent there would be no Israel were it not for British support (Segev, 2001).

In many respects then the fate of Palestine would be determined by events and powers external to this arena. The events of the First World War, anti-Semitism in Europe, Western theories of nation and nationalism, romanticism and sympathy for the Zionist cause, and colonial indifference to native peoples determined the future of Palestine's inhabitants. High power elite politics of the type that seems inconceivable in the twenty-first century allowed the Zionists important access to key individuals who in turn would largely determine the future of entire nations and regions of the globe (Smith, 2004: 84). The 'natural rights' of colonial statesmen to determine the future of Palestine was, however, resisted locally and led to an era of increasing resistance and drama as the unfolding of the Israeli– Palestinian conflict occurred.

Further reading

As noted in the introduction to this book 'writing the conflict' has generated pretty much an open war between academics themselves over the ways in which to record the history of the conflict, its roots, and the facts and the fictions that contribute to the many ways in which the conflict can be analysed in the present day. Offering recommendations for further reading is another site of contest and battle. If anyone sits down at a computer and 'Googles' recommended reading for the Israeli–Palestinian conflict they will see what I mean! This further reading section, then, is subject-specific in its recommendations but includes materials that are viewed, by one side or another, as provocative or just plain wrong!

Stories and analysis in the English language of late Ottoman society and politics in Palestine is largely framed by the scholarly writings of Israeli, Western and latterly Palestinian scholars. Such accounts have changed in tenor and analysis over the past 30 years. Writings from the 1970s are often quite different from those in the present day. This may be because the authors are using different sources, looking at different aspects of the organization of life in late Ottoman Palestine, or because within their studied 'neutrality' others discern degrees of bias or prejudice. Some of the work cited is deliberately designed to make a case for one perspective or another, others are a response or reaction to the absence of the 'stories' or 'history' of their own societies in the accounts of others. In terms of offering a general historical account of this period it is first worth looking at the late Albert Hourani's *History of the Arab people* and his chapters on the Ottoman period of reform (Cambridge, MA: Harvard University Press, 2003) because this eases the reader into the subject matter more generally. Along with Hourani's selected chapters other books that are worth consulting for this period include: Mark Tessler's book (Bloomington, IN: Indiana University Press, 1994), Pappe (Cambridge: Cambridge University Press, 2004) and Charles Smith (Boston, MA: Beford/St. Martins, 2004). These historical works detail the political as well as social and economic issues that prevailed in Palestine during this period. The account by journalist David Hirst (New York: Nation Books, 2003) is also a very useful introductory text to the period and the roots of the conflict and its linkages to the present day.

On the construction of Zionism a number of books are worth reading at this juncture and they include: Walter Laqueur's work helpfully entitled *A history of Zionism* (New York: Schocken, 2003). You can read Herzl's book on the Jewish state (New York: Filiquarian Publishing, 2006) along with some more controversial accounts of Zionism such as O'Brien's *The Siege* (London: Weidenfeld and Nicolson, 1986), John Rose's *Myths of Zionism* (London: Pluto Books, 2004) and Jacqueline Rose's *The question of Zion* (Princeton, NJ: Princeton University Press, 2005). Hertzberg's Reader on Zionism printed by the Jewish Publication Society of America provides documentation that addresses this early period in the Zionist movement (New York: Jewish Publication Society of America, 1997). Also Benny Morris's work entitled *Righteous victims: A history of the Zionist–Arab conflict* is worth considering (New York: Knopf, 2001a). It should be noted that the reviews of this book, and many of the others featured in the further reading section often question the political nature of the scholarship undertaken by the author. Further reading on Zionism can be found in Sacher (New York: Knopf, 1996), Sternhell (Princeton, NJ: Princeton University Press, 1998) and Vital (Oxford: Clarendon Press, 1982) though some of these books may be more difficult to acquire than others.

Some interesting counter-narratives and analyses on this period can be found in Said (London: Routledge and Kegan Paul, 1980) who rebuts many of the founding 'myths' of Zionism, Rashid Khalidi (New York: Columbia University Press, 1997) and Muslih (New York: Columbia University Press, 1988). Edward Said's work usually invokes the ire of the pro-Israel lobby who criticize his work almost in its entirety. Also worthy of further serious study is Walid Khalidi's edited collection entitled *From haven to conquest: Readings in Zionism and the Palestine problem until 1948* (Washington, DC: Institute of Palestine Studies, 1987). Finally two more books which are worth following up from this chapter are Kimmerling and Migdal (Cambridge, MA.: Harvard University Press, 2003), and Tom Segev (New York: Abacus Books, 2001) – who I'll recommend again in the following chapter. If you are looking to access Internet materials to supplement the books recommended in this section then there is a wide choice available. You should be aware, however, that most of the content mined from Google or Yahoo searches using key words such as Palestine-Israel, roots, conflict, etc., is highly partisan and should come with warnings to that effect. Most mainstream international media organizations also offer online timelines, background reading and information to the conflict but little in terms of the actual detail around the roots of the conflict covered in this chapter.

Hertzberg, A. (1997) *The Zionist Idea: A historical analysis and reader*, New York: Jewish Publication Society of America.

Herzl, T. (2006) *The Jewish State*, New York: Filiquarian Publishing.

Hirst, D. (2003) *The gun and the olive branch: The roots of violence in the Middle East*, 3rd edn, New York: Nation Books.

Hourani, A. (2003) *A history of the Arab people*, Cambridge, MA: Harvard University Press.

Khalidi, R. (1998) *Palestinian identity: The construction of modern national consciousness*, New York: Columbia University Press.

Khalidi, W. (1987) *From haven to conquest: Readings in Zionism and the Palestine problem until 1948*, Washington, DC: Institute of Palestine Studies.

Kimmerling, B. and Migdal, J.S. (2003) *The Palestinian people: A history*, Cambridge, MA: Harvard University Press.

Laqueur, W. (2003) *A history of Zionism: From the French revolution to the establishment of the state of Israel*, New York: Schocken.

Morris, B. (2001a) *Righteous victims: A history of the Zionist–Arab conflict, 1881–2001*, New York: Knopf.

Muslih, M. (1988) *The origins of Palestinian nationalism*, New York: Columbia University Press.

O'Brien, C.C. (1986) *The siege: The saga of Israel and Zion*, London: Weidenfeld and Nicolson.

Pappe, I. (2004) *A history of modern Palestine: One land, two peoples*, Cambridge: Cambridge University Press.

Rose, Jacqueline (2005) *The question of Zion*, Princeton, NJ: Princeton University Press.

Rose, John (2004) *The myths of Zionism*, London: Pluto Books.

Sacher H.M. (1996) *A history of Israel: From the rise of Zionism to our time*, 2nd edn, New York: Knopf.

Said, E. (1980) *The question of Palestine*, London: Routledge and Kegan Paul.

Segev, T. (2001) *One Palestine, complete: Jews and Arabs under the British*, New York: Abacus Books.

Smith, C.D. (2004) *Palestine and the Arab–Israeli conflict*, Boston, MA: Beford/St. Martins.

Sternhell, Z. (1998) *The founding myths of Israel: Nationalism, socialism, and the making of the Jewish State*. Translated by David Maisel. Princeton, NJ: Princeton University Press.

Tessler, M. (1994) *A history of the Arab–Israeli conflict*, Bloomington, IN: Indiana University Press.

Vital, D. (1982) *Zionism: The formative years*, Oxford: Clarendon Press.

2 Between the wars

Chapter outline

- The gloves are off: determining the future of Palestine   33
- The mandate   35
- Ascendance   39
- Prelude to revolt   40
- Sheikh, rattle and revolt   41
- The Palestinian revolt   43
- Resistance   45
- The Peel Commission: partition of Palestine   47
- The revolt and the Zionists   48
- End of an era   49
- World war and rethinking the mandate   51
- Further reading   52

At the end of the First World War in 1918 a series of peace conferences were held to determine the future of the territories that the Allied powers had won from the German and Axis powers. At these conferences the fate of millions of people were to be decided in a series of deals, compromises, agreements and treaties that created new states, new regimes, new political orders, new strategic and economic realities in the Middle East. After the war it was not difficult for Britain and France to persuade the members of the newly constituted international body of the League of Nations, in which they were the dominant powers, to give them authority over the former Ottoman territories in the Middle East that had fallen into their hands.

In this chapter the powerful governments and their policies – rather than the principle of the mandate system – that would, in reality, determine the future of Palestine will be examined. These new British and French regimes were known as mandates and protectorates. Britain obtained the Mandate for Palestine, plus the newly established states of Transjordan and Iraq. Britain then tried to persuade the Arabs to embrace the idea of a Jewish homeland in Palestine as underscored in the mandate of 1920. The incompatible promises made as a result of wartime expediency began to cause problems for the British.

The effects of the rise of Nazism in Hitler's Germany, new waves of Jewish immigration, and restive Palestinian nationalism leading to the outbreak of the 1936–39 Palestinian General Strike and Uprising will also be analysed in this chapter. British responses – including the Peel Commission of 1935 – and the context of Palestine during the Second World War 1939–45 will also be surveyed to highlight the growing difficulties with which Britain was faced not just from Palestinian nationalists but restive Jewish nationalists who grew to resent the British presence. 'Re-thinking the mandate' will be the theme with which the chapter concludes.

The gloves are off: determining the future of Palestine

In the wake of the First World War and territorial victories in the Middle East the British were a dominant power. This new dominance in Palestine presented the British with a dilemma – if it were to honour all of the promises it had made to the Arabs, the Zionists and other actors during the war. The British were compelled to face up to the contradictory promises they had made over Palestine. Despite attempts to keep some deals secret, by the end of the war the extent of Britain's promises to various parties had already been made public. Attempts to reassure the Arabs that the Balfour Declaration would not harm their political rights in respect of self-determination and independence largely turned out to be hollow words as the Great Powers convened at the peace conferences. Britain's goal was to preserve its own national interest even if it meant sacrificing the national interest of others and reneging on wartime promises. To a certain extent Britain achieved this goal in a series of secret meetings with the French even before the official peace conferences began. At the official 1919 Paris Peace Conference the Arabs were out-manoeuvred as the alliance between the British and the Zionists was also shored up. As Smith notes, 'the Zionist delegation to the peace Conference had submitted a memorandum to the British . . . asking that Palestine be acknowledged as the Jewish National Home under the aegis of Great Britain' (Smith, 2004: 79). Arab energies were dissipated in the struggle in negotiations to win their rights in other territories in the Middle East. Sharif Hussein's son and the leader of the Arab revolt, Faisal of Syria, for example, saw his throne in Damascus taken away from him. He was eventually offered British Mandate controlled Iraq as a consolation prize.

Moreover the British had to reconcile their desire for control in the Middle East with the American demand that principles of self-determination for the people of the region be truly respected. On the issue of Palestine, however, the British, and more specifically Balfour, were increasingly reluctant to concede that the rights of the native population should be paramount. By the time of the following peace conference in San Remo in 1920 it had been decided that the British and the French would be awarded mandate power in much of the Middle East including Palestine.

In the case of Palestine the British Mandate terms enshrined the promises outlined to the Zionists in the Balfour Declaration. Hence if the British had at any point wanted to renege on its promises to the Zionists, in the way that it did to the Arabs as far as Palestine was concerned, the drawing of the terms of the Mandate for Palestine would have been the opportunity to wriggle out. The British came under the concerted efforts of the Zionist movement at this time, however, to ensure that the mandate enshrined their aspirations. In advance of the conference the Zionists had mobilized themselves and formulated their demands. These demands were that:

> Palestine shall again become a Jewish commonwealth, and that world Jewry should have predominance in the government and administration of Palestine . . . that the Powers should nominate Great Britain as their representative . . . and should confer on it government of Palestine with a view to aiding the Jewish people.
>
> (Jannaway, n.d.: 157–58)

At the San Remo Peace Conference Zionist leader Weizmann was there in person to ensure that the British line on the Zionists did not waver and that the French could be persuaded to abandon their reluctance for the Zionist project (Reinharz, 1993: 317).

Balfour had been recruited to head up the Anglo-Zionist committee and by and large he was successful. The only division within the house of Zionism came when the British determined that the boundaries of Mandate Palestine (and hence the future Jewish national homeland) would stop at the frontier of the new British-inspired state of Transjordan headed by another of Sharif Hussein's sons Abdullah (Milton-Edwards and Hinchcliffe, 2001: 20). This led those who became known as the revisionist Zionists to breakaway. Instead the terms of the mandate ensured British protection and support for Zionist immigration to Palestine and its goals in terms of nation, territoriality and, some would argue, ultimately statehood, and kept the French out.

The organization of Palestinian Arab demands for their rights, the public meetings, protests, newspaper editorials, petitions and denunciations of the Balfour Declaration counted for very little if anything in British quarters during the peace conferences. Of course matters were not helped much by the fact that the British authorities in Palestine actually refused permission for a Palestinian delegation to travel to the Paris Peace Conference to present their case. The Palestinian Arabs then authorized King Faisal of Syria to argue their case in Paris for them.

Although Sharif Hussein's son, Faisal, had won Damascus for the Allies during the war, this did not, as he had hoped, guarantee him a place at the peace negotiations. Nevertheless he was determined to act as the agent for Arab rights. In early 1919 he submitted his outline for the future of the Middle East to the delegates at the Paris Peace Conference. He acknowledged that though the majority of Palestine's population was Arab, the future of the country might be assured under a trustee 'so long as a representative local administration commended itself by actively promoting the material prosperity of the country' (Black, 2004).

French intransigence and the absence of British support for Arab demands for independence hit a further setback when in March 1920 at the Second General Syria Congress the Arab nationalists declared independence in their own territories (including Palestine). At the San Remo Peace Conference a month later the British and French mandate system was arranged and earlier Arab declarations of independence simply ignored. King Faisal issued a protest to the peace conference and protests in the Middle East erupted at the news of the British and French Mandates. But the die had been cast against Faisal. By the middle of 1920 the French had issued an ultimatum to Faisal – to support France or else. On 24 July the French entered Damascus, Faisal was deposed and the French mandate system imposed by force. The symbol of Arab aspirations and rights to self-determination including that of the Palestinians had been thrown from his throne. Around the same time the British appointed 'declared Zionist Jew', Sir Herbert Samuel, as the new High Commissioner of Palestine (Kimmerling, 2001: 29). With his mandate to support the Jewish national home in Palestine things looked bleak in terms of Palestinian Arab aspirations and the early hopes of self-determination that they had had at the end of the war following the Turkish capitulation in the Middle East.

The mandate

The mandate system – formally approved by the League of Nations in 1922 – outlined that the British should foster and support the indigenous population to independence and freedom. It was agreed that the British would also 'fix the boundaries' of Palestine. The mandate made clear the following provisions:

> The Mandatory should be responsible for putting into effect the declaration originally made on November 2, 1917 . . . in favour of the establishment in Palestine of a national home for the Jewish people . . .
>
> . . . The Mandatory shall have full powers of legislation and administration . . .
>
> . . . The Mandatory shall be responsible for placing the country under such political, administrative and economic conditions as will secure the establishment of the Jewish National Home . . . and the development of self-governing institutions, and also for safeguarding the civil and religious rights of all the inhabitants of Palestine . . .
>
> . . . The Mandatory shall, so far as circumstances permit, encourage local autonomy . . .
>
> . . . An appropriate Jewish Agency shall be recognized as a public body for the purpose of advising and co-operating with the Administration of Palestine . . .
>
> The Administration of Palestine, while ensuring that the rights and position of other sections of the population are not prejudiced, shall facilitate

Jewish immigration . . . and shall encourage . . . close settlement by Jews on the land, including State lands and waste lands not required for public purposes.

(AACI, 1946: 36–37)

There was much in the text of the mandate that would give succour to the Zionists and little to the Palestinian Arabs. By 1920 the British had moved from military to civil administration in Palestine, Herbert Samuel the first British High Commissioner was ensconced in Jerusalem and a real battle for influence between the Palestinian Arabs and the Zionists broke out in earnest. The sympathies of the British have been described as pro-Zionist at this time though it has to be said that there were many local officers of the mandate who were either pro-Palestinian, or anti-Semitic. Moreover the private sympathies of the Mandate officials were tempered by the public tactic of diplomatically coercing the Palestinian Arab elite into their hands and of playing the ultimate game of British colonial policy: divide and rule. The terms of the mandate gave the British decisive authority over the affairs of Palestine.

The British set about the usual colonial tasks of developing the country: organizing a survey of the land, setting boundaries, creating administrative structures, engaging in infrastructure projects, organizing a civil service employing members of the local population, promoting law and order through the establishment of its own Mandate police force and seeking to replicate the British way of doing things. In many respects it would have been difficult to distinguish between a mandate and full-blown colonialism. Such tasks, of course, were often undertaken at the expense of the local population who viewed such changes with deep-seated and ultimately well-founded suspicions. The British may have contributed to the inception and building of aqueducts, sanitation, roads, education, irrigation and public health but they did not herald an era of peace, harmony and public order among its inhabitants. They failed to realize that the Palestinian Arabs would not be so easily pacified and nor later that they could halt the inexorable rise of Zionism, which was largely abetted by rapidly increasing levels of Jewish immigration. The majority Palestinian Arab population was faced with the task of having to resist a foreign authority ruling their territories and facilitating the immigration of other foreigners engaged in a settlement project.

As noted in the previous chapter the formation of a Palestinian Arab leadership and national consciousness-raising had been, in many ways, congruent with the rising force of Zionism and the impact of Zionist settlement in Palestine. The advent of British rule through the mandate left the nascent Palestinian national movement with a formidable task. Its leaders – mostly from the notable classes – were ill-prepared for the organization of national resistance and were susceptible to British machinations. Moreover they faced a dual struggle: against the British colonial occupier and the Zionist settler movement. Both were intent on denying the Palestinian people their right to self-determination and independence in their own lands. Khalidi also argues that it was during this period that 'the sense of political and national identification of most politically conscious, literate, and urban

Palestinians underwent a sequence of major transformations. The end result was a strong and growing national identification with Palestine' (Khalidi, 1997: 149).

The Palestinian elite was presented with the challenge of needing to be part of the system of the British Mandate while opposing its positions on the Palestinian people and the irreconcilable promises to the Zionists contained in the mandate. The British, in turn, sought to exert their control over the local elite of families such as the Husseini, Nashashibi and Khalidi. What emerged from this control was a series of internal tensions between and among the notables as the British tended to favour one family, in terms of allocating so-called positions of power, over others. The one family the British tended to favour over others were the Husseini family from Jerusalem. Their leading males were appointed by the British into positions and posts such as Mufti of Jerusalem and head of the British-established Supreme Muslim Council. In this way local power networks based on family and the all-important faith of Islam tended to bend to the British viewpoint. The British, in turn, saw the creation of such posts and institutions as a necessary balance to the burgeoning Zionist movement and its growing strength within Palestine. From these tensions and rivalries emerged opposition elements, groupings, factions and small political parties who vied with each other in working against and resisting the threat so explicit to the Palestinians that was posed by the Zionists and their British supporters.

The British were only prepared to let the Palestinians participate in governance if it was alongside the Zionists. In the early years of the mandate this arrangement was largely viewed in Palestinian circles as unacceptable and unworkable but in the late 1920s they ceded the principle of power-sharing with the Zionists. This climb down occurred because of a growing sense of impotency and frustration at the realities of the mandate structure which included – at this stage – largely unrestricted Jewish immigration and settlement in Palestine. In fact during the 1920s nearly 100,000 Jews entered Palestine and, according to British statistics at the time, registered as immigrants. There was also a growing sense that Palestinians were literally losing grip on their society, their lands and thus their status, power and economic prosperity.

Places of worships, holy sites and shrines became the focus of identity for both Jews and Palestinian Muslims, as epitomized in 1929 at sites in both Jerusalem and Hebron. In Jerusalem's Old City the proximity of the most holy place in Judaism (the Western Wall) to one of the most holy sites in Islam (Haram al-Sharif the al-Aqsa mosque and Dome of the Rock) became the focus of rising tensions which culminated in the 'Western Wall riots' in 1929. By the summer of 1929 a long-running dispute between Jews and Muslims over the site, its access and use escalated and finally erupted into violent demonstrations and riots, which spread from Jerusalem to other towns in Palestine. The violence in Jerusalem and Hebron resulted in the deaths of hundreds and appeared to further deepen the chasm between now opposing faith communities – while each struggled against the other in an assertion of supreme and ultimate identity. Some 133 Jews and 116 Arabs were killed as each side fought with the other and the British tried to intervene to restore law and order.

In Hebron, where the Jewish community had resided, the Arab violence led to more than 60 Jews being murdered and the rest of the community leaving the city in the wake of the riot. In 2006 when descendents of Jewish survivors of the Hebron riots of 1929 met in the city to commemorate the events they remained divided over its future. Some argued that the Jewish presence should be maintained in Hebron at any cost to the local Palestinian community while another descendent maintained, 'I'm not saying what happened here [in 1929] was right . . . I'm saying that one wrong doesn't justify another' (Lazaroff, 2006: 3). Today the Jewish settlement of the Old City of Hebron is often explained in terms of the symbolic right to seek restitution after the killings of the Jewish inhabitants and the evacuation of survivors of the city in 1929.

External intervention – commissions of inquiry, international committees and rulings from the Mandate authorities – only seemed to worsen the situation. In the wake of the 1929 violence, for example, the British authorities drew up a series of highly complicated rules and regulations regarding the holy places and areas around the Haram al-Sharif and the Western Wall that satisfied neither party keen to assert their rights to worship in Jerusalem, the holy city.

What the British failed to grasp from such incidents was that the potent mix of politics and faith was espoused in the new nationalisms of the Zionists and the Palestinians; their employment of the symbols of faith in their political programmes was bound to disrupt the relative harmony that had previously existed in terms of religious tolerance of faith communities in Palestine. The British were as responsible as any other party for this state of affairs. They too used religion as a political tool for control and the extension of power for their own interests. They used their own faith as justification for embarking on a project in support of Zionism and they used other faiths and invented posts and positions within them to manipulate local elements. Nevertheless, as one author notes, the 'riots marked a decisive turning point in the history of Palestine: the end of any realistic hope of Arab-Jewish peace under the British mandate' (Wasserstein, 2001: 327). A growing sense of estrangement and hostility marked Palestinian Arab and Zionist relations. Neither side trusted the other and the idea that the two sides could work together, govern and live together in one sovereign state became increasingly untenable.

Relations would only worsen when, in the wake of the 1929 violence, two subsequent commissions suggested immigration controls to stem the land sales leading to dispossession of the Palestinian peasant class and address their disbarring by the Jewish colonies and other enterprises from local employment. The Commission of Inquiry into the violence of 1929 – the Shaw Report – blamed the Arabs for the violence but recommended that the British government rethink its policies on Jewish immigration and land sales to Jews. This directly resulted in the convening in 1930 of the Hope Simpson Royal Commission, which also recommended imposing limits on Jewish immigration to Palestine amid practical concerns regarding territorial absorption in rural and agricultural areas. Zionist fury at British government proposals to act on such recommendations led to a pretty rapid climbdown from the British and further disappointment for the Palestinians. Clearly Zionist pressure was winning the day.

Ascendance

For the Palestinian Arab leadership of Palestine the first decade of the British Mandate (1920–30) appeared to bring little by way of political autonomy or cohesion as a unified national group. The same was not true for the Zionists. By the late 1920s the Zionists had succeeded in the organization of successive waves of immigration and settlement to Palestine, designed to further the sole goal of Jewish statehood or 'commonwealth' in the Holy Land. The dynamic political leadership of the Zionist movement in Palestine and the Diaspora ensured that the political momentum created in the establishment of the British Mandate was maintained.

The new settlements and communities became a focus for the fashioning of a new national identity for the Jewish people in Palestine that was forged on exclusive notions. In the absence of a state the Zionists were creating organizations and structures that would mirror state provision. Education, language, employment, community life, culture, economy and politics were fashioned in terms of the new identity. As Pappe notes:

> Their greatest success was in extracting the Zionist community from the colonial state in significant spheres of life, to the extent that even non-Zionist Jewish sections, such as the ultra-orthodox Jews, were subject to the Zionist leadership's executive and legislative bodies.
>
> (Pappe, 2004: 88)

It has been noted that the Palestinians under the PLO in both Jordan in the late 1960s and Lebanon in the 1970s also acted as a state within a state in terms of building infrastructures and institutions for the people it represented. Perceived as a threat to the command and control of the state such activities were barely tolerated. The Zionist leadership of Palestine in the 1920s did, however, succeed in building its own institutions and services in preparation for statehood. It established autonomy and independence (including its own coercive and paramilitary forces – Haganah) not only from the existing indigenous community and the British authorities as well but increasingly from the Zionist organizations of the Diaspora who ultimately became handmaidens to the centralizing tendencies of the Zionist leadership in Palestine.

This Zionist organization of the 'state in the making' as Kimmerling refers to it provided sustenance to the vision of Zionism as a nation state for the Jewish people (Kimmerling, 2001). It would be propelled by ideological rhetoric rooted in the European movements of socialism and organized labour and would ultimately act as the foundation stone of the state of Israel when it was established in 1948. Internal rivalries within the Zionist movement existed. As Pappe highlights 'four major ideological interpretations of Zionism' vied with each other to lead the movement but the most significant of these actors was 'the Labour movement, followed by the more socialist Hashomer Hazair, the religious national Mizrahi movement and finally the right-wing revisionists' (Pappe, 2004: 90). Reconciling idealized notions of the Jewish utopia in Palestine with the reality of an already present indigenous population with an alternative culture, history, language and national identity would prove to be an obstacle that the Zionists sought a number of ways and means to overcome (Masalha, 1992).

By 1930, in the wake of growing tensions and violence as Palestinian Arabs opposed the Zionist expansion in their land, Zionist leader, Chaim Weizmann, who would later become the first president of Israel, 'actively began promoting ideas for Arab transfer' among British officials (Masalha, 1992: 34). Although the British appeared to be prepared to give such schemes a hearing they did not sanction such proposals. Indeed, as previously noted, the 1930 Hope Simpson Commission resulting in the Passfield White Paper issued by the government in the wake of the 1929 riot, proposed limiting Jewish immigration rather than Arab transfer. Such decision-making led to a further hardening of attitudes within the Zionist movement in their dealings with the British authorities. Some Zionists came to perceive the British as becoming pro-Arab and thus anti-Zionist. In this conflict there would be no place for neutrality, fence-sitting or the middle road as the enmity between the Zionists and the Palestinians grew.

Prelude to revolt

If the Zionists had believed, in the wake of the 1930 Passfield White Paper, that the British government had begun to waver in their support for them, they recovered their position when they achieved a climb-down over immigration cuts from the British government led by Ramsey MacDonald. In 1931 MacDonald wrote a letter to Chaim Weizmann denying the intention of the British government (despite the Passfield White Paper) to limit Jewish immigration to Palestine. MacDonald stated that, 'His Majesty's Government did not prescribe and do not contemplate any stoppage or prohibition of Jewish immigration in any of its categories'. Segev argues that:

> [there] is no rational explanation for this stunning turn of events. The government's panicked retreat from Passfield's White Paper reflected fear. MacDonald had been intimidated by the Jews . . . The world economic crisis required special caution; who wanted at this juncture to get in trouble with 'world Jewry'?
>
> (Segev, 2001: 337)

For Palestinians it was as though the tide was turning inexorably against them. Their strategies of 'gentlemanly' politics were simply failing to persuade the British government of their arguments, their leadership was increasingly ineffective in terms of influencing the British and popular support for them began to wane. In the rural communities of Palestine the harsh realities of the failures of the Palestinian leadership were being experienced as more land was being lost to Jewish sale, more peasants were dispossessed and the certainties of the old way of life were disrupted by the introduction of new taxes and plans by the Mandate authorities for agricultural reform and development. New voices were raised in protest against the notable and established leadership.

A new regime of economic inequality undoubtedly penalized the Palestinian Arabs and favoured Jewish workers. In the rural economy incomes declined, indebtedness increased, taxes were imposed, peasants were forced to migrate into poorly paid work in the cities and even in those poorly paid jobs their earnings were comparably lower than those of Jewish workers. It has been noted that: 'Clearly then, Jewish immigration and the transformation of the Palestinian economy from an essentially Arab agricultural economy to an industrial economy dominated by Jewish capital, affected primarily the small Palestinian Arab peasants' (Kanafani, 1972). Sheer despair and impoverishment propelled the peasant and working classes of Palestine to revolt at an unjust regime and its practices of supporting Zionist goals irrespective of their effects on the indigenous population.

The Palestinian Arab political landscape was also changed. In part the changes could be accounted for by the failure of the traditional notable and established leadership to win major concessions. Another reason for change lay with the rise of a younger generation of nationalists (many of whom were drawn from the old notable and established classes), who were critical of the old leadership and its methods. These new leaders promoted an agenda of militant and active opposition to both the Zionists and the British authorities. They objected to the mandate structures and their biases against the indigenous population, and called for its termination. They wanted Palestinian self-determination and self-government, not British rule and a Zionist state within a state. These radical elements motivated the public to action by organizing new political parties and groupings such as the National Defence Party, the Palestine Arab Party, the Communists, the Youth Congress, the Reform Party, Young Men's Muslim Association, the Independence Party, and the National Bloc Party. Their initiatives and proposed activities were not always warmly received from within the Palestinian fold. Many elements from the notable class, who by that time had been co-opted into the structure of the mandate and held salaried posts and positions, sought to head off such discontent. One area where opposition grew from within, however, was among the Muslim religious figures and leaders.

Sheikh, rattle and revolt

The key players in this powerful mix of faith and politics were Muslim and represented both establishment Islam, epitomized by the Mufti of Jerusalem, Hajj Amin al-Husseini, and the politics of oppositional Islam, led by a populist Syrian Sheikh called Izz-a-din al-Qassam (Milton-Edwards, 1999). Sheikh al-Qassam had arrived in Palestine in the early 1920s and preached among the urban poor and peasant peoples of northern Palestine. Sheikh al-Qassam and his supporters preached a message of Muslim resurgence and identity, re-asserted in the face of opposition from the British and the Zionists. Al-Qassam believed that through the framework of Islam, Palestinian opposition could be effectively mustered into direct action and resistance against those who sought to dispossess the people. Al-Qassam believed in the same message as that of the Islamic reform movement based in Egypt in the 1920s and led by figures such as Mohammed Abduh and his disciple, Rashid al-Rida. Al-Rida, as noted in Chapter 1, was vehemently opposed to the Zionist project in Palestine and called for Muslims to rally in defence of its Muslim inhabitants. Sheikh al-Qassam had already been involved in the Syrian revolt against the French in 1921 and had been sentenced to death by the authorities there *in absentia*. Once in Palestine he organized his activities in a form of outreach – teaching the rural and urban poor to read, teaching the Koran, and running evening classes. In Haifa the Sheikh was involved in the Young Men's Muslim Association (YMMA) and he became one of its more prominent members.

By 1929 Sheikh al-Qassam had been appointed to the post of marriage registrar by the Shari'a court in Haifa, was head of the YMMA and had become a popular preacher in the al-Istiklal mosque in Haifa. The appointment as marriage registrar provided ample opportunity for the Sheikh to travel around the surrounding countryside and form a series of important relations with local Palestinian Arab communities. His work among the rural poor included a project to establish agricultural cooperatives as well as the literacy programmes that he ran in Haifa. Through the platform of both his official role as marriage registrar and his unofficial role of social activist, Sheikh al-Qassam also promoted his religious perspective. His reformist beliefs led him to complain locally of the dissipation of the faith through what he referred to as 'folkish practices'. Although he had grown up in a Sufi Muslim family he did not believe that the faith structure of Palestine at the time was best served by what he considered to be improper faith practices. Instead he believed that the recovery of Muslim Palestinian identity would be achieved through what might today be termed as a form of striving or jihad.

Sheikh al-Qassam was also reputedly different from other Muslim leaders associated with establishment Islam at the time and led by the notable families of Jerusalem because he did not distinguish himself or his lifestyle from the people he worked among. This was quite different from the studied aloofness of the Mufti of Jerusalem and leader of the Supreme Muslim Council, Hajj Amin al-Husseini. As a leading member of one of the more notable families in Palestine and salaried high ranker of the Mandate authorities, Hajj Amin's status dictated distance rather than familiarity. Sheikh al-Qassam, on the other hand, was an outsider and although from a notable clerical family in Syria was renowned for living simply in Palestine.

The notion of striving to achieve the purest practice of Islam, to defend it, its adherents and its holy territories (waqf) was espoused by al-Qassam. This form of striving is known in Islam as jihad (Milton-Edwards, 1992). Sheikh al-Qassam preached the message of jihad as a form of resistance against the British Mandate authorities and the Zionist settlements of Palestinian lands. From his experiences in his native Syria he knew that foreign occupation and foreign settlement would not deliver the Arabs their rights but only deny them. This was the message he brought to Palestine and made public in his sermons and other public speeches. Such political postures and hostility brought him to the attention of the authorities and his Zionist opponents.

News reports, memoirs, memorandums and accounts from the period indicate that at some point in 1935 Sheikh al-Qassam decided to combine his arguments and sermons for resistance into actual armed action. With a small group of supporters Sheikh al-Qassam took to the hills and villages of northern Palestine in readiness to launch a series of attacks on their enemies. Such attacks culminated in a shoot-out between al-Qassam and the British police in November 1935. Al-Qassam was killed by British bullets and news of his death galvanized the Palestinian masses. His death was not much remarked on by the British but as news spread across Palestine demonstrations and protest broke out. At his funeral in Haifa thousands of people mourned his loss and proclaimed him as a new symbol of Palestinian resistance. British High Commissioner, Sir Arthur Wauchope, remarked that:

> One day it might be that every Palestinian would become as one of those who were killed a few days ago near Jenin [Sheikh al-Qassam]. A sense of hopelessness was widespread throughout the country and this feeling has been expressed by different symptoms.
>
> (Wauchope, 1935)

In the wake of al-Qassam's death small armed groups sprung up in his name, in prelude to the larger revolt that broke out some months later in 1936. In death Al-Qassam had become a symbol of national resistance for all Palestinians – irrespective of their ideological hue. He had challenged the traditional Muslim leadership of Palestine; he had preached a message of resistance and steadfastness to the dispossessed and the poor in echo to the loss of their rights and independence. He had shown up the failings and weaknesses of the traditional leadership and left them undermined by their own failure to understand that the peasant and newly urban Palestinian Arab classes of Palestine wanted action and a meaningful challenge to the events that were taking place around them. His legacy found almost instant expression in the outbreak of the revolt and up until the present day he is a symbol of resistance and jihad in the Palestinian milieu. The Palestinian Islamic resistance movement Hamas has named not only their armed wing in his honour – the Izz-a-din al-Qassam Brigades – but their missiles, which they fire on Israel, are also called 'al-Qassams'.

Was al-Qassam's death at the hands of the British the spark for the revolt? Some historians and myth-makers of the period claim it was so. Others believe that different factors account for the outbreak of violence that spread through Palestine from 1936 onwards.

The Palestinian revolt

In April 1936 a band of al-Qassam's armed followers launched an ambush and killed two Jews. In retaliation the Jewish resistance (Haganah) attacked and killed two Palestinian Arabs. Then in the coastal city of Jaffa tensions rose to fever pitch as sporadic violence between Palestinian Arabs and Jews broke out and the British, fighting to maintain control, declared a state of emergency. Later that month

Palestinian leaders called for a general strike and all sectors of society banded together in solidarity to protest against British measures and Zionist encroachment. Political impulses were quickly harnessed by the local elite in the establishment of the Arab Higher Committee (AHC), led by Hajj Amin al-Husseini, 'who although appointed and beholden to the British authorities, had no alternative but to join the militants' (Farsoun with Zacharia, 1997: 106). The AHC issued a series of well-rehearsed demands: cessation of Jewish immigration to Palestine, an end to land sales to the Zionists and the foundation of a Palestinian Arab government. None of these demands was new but the context in which they were made was. It appeared that the ordinary Palestinian Arab people had had enough. Their livelihoods, their society, their structures of power, their sense of place, space and dimension were all under threat and a collective sense of despair now propelled people into action.

At first the revolt was not really a revolt. The main expression of discontent was the general strike. Palestinian businesses and shops were closed. Trade unions organized Palestinian labour in support of the strike and the Palestinian economic sector as a whole was deeply affected by the action. Violence also continued to mark relations between the Palestinian Arabs, the Jews and the British. The strike lasted six months but was then replaced with a widespread violent revolt or uprising that lasted until 1939.

The revolt consisted of armed Palestinian militants who launched attacks against both British and Jewish targets. The militants enjoyed widespread popular support. Their grievances were as deeply held against the British as the Zionists. They held the British responsible for allowing the Zionists to pursue their goals in Palestine with little regard for the indigenous population. They were increasingly incensed at the British unwillingness to limit Jewish immigration or land sales. It appeared that no matter how many ways and how many times they got their leaders to pressure the British nothing happened to stop the influx of Jews into the ports of Haifa and Jaffa. Every month brought more and more immigrants and by the early 1930s there was a significant increase in Jewish arrivals to the country as the spectre of Nazism and Fascism loomed over Europe. Official statistics were recorded detailing the fact that 367,845 Jews immigrated legally between 1920 and 1945. It was also estimated that an additional 50,000–60,000 Jews immigrated illegally during this period. Immigration accounted for the rapid increase of the Jewish population.

The revolt developed a cyclical character defined by periods of intense violence followed by increasingly severe repression from the British authorities and retaliation by the Jewish militants of the Haganah and Irgun. Attacks were sectarian and indiscriminate in nature: if someone looked like a Jew, worked in a Jewish occupation or lived in a Jewish settlement then they were a potential target. The same reasoning was visited on the house of the Palestinian Arabs in revenge for Jewish losses:

> These outrageous incidents triggered off Jewish reprisals committed by the Irgun which were no less murderous. Bombs were planted in the Arab

market-places of Jerusalem and Haifa and passengers on the roads were indiscriminately attacked. These Irgun reprisals further incited the Arab bands to attack Jews and drove more moderate elements to their fold, a fact from which the leaders of the Arab terror derived much satisfaction.

(Porath, 1977: 238)

The British authorities failed to anticipate that the Palestinians would respond with fury at the events around them and then rise in rebellion at their subordination. One leader of the rebellion is quoted as saying:

> We felt we had to do something to force the British the change their policy, otherwise we would lose Palestine to the Zionists. So we decided on the General Strike. It was a great step for us and daunting to take on the British Empire, can you imagine? But we believed that the strike would bring about a peaceful revolution. That with every single person on strike in Palestine it must lead to that. So we called for an indefinite strike until the British changed their policy.
>
> (Dimbleby and McCullin, 1979: 67)

The British authorities quickly lost control of public order and also became targets of the rebels. Their posts, patrols and police stations sustained attacks by the rebels. Their soldiers and police officers were killed or injured and their attempts to manipulate those Palestinian notables in their pay failed. There seemed to be only one option open to them: repression and suppression. Surely, the British must have figured, if these tactics had worked in their other domains (Iraq, Ireland and India) then they would stand a good chance of asserting their authority over the rebellious Palestinians? Strong counter-insurgency tactics became the order of the day and included: curfews, house demolitions, extending the state of emergency, military trials, executions, mass arrests and the deportation of much of the Palestinian national leadership abroad to Egypt and the Seychelles. The British also organized their own 'special' forces in the attempt to quell the revolt. The squads, consisting of British soldiers and partisan Jewish recruits, gained an unpopular reputation for their 'gang' attacks (Bowden, 1977).

Resistance

From 1936–39, in both rural and urban areas, Palestinian Arabs took up arms and engaged in acts of violence as a means of advancing their political demands on the British authorities. The rural–urban divide appeared to melt as the peasant class and the newly urban working classes of Palestine engaged in their fight. Men were often motivated to join the rebellion and lead armed groups or cells because they had experienced directly the effects of being dispossessed through land sales to the Zionists. Such people were compelled to turn their backs on their former livelihoods, their life and family structure in the village and to seek work in the docks and burgeoning industries around Haifa that would permit employment for

Arabs. Other activists sought to resist the British through their participation and agitation in the newly formed Arab Higher Committee led by Hajj Amin al-Husseini.

As noted earlier, Hajj Amin al-Husseini, although in the pay of the British and an appointee of some status through their patronage, had been compelled into a leading role once it became apparent to the notable classes of Palestine that the revolt was widely supported among the Palestinian Arab masses. Hajj Amin and his supporters, however, though initially believing they could harness and direct the ire and energies of the people, quickly discovered that the malleability of the general population was no longer guaranteed. Members and activists of the Palestinian Communist Party, for example, used their leadership positions within the command structure of the revolt to agitate not only against the British but their own traditional leadership too. Such populist elements also worked in the local areas and regions of Palestine to form popular committees for the rebellion or uprising. The organization of the popular committees empowered new elements within Palestinian society and were part of an internal challenge. It was the popular committees, for example, that not only reiterated the basic demands of the uprising but in an act of civil disobedience designed to deny legitimacy to the British authorities declared a boycott of the British courts and the setting up of alternative people's courts and judicial structures.

It is fair to say, and with some irony, that resisting the Zionist settlement enterprise was not the immediate priority of those engaged in the Palestinian revolt of 1936–39. This is not to say that Jewish targets did not fall into Palestinian sights but rather that the Zionist movement per se was not the sole target of Palestinian antipathies as stated in the demands of the leadership of the uprising. It was the failure of the British authorities to stop the Zionists that drew the deep-seated resentment of the Palestinians. Of course, the armed bands attacked the new Jewish enterprises where former Palestinian farming and other settlements had previously existed and indiscriminate tit-for-tat killings became an increasingly regular occurrence. But the Palestinian political leadership and their followers persisted in believing it was the British who were key to their misfortunes and disempowerment.

As the spiral of violence intensified, the British responded with increased state force and coercion. But for all their expressions of coercive power – the mass arrests, the internment camps, house demolitions, deportations, military trials, mass leafleting and brute force – they were still initially unable to restore order in Palestine. By September 1936 the British government sent a further 20,000 soldiers to supplement the pre-existing British presence in a further attempt to quell the rebellion. In the following months these well-equipped, well-trained and highly experienced troops arrived in Palestine to put down the native insurgents. The Palestinian armed rebels remained undeterred but the death tolls rose on all sides. The British introduced another strategy for resolving the conflict: they proposed a new commission.

The Peel Commission: partition of Palestine

The prospect of yet another British government commission in Palestine would have alarmed rather than reassured the Palestinians. One cause of their growing ire and frustration in the early 1930s had been the fact that, despite the recommendations of the commission formed in the wake of the 1929 riots to limit lands sales and immigration to the Jews and take account of the rights of the Palestinians, the Labour Prime Minister of the day had written a letter to Zionist leaders, in the wake of the commission, promising to support the Zionist enterprise including discriminatory labour practices, land sales and immigration. This support is epitomized on the issue of the Histadrut policy of exclusive Jewish employment rights. In his letter the Prime Minister declares:

> in all the works or undertakings carried out or furthered by the [Jewish] Agency it shall be deemed to be a matter of principle that Jewish labour shall be employed . . . The principle of preferential, or indeed exclusive, employment of Jewish labour by Jewish organisations is a principle which the Jewish Agency are entitled to affirm.
>
> (Laqueur and Rubin, 2001: 41)

The letter clearly endorsed racially discriminatory labour practices against the Arabs.

The Commission, which was officially entitled the Palestine Royal Commission, was supposed to inquire into the cause of the Palestinian rebellion and was headed by Lord Peel. Peel arrived in Palestine, resplendent in his top hat and tails and a fresh flower in his buttonhole, to review the prevailing situation of chaos and disorder, at the same time that more troops were being dispatched from London. How this colonial figure must have jarred against the impoverished landscape of Palestine and the paltry attire and equipment of the rebels. Representatives from both sides of the Zionist–Arab divide were called to give testimony – the Zionists responded with alacrity to the opportunity while the Arabs officially boycotted the commission and merely publicly repeated their demands for a halt to immigration, an end to land sales and independence for the Palestinians. Peel's report was issued in July 1937. He called for a termination of the mandate and the partition of Palestine between the Jewish and Arab population in pursuance of the establishment of two independent states, including territorial exchanges and population transfer.

The text of the report succinctly summed up the situation:

> After examining this and other evidence and studying the course of events in Palestine since the War, we have no doubt as to what were 'the underlying causes of the disturbances' of last year. They were:
>
> The desire of the Arabs for national independence
> Their hatred and fear of the establishment of the Jewish National Home.

An irrepressible conflict has arisen between two national communities within the narrow bounds of one small country . . . There is no common ground between them. National assimilation between Arabs and Jews is thus ruled out . . . neither Arab nor Jew has any sense of service to a single State.

(Verdery, 1971: 298; Laqueur and Rubin, 2001: 42–43)

Partition is supposed to be a solution to conflict, a means of ending a conflict by divorcing people from each other through territorial separation while still maintaining respect for the principle of self-determination. The method of partition can vary and in the case of Peel's proposal what we see is not an agreement by parties to territorial separation, or the ceding of territory by a core state to a minority group but the dismemberment of territory through imposed external decision. The Palestinian Arabs of Palestine were not secessionists seeking divorce through statehood but simply demanding their rights to self-determination over the whole of their territory. Their wishes and rights, in this instance, were clearly ignored. Peel was proposing to solve a British-created problem in Palestine by ceding Palestinian territory to the Zionists. Palestinian Arabs were being asked to envision future independence but without the territorial integrity of statehood on the lands that they had lived on for hundreds of years.

Hearing the news of the partition proposal the Arab leadership immediately rejected the Peel recommendations for the formal dispossession of their land and denial of statehood in all of Palestine. The response of the Zionists was more equivocal – some perceived it as an opportunity and others did not. The man who was to become first Prime Minster of Israel, David Ben Gurion, wrote in his diaries of the Peel proposals:

The compulsory transfer of the Arabs from the valleys of the proposed Jewish state could give us something which we have never had . . . We are being given an opportunity which we never dared to dream of in our wildest imagination.

(Teveth, 1985: 180)

The Peel report only served to intensify the Arab revolt and this was further exacerbated a year later in the wake of the British government's formal response to the proposals for partition. By this point the balance of influence had firmly tipped in favour of the Zionists and against the Palestinian leaders of the national movement in terms of the British Mandate and any form of relationship with the Palestinian parties in Palestine.

The revolt and the Zionists

During the period of the revolt, events in both Palestine and abroad served to alter the relationship between the British authorities and the Zionist movement. Within Palestine the dual threat posed by the revolt to British and Zionist interests and ambition forged an alliance that centred on security cooperation and intelligence sharing. This proved to be an important relationship in terms of undermining Palestinian unity. The Zionists served British interests in terms of 'provid[ing] the [British] army with intelligence reports and situation evaluations, and . . . This cooperation dwarfs almost to insignificance any claims that the military administration acted in opposition to Zionist concerns; the mutual intelligence work was directed against Arab national interests' (Segev, 2001: 429–32). Moreover, the Haganah trained and served with British units and squads (the Special Night Squads) that were formed with a specific counter-insurgency brief. The lessons acquired under the stewardship of British officers such as Orde Wingate, whom the Haganah nicknamed *hayedid* (friend), were often brutal and would contravene accepted laws and norms regarding civil rights both at the time and today. It has been remarked that, 'the Haganah's best officers were trained in the night squads, and Wingate's doctrines were taken over by the Israeli Defence Force', formed after Israel's independence in 1948 (Segev, 2001: 432). The spiral of viciousness and increasing lack of respect for basic human values that should have kept civilians out of the burgeoning conflict simply increased.

By 1938 the Palestinians had turned their ire on Jewish civilian targets as well as the soldiers of the Mandate and the Jewish paramilitary forces. Every day more and more ordinary people, on both sides of the divide, were being caught up in the conflict. Unarmed Palestinian villagers were subjected to the brutal tactics of the British forces while at the same time Jewish civilians in towns like Tiberias were killed by the Palestinian armed elements. The political control and restraint that had been exercised over the Palestinians in the early months and years of the revolt by the notable leadership, political parties and committees had been forcefully exterminated by the British policy:

> [of] arrest and detention by administrative order of some two to three hundred notables . . . those . . . who could be found were arrested in their beds and deported to the Seychelles . . . those who were abroad were forbidden to return to Palestine . . . Disorder [is] reported throughout the country.
>
> (Barbour, 1946: 190)

A Rubicon had been crossed and, although there were acts of individual kindness, protection and friendships sustained through times of trouble, a true sense of enmity began to spring up between the Jews and Palestinian Arabs. Although the initial target of the revolt had been the British authorities and their policies in Palestine, the dynamic of the revolt and the way in which it drew in the Zionists and altered the face of leadership within the Palestinian Arab community meant that Zionists became direct targets of Palestinian resistance, violence and loathing. The Zionists were no longer buffered by the British authorities.

End of an era

By the closing months of 1938 the Palestinian revolt was in decline. The armed gangs that roamed the highways and byways of the countryside were as often engaged in attacks and struggles with each other as they were in the 'jihad' against the British. In the absence of a strong national leadership the ideals and momentum of the revolt was being lost to personal greed and ambition. Nevertheless the British were forced to concede that in areas such as Gaza and Beersheba 'villages [are] under control of local rebel leaders and visiting gangsters . . . there are no British officials' (Colonial Office, CO733/1939). Rivalries among the Palestinians were still exploited by the British but not to the extent that divide and rule policies could recover the situation as a whole. There seemed to be little in terms of the British–Palestinian Arab relationship to recover. As a result of its own policies the British had denied legitimacy to any faction of the Palestinian leadership – including their own appointed Mufti and head of the Supreme Muslim Council, who by 1937 they had forced into exile and stripped of all official office. Despite the dissipation of the revolt the British re-assessed policy in Palestine once again. This led to the outlining of the 1939 White Paper.

The British government's 1939 White Paper went some way in reversing 'its previous policy and responded to Palestinian concerns' (Farsoun with Zacharia, 1997: 107). Whether this can be regarded as a major achievement of the revolt is difficult to tell but the British did at last appear to be taking seriously the long-standing concerns of the Palestinians in relation to their rights as indigenous people. The White Paper put aside partition as a form of solution to the troubles in Palestine. Instead the British proposed self-rule tied by treaty to London. This was an option popular in British-ruled Transjordan and Iraq. On the thorny issue of immigration the British outlined an immigration quota of 75,000 per annum and the inauguration of an Arab consent mechanism for further Jewish immigration. Land sales, moreover, would also be subject to new restrictions.

Neither the Arab nor Zionist leadership was prepared to embrace the proposals outlined in the 1939 White Paper. The Zionists had to contend with the consequences of a five-year limit on immigration to Palestine. The Palestinians had, once again, to contend with a denial of their right to independence from an occupying power. In sum the White Paper failed to resolve anything. It may well have been the end of an era in terms of Britain's future in Palestine and its relationships with both sides to the conflict but Palestinian hopes and aspirations remained on a collision course with the Zionist plan for statehood in Palestine.

The interwar period from 1918–39 had succeeded in both uniting the Palestinian Arabs in terms of national identity and fracturing this identity in ways which still characterize it in the present day. The motif of unity, resistance, factionalism and steadfastness forged by the rebel bands and leaders, peasant farmers, urban workers and notable national leadership has been woven into the tapestry of Palestinian identity. For the Zionists:

> [they] emerged from the revolt fortified and more determined than before. More than anything else their leaders were mesmerized by the power of military force. These were the days when military solutions to the Palestine problem received precedence over negotiated solutions.
>
> (Pappe, 2004: 108)

From this point on the prospect of reconciling the indigenous rights of the Palestinian Arab people with the demands of a new Jewish nation and their colonization of new territories was very dim indeed. British policy toward Palestine had resulted in the chaos of mutually exclusive demands and a lesson in the arrogance of power in the modern age. Although it was true that individual sympathies for the Palestinian people existed among the officers of the Mandate, most historians agree that official policy and high-ranking officials themselves remained swayed by their compassion for the Zionist cause, which was allied to a formal policy of encouraging Zionism as an extension of the Western enlightenment policy in the native lands of Palestine.

World war and rethinking the mandate

The Second World War, as the following chapter outlines, would have a profound effect on the future of Palestine. Yet one still has to wonder whether the mandate would eventually have fallen apart even without the war. The Palestinian revolt had turned the British presence in Palestine into an increasingly costly affair; one that the government back in London may no longer have felt strictly necessary. The Jewish militias were growing in strength and organization and the British had not been terribly successful at stemming the flow of arms to support such groups. British soldiers stationed in the country during their war had their attention drawn to the battles of North Africa, including events in the deserts of Egypt and Libya. Of course, in the wake of the war, there were some elements of the British forces present that were used to run arms to the Arab Legion through Lebanon and into Transjordan (or the Hashemite Kingdom of Jordan as it had become on achieving independence in 1946). Born of war the mandate would thus end as a result of another global implosion that would grip the region and hold it in a stranglehold for the best part of 60 years.

The mandate, as a form of international intervention in the Middle East region could not truly be deemed a success. The Mandate authorities, the British, had established a functioning system of administrative authority over Mandate Palestine and some of their policies and practices had assisted the Zionists in their goals to settle the land. But the Zionists were not, ultimately, looking for benign political patronage from a higher British authority but independence and statehood. As it became clear that the British would resist them, enmity grew and violence by the Zionists against the British was almost inevitable. With respect to Arab wishes or the pre-existing rights of the indigenous population the Mandate authorities did little by way of assisting these people in the protection of their rights or in recognizing the parity of their political rights with respect to self-determination and independence. In some respect the British governors and functionaries of the mandate in Palestine were treading a well-worn path that had been tried in Ireland and would follow almost simultaneously in India, and later Iraq. The legacy of this period of rule was a historic mistrust of British motives in the Middle East that has coloured relations to the present. The Palestinians blame the British for their predicament. Israel, strengthened by statehood and the special relationship with the USA, has little, if anything, to feel beholden to the British for. The Israeli founding myth begins, not with Balfour or the decision at the United Nations in the wake of collective guilt at the horrors of the holocaust to promote a new state, but with the Zionist settlers who built their new moshav, towns and kibbutzim and a dream of a Jewish state that was inspired by Herzl and not Lloyd George or Arthur Balfour. If there were an attempt to rethink the mandate there is little by way of evidence to suggest that British officials were systematically inclined to do so. On the eve of their departure the British Chief Secretary still believed that Britain had done good in Palestine: 'Palestine had become rich. It had first-class roads and water supplies, schools, hospitals, and electric power', but it was 'an edifice built on sand' (Segev, 2001: 514). The mandate had secured British interests at a time, however, when wartime expediency and British national interests far outweighed those of the native population of the Middle East and in particular those territories that would become subject to British authority anew.

Further reading

The readings that are recommended for this period tend to cover the same ground in terms of the events that are judged worthy of mention but, of course, differ in terms of interpretation of events, the motives of the actors and the outcomes for those involved. Some of the recommendations for further reading appearing in this section have already been mentioned in Chapter 1. They include Pappe's book (Cambridge: Cambridge University Press, 2004) and Tessler's (Bloomington, IN: Indiana University Press, 1994) account as well. The book by Kimmerling and Migdal (New York: The Free Press, 1993) has a number of chapters in part one that account for the nature of Palestinian society between the First and Second World Wars and the impact of both Zionism and the British Mandate. Wasserstein (London: Profile Books, 2004) in his overviews of people, territory and society, draws out the Zionist motive and imperative to settle in Israel and establish a nation of Jews in one land. Halpern and Reinharz (Oxford: Oxford University Press, 2000) also offer a meaningful insight into the history of Zionism and the concurrent emergence of the state of Israel. These issues are more controversially presented in Finkelstein's book (London: Verso, 2003). British motives are worth examining by reading Segev's book (New York: Abacus Books, 2001). The challenges presented to local society during this period can be further unearthed by reading Beit-Hallahmi (Concord, MA: Pluto Press, 1992) and Flapan (New York: Pantheon Books, 1987). Also recommended are Avineri's book on the intellectual roots of Zionism (New York: Wiedenfeld, 1981) and Shafir (Berkeley, CA: University of California Press, 1996). Most of these books present a challenging and critical perspective of Zionism and British policy in the country. Further consideration should be made of books such as Khalidi (New York: Columbia University Press, 1998) that explore rising Palestinian national identity and consciousness.

Avineri, S. (1981) *The making of modern Zionism: Intellectual origins of the Jewish state*, New York: Wiedenfeld.

Beit-Hallahmi, B. (1992) *Original sins: Reflections on the history of Zionism and Israel*, Concord, MA: Pluto Press; reprint, New York: Olive Branch Press, 1993.

Finkelstein, N.G. (2003) *Image and reality of the Israel–Palestine conflict*, 2nd edn, London: Verso.

Flapan, S. (1987) *The birth of Israel: Myths and realities*, New York: Pantheon Books.

Halpern, B. and Reinharz, J. (2000) *Zionism and the creation of a new society*, Oxford: Oxford University Press.

Khalidi, R. (1998) *Palestinian identity: The construction of modern national consciousness*, New York: Columbia University Press.

Kimmerling, B. and Migdal, J. (1993) *Palestinians, the making of a people*, New York: The Free Press.

Pappe, I. (2004) *A history of modern Palestine: One land, two peoples*, Cambridge: Cambridge University Press.

Segev, T. (2001) *One Palestine, complete: Jews and Arabs under the British*, New York: Abacus Books.

Shafir, G. (1996) *Land, labour and the origins of the Israeli-Palestinian conflict, 1882–1914*, Berkeley, CA: University of California Press.

Tessler, M. (1994) *A history of the Arab–Israeli conflict*, Bloomington, IN: Indiana University Press.

Wasserstein, B. (2004) *Israel and Palestine, why they fight and can they stop?*, London: Profile Books.

3 Palestine after the Holocaust

Chapter outline

- War clouds   55
- After the dust has settled   57
- The UN Partition Plan of 1947   59
- The future decided   63
- British blight?   66
- What came next   68
- Whose history? The events of 1947–48   70
- Legacy   72
- Further reading   73

> I was not well-versed on matters of saving the Jews of Nazi-occupied Europe . . .
> The heart of my activity was enlisting Jewry in the demand to establish a Jewish
> state.
>
> David Ben Gurion (Segev, 2001: 461)

In this chapter the process of British withdrawal from Palestine as it sought an exit
strategy from the conflict between the Jews and the Arabs will be examined within
the framework of the wider international environment after the Second World
War and the perpetration of the Holocaust. The focus, therefore, will be on issues
of immigration, political development of opposing elements, the military
campaign waged by the Zionists against the British and developments within the
Zionist movement with respect to Jewish statehood. The UN Partition Plan will be
examined along with Zionist acceptance and Arab rejection. The prelude to war –
including the controversial Zionist massacres of 1947–48 – will be debated within
the framework of contemporary analysis of ethnic cleansing, population transfer
and other dimensions of ethnic and national politics. The issue of international
intervention also needs to be explained in terms of the Second World War, the
Holocaust and Western guilt and reparation issues to the Jewish people. The
British decision to withdraw from Palestine and relinquish its mandate will be
explored in terms of domestic and foreign factors.

War clouds

The outbreak of the Second World War and events in Europe inevitably impacted on Palestine and its population, further polarizing antipathies between Jew and Arab. While it was the case that during the war the Middle East itself became a battleground it was the consequence of events in Europe that would have an impact in determining the future of Palestine. The Nazi plan for the extermination of the Jewish people and the perpetration of the Holocaust established a trauma and series of scars that disfigures the landscape of distant Palestine to this day. Although other categories of people were singled out by the Nazi regime it was the systematic annihilation of the Jewish people in concentration camps, labour camps, death marches and ghettoes that by the end of the war had led to the deaths of some 6 million Jews. The Holocaust and Western guilt at not stopping the genocide against the Jews perpetrated by the Nazis led to heightened political and diplomatic sympathies for the Zionist cause and the goal of establishing a state for the Jewish people in Palestine. This sympathy, according to Orr, was, on occasion, exploited by the Zionists who 'contrary to accepted opinion . . . [were] not keen to rescue Jews from the Nazis' but were willing to exploit the notion of the Jews as a persecuted race in order to win support for Jewish statehood in Palestine (Orr, 1994: 67).

By 1939 the Palestinian revolt had all but come to an end and the British had issued yet another policy White Paper regarding the situation. The 1939 White Paper addressed the issue of the 'national home for the Jewish people' noting that, with 450,000 Jewish immigrants to Palestine, an independent state – jointly governed by the Jews and Arabs – should be established within a decade. The idea of an exclusively Jewish state in Palestine was dismissed:

> His Majesty's Government believe that the framers of the Mandate in which the Balfour Declaration was embodied could not have intended that Palestine should be converted into a Jewish State against the will of the Arab population of the country. [. . .] His Majesty's Government therefore now declare unequivocally that it is not part of their policy that Palestine should become a Jewish State.
>
> (Civic heads, n.d.)

The White Paper also addressed the issue of Jewish immigration and announced a limit of 75,000 for the following five years and 'Arab consent' for further waves of Jewish immigrants to the country: 'After the period of five years, no further Jewish immigration will be permitted unless the Arabs of Palestine are prepared to acquiesce in it.' The British cited both 'adverse' economic and political reasons for limiting the flow of Jews settling in the country. Clearly the prospect of Jewish demographic domination of the Arabs was finally being addressed by the British. The British thus sought to curb immigration to allow for the Jews to eventually constitute one-third of the total population. The White Paper also tackled the highly contentious issue of land sales or 'land transfer' to the Jews. The announced policy focused on a means of prohibiting or regulating land sales from Arabs/ Turks to Jews in order to allow the Palestinian peasant population to remain in sustainable occupation on the land. In London the proposals outlined in the paper met with parliament's approval but in Palestine both Jews and Arabs denounced the new British agenda. For the Zionists the paper was a setback in terms of their aspirations for statehood, Jewish immigration and the ability of the Jews to settle the land and establish their own colonies and communities. When the Second World War broke out in September 1939 Jewish opposition remained implacable, 'We will fight the White Paper as if there is no war, and fight the war as if there is no White Paper' declared Israel's future Prime Minister, David Ben Gurion. The Palestinian Arab Higher Committee (AHC) argued that the notion of a power-sharing government with the Jews would never work. They knew the Jews would boycott such a structure and that ultimate authority would still rest with the British. The AHC called for a complete cessation of Jewish immigration, declaring that mere British-inspired limits on the numbers of immigrants would not be enough to stop the Zionists.

The war itself would impact on Palestine as well as the principal actors in the increasing dispute over its territory. Palestine itself was part of the British Middle East Command headquartered in Cairo and a base, along with neighbouring Egypt, for the thousands of British and Commonwealth troops who would later engage with Rommel's German soldiers in the Western Desert of Egypt (1940–43). The presence of so many troops contributed to a wartime economic boom:

> The British devised an economic plan . . . to mobilize local and regional . . . production for both military and civilian needs in order to reduce dependence on external sources of supply. This successful strategy resulted in economic development of nearly all sectors of Palestine's economy.
>
> (Farsoun with Zacharia, 1997: 93–94)

Throughout the war, however, both the Zionists and the Palestinian Arabs continued to vie with each other in terms of the grander political imperatives of the conflict, including the making and breaking of important strategic alliances.

For the Palestinians the alliance between their former Mufti and national leader, Hajj Amin al-Husseini, and the Axis powers proved to be more detrimental than beneficial to their cause (Fisk, 2006; Morse, 2003; Mattar, 1988). Following his self-imposed exile in the wake of the Palestinian uprising of 1936–39 and his rejection of the 1939 White Paper, the Mufti courted the Nazi regime in Germany. In 1941 he went to Berlin and was received by Hitler. The Mufti, many scholars allege, then formed a close alliance with the Nazis and subscribed to their programme of Jewish extermination. Back home such alliances failed to win him much support. As one British official reported at the time: 'The [Palestinian] public is now resigned to intransigence on the part of Haj Amin towards the British government, and on the part of the British government towards Haj Amin.' (Colonial Office, CO733/398/11 1939). Hajj Amin al-Husseini's alliance with Berlin left him even further marginalized from the centre of decision-making after the war than before it – whether that centre was in Jerusalem, Tel Aviv or London.

For the Zionists their mobilization of American, including American Jewry, support during the war, would prove decisive in the post-war period. During the war, however, British–Jewish relations in Palestine would disintegrate further, culminating in a Jewish-waged terror campaign against British targets including personnel and institutions. Jewish immigration to Palestine continued throughout the early 1940s as the Nazi occupation of Europe intensified. The immigration was often illegal and was encouraged by local Zionists in defiance of the official British limits and controls. In 1942 Zionist ire at the British intensified in the wake of the sinking of the Struma. The ship, carrying Jewish refugees, had been denied entry to Palestine by the British and subsequently sank killing all but two of its passengers. By the mid-1940s, when news of the concentration camps and the Nazi plan for the annihilation of the Jewish people started to filter out of occupied Europe, both the Diaspora community and the Zionists in Palestine began to pressure the Allied powers to take action. They wanted movement on both the issue of the refugees and statehood. As far as the Zionists were concerned the imperative for Jewish statehood in Palestine became all the more pressing. They simply would not budge on the issue and saw the resolution of the Jewish refugee crisis as now inextricably tied to the realization of a plan for Jewish statehood in Palestine. The Zionists became frustrated at what they perceived to be British intransigence on this issue and unwillingness, throughout the war, to fully extend British support to Zionist goals in Palestine. The relationship between Britain and the Zionists soured and a deep and violent rift emerged. By the end of the war and the Allied victory in Europe the rift was beyond repair in Palestine. New allies of the Zionists would emerge, however, in the form of the US government. Abroad, the Zionist campaign had gained a new momentum in the USA. In May 1942 the World Zionist Congress meeting in New York agreed on a strategy, the major platform of which was the Jewish demand for the establishment of a Jewish state in Palestine. To this end it was decided that the Zionist movement in Palestine should establish its own national armed structures, that Jewish immigration should be unrestricted and organized by the Jewish Agency, who would in turn handle the absorption of the new immigrants and their settlement in Palestine.

After the dust has settled

The defeat of the Nazis and the Allied victory in Europe was a portent of a re-alignment of the international order that would irrevocably alter the fate of the Zionist movement and the future of the Palestinian Arabs. The Holocaust had established a moral imperative to create a safe haven for surviving European Jewry. The British moreover were in a severely weakened state as they emerged from war against the Axis powers; in some respects they simply did not have the energies to expend on the 'local difficulties' in Palestine.

Chiefly, the following factors would play a part in determining what would unfold in Palestine:

- The emergence of the USA and the USSR as the principle superpowers in contest with each other post-war.
- The legacy of the Holocaust as perpetrated against the Jews of Europe and Western guilt.
- The founding of the United Nations.
- The waning of Europe on the international stage and decline of European powers such as Britain and France in the Middle East region.

In the immediate aftermath of the war it was impossible to predict that the rivalry between the USA and the USSR would develop into a Cold War in which the Middle East would become one theatre of struggle between them. Yet the development of superpower rivalry in the region had a significant impact on the dynamic of the conflict between Israel and the Palestinians and surrounding Arab states. Both the USA and USSR would play a part in exacerbating as well as resolving the conflict at various points (Milton-Edwards and Hinchcliffe, 2003). Israel would come to enjoy the status of a 'special relationship' with the USA, with the state being in receipt of unprecedented amounts of US aid, loans and military assistance. The Palestinians, through representative organizations such as the PLO and alliances with Arab states such as Syria, managed to win support from the Soviet side as they later pursued their liberation struggle.

In the aftermath of the Holocaust the international community, and especially the European 'powers', demonstrated a strong responsibility with respect to the Jewish people. The Allied powers had failed to prevent the Holocaust and their collective guilt obligated them to address the issue of compensation to the Jews. Some thus argue that this 'guilt' and need to re-settle the more than 250,000 surviving and displaced European Jews inevitably led to a support for the creation of the state of Israel three years later in 1948. Others dispute this argument and counter that the Holocaust was not the determining factor behind Israel's establishment, pointing to the inexorable growth of the Zionist movement and immigration before the Holocaust and natural demographics after the settlement of Jews in Palestine in the decades before the outbreak of the Second World War.

The Palestinians, however, were at a loss to know why they had to pay the price for the Holocaust or European guilt in the wake of the genocide committed by the Nazis (Kimmerling, 2001: 36–37). Nevertheless Zionist leaders sought to exploit this guilt. 'The leading diplomats of the Yishuv claimed that only a future Jewish state could be a haven . . . and a buffer against another Holocaust' (Pappe, 2004: 119). The notion that the Holocaust could serve as a form of 'ideological weapon' or a 'political football' employed by competing Zionist factions of the Yishuv in Palestine became apparent in both their use and misuse of events in Europe from 1939–45 vis-à-vis their goal of statehood and independence (Segev, 2000; Finkelstein, 2001). The majority of Jewish survivors of the Holocaust, however, did not want to settle in Palestine and this in itself became another obstacle for the Zionists to overcome.

Palestine's future, however, would be determined by the United Nations and not its indigenous Palestinian population. Their right to shape their own fate was again taken from their hands. In February 1947 the British turned the 'problem' over to the United Nations. Yet the proposed solution was, in so many respects, a very British and colonial one: partition (Brown, 2003: 62). Britain had extricated itself from Ireland in 1921 through partition and in India partition was also being employed as the British sought to extricate themselves from the ruins of the Raj. Partition would present the Zionists with an opportunity for statehood realized.

One reason why Britain turned Palestine over to the United Nations was its own status post-war. After the war the major European powers had to re-think their foreign policies and imperial stretch particularly as it pertained to the Middle East. The coffers of the British treasury could no longer sustain British ex-territorial engagements such as Palestine because they were uneconomic and a drain on national resources. Palestine was 'costing' Britain £30 million per annum and thousands of troops were also deployed to the country at a time when recovery of a war-shattered nation had become the priority. Britain and France, along with other European powers, were also compelled to acknowledge their diminished presence on the world stage post-war. They had to come to terms, moreover, with the fact that they were being replaced by the two new superpowers and a new international organization – the United Nations – that in its General Assembly would decide the fate of nations.

The UN Partition Plan of 1947

> As soon as partition had been announced . . . our friends spoke of scenes of wild jubilation in the Jewish areas as they celebrated . . . 'We have a state! We have a state!' they sang.
>
> (Karmi, 2001: 76)

The beginning of the process of Palestinian loss of the territory that they had called their own for centuries lies in the passing of the UN resolution for the partition of Palestine in November 1947 and ends in May 1948 when the newly established state of Israel found itself at war with its Arab neighbours. This period is referred to by Palestinians as the *nakbah* (the disaster) and is regarded by some scholars as an era of 'unofficial' war waged by the armed Zionist groups against the Palestinian Arab population of Palestine (Shlaim, 2000: 28). Certainly the process of accelerated dispossession and the acts of brutal violence committed against the Palestinian Arab population played their part in creating a refugee issue that remains core to the resolution of the Israeli–Palestinian conflict in the present day. But it is not the sole reason why Palestinians fled their home and lands.

During this period – from November 1947 to May 1948 – more than half of the Palestinian Arab population fled or left the country voluntarily, believing that they would return to their homes shortly after the end of any conflict. Their lands and homes were abandoned and their status as the majority population of historic Palestine would be irreversibly altered. In the wake of the war of 1948 the new state of Israel would come to constitute 77 per cent of the former territory of Mandate Palestine and those Arabs living within the boundaries of the new Jewish state would become a permanent minority. Israeli officials and their supporters vehemently deny such assertions contending that before 1947 the Palestinians were not citizens of their own state to be dispossessed from.

Palestinian Arabs living in territories of Mandate Palestine that became known as the Gaza Strip and the West Bank found their lives subject to the administrative and latterly political control of the Jordanian and Egyptian authorities. I will outline the various reasons for these events later in this chapter but for now let us look at the series of events that directly preceded and then followed the Partition Plan and its acceptance by the United Nations in a General Assembly vote in November 1947.

We already know that by the end of the Second World War Britain was struggling with its responsibilities in Palestine and had already proposed partition (in the 1939 White Paper) as a means of divesting itself of its responsibility for the country. Its many soldiers and officials stationed in the country were becoming the target of 'a terror campaign waged by Zionist extremists, the most notorious being the Stern Gang' (Pappe 2004: 121). In November 1944, for example, in the wake of a Stern Gang assassination of the British Minister for the Middle East, Lord Moyne, the Prime Minister declared to Parliament in London that:

> If our dreams for Zionism are to end in the smoke of assassins' pistols and our labours for its future are to produce a new set of gangsters worthy of Nazi Germany, many like myself will have to reconsider the position we have maintained so consistently and so long in the past. If there is to be any hope of a peaceful and successful future for Zionism these wicked activities must cease and those responsible for them must be destroyed, root and branch.
>
> (AAIC, 1946: 73)

Former Israeli Prime Minister and Stern Gang member, Yitzhak Shamir, defended the decision to assassinate Lord Moyne claiming he had been responsible for the benighted fate of Jewish refugees who had been turned back from Palestine's shores (Cohen, 1979).

The most ferocious and deadly assault by the Zionist militants was the bombing of the King David Hotel. The King David Hotel in Jerusalem is a rectangular monolith that dominates the western side of Jerusalem outside the fortified walls of the Old City. Even today its reception rooms and restaurants echo to an earlier era where the rich, royal and powerful came to stay for business and pleasure. In 1938 the British had commandeered one wing of this 'hotel of heads of state' as headquarters for the military command and government secretariat. The British would become major targets of the Zionist armed groups, including the Irgun group who, on 22 July 1946 detonated a bomb at the hotel killing a total of 91 people. The bombing was described by one local as jarring 'England's memory, reminding this ailing dowager that her unruly offspring were determined to exercise their proclaimed God-given right of unconditional inheritance' (Toubbeh, 1998: 22). After the bombing there was a sense that British-ruled Palestine was becoming untenable. Toubbeh argues:

England experienced increased attacks by Jewish terror gangs on its citizens in Palestine. With each attack, with each death, the country weighed its losses against relinquishing a piece of territory that was not its property to cede in the first place.

(Toubbeh, 1998: 22)

By January 1947 the British were proposing once again that Palestinian and Zionist autonomy should be granted, with the British maintaining direct power only in a limited number of areas. This proposal was rejected, once again, by both sides. The Zionists rejected it because by this point they were determined to achieve nothing short of an independent Jewish state in Palestine and the Palestinian Arab leadership rejected it because it denied them their rights to an independent Palestinian state in Palestine.

By February 1947, convinced that they could do nothing further to resolve the situation, the British handed over the issue to the United Nations for a solution. The fate of Palestine would largely be decided by members of a special UN committee (UNSCOP). UNSCOP started its work in May 1947 and the committee was made up of members from 11 states. The committee held a series of hearings to which Arab and Jewish representatives were invited to make their case. As part of their activities UNSCOP members also made a short visit to Palestine. The recommendations of the committee were made public in August 1947. During their investigations of the issue they largely determined and agreed that a form of partition was the only way in which to meet the competing claims and demands of Arabs and Jews. Only a few members of the committee proposed the alternative of a single binational federal state solution. It is notable that two of the states supporting this proposal were India, which had been subject to proposed partition, and Yugoslavia, which was a multi-ethnic federal state in the post-war era. The British Mandate for Palestine would be terminated, two independent states would be proposed as a solution and Jerusalem, including areas that would reach as far as Bethlehem to the south, would enjoy special international status.

The UNSCOP recommendation was translated into a resolution proposed to the United Nations. The implications of the proposal in terms of the territories planned for the two new states caused immense fear and further domestic tensions back in Palestine. Indeed between November 1947 and May 1948 hundreds of Jews and Arabs were killed by opposing armed elements. In Haifa, on 30 December 1947, 39 Jews were killed during Palestinian riots against the Partition Plan. In April 1948 the Irgun and others killed an estimated 100 Palestinians in the village of Deir Yassin. Zionist fears centred on demographic and security issues and the Palestinians had simply rejected the issue out of hand. The vote to determine the future took place on 29 November 1947 and the UN General Assembly voted 33 to 13, with 10 abstentions, in favour of the Partition Plan, as contained in Resolution 181. The actual partition would take place as soon as the British withdrew from Palestine and terminated its Mandate. The partition was also backed by powerful post-war states such as the USSR and the USA. In agreeing to the resolution they were both seeking to influence and shape policy in the Middle

East. It should have been no surprise that of the 13 member states that voted against the resolution the majority of them were from the Middle East and included: Egypt, Iran, Iraq, Lebanon, Syria, Saudi Arabia and Yemen. Also voting against the partition were several member states with ongoing experience of the effects on their own territories, including Greece and India. The Arab member states also called on the International Court of Justice to investigate the validity of a partition against the wishes of the majority Palestinian Arab population.

If partition was to be inevitable, what would the division of territory actually look like? The members of UNSCOP had determined that the Jews, although they only owned 8 per cent of the land, would receive 55 per cent of the land that constituted the Mandate territory of Palestine. In this new nation state the Jews would enjoy territories that included areas of coastline, desert, the Red Sea and the Sea of Galilee. The territory of the proposed state also included those areas that by the late 1940s were most densely populated by Jewish settlers. One problem was that it also included 'more than 45 per cent of the Arab population in the designated Jewish state, but the committee believed this demographic reality to be temporary' as they believed that accelerated Jewish immigration to the new state would soon tip the balance against Arab demographics in Israel (Pappe, 1994: 31). For those elements of the Zionist movement that believed that the imperative of statehood at any cost had grown out of the horrors of the Holocaust the prospect of statehood offered by the UNSCOP proposal and subsequent UN resolution was a victory of sorts. Shlaim even states that, 'despite all its limitations and anomalies, the UN resolution represented a major triumph for Zionist diplomacy' (Shlaim, 2000: 24). For many within the movement, however, the UN proposal was not the end to the aspirations for legitimate statehood but the beginning of the realization of the wider dream of the establishment of Eretz Israel in Arab territories that included the whole of Palestine and lands beyond it.

Although a two-state solution was proposed, inter-state cooperation was enshrined in a plan for economic union. It was proposed that the Palestinian Arab state would be situated on the lands of the Jordan valley, Gaza, Jaffa and Majdal area, and the Galilee. The fate of the Palestinians was placed in Arab hands. The Arab League made a series of representations to the UNSCOP delegation and they were vehemently opposed to the proposed partition. One local notable Palestinian figure writing a private note commented that: 'They [the Arabs] refused at any time to sign their own death warrant' (Segev, 2001: 496).

There was one small problem in terms of the Arab line because of the secret negotiations that had already taken place between Jordan's King Abdullah I and the Jewish Agency. Since the early 1920s the Zionists and King Abdullah I had been in secret talks and negotiations. King Abdullah I appeared to be the only leader in the Arab world who had been willing to deal with the Zionists – though the purpose and ends of such deals remain open to very varied interpretation (Salibi, 1998: 124–25, Shlaim, 2000: 29 or George, 2005: 17). King Abdullah's dialogue and dealings with the Jewish Agency are variously described as 'discreet links', 'no harm' persuasion, or 'friendly relations' that meant that the Zionists could substitute a Palestinian partner for a Jordanian one in seeking to shape and decide on the future of Palestine's indigenous Arab inhabitants. It has been written that Abdullah was perhaps the one Arab leader at the time that had made 'a realistic appraisal of the balance of power between the Zionist movement and the Arab national movement' (Shlaim, 2000: 29). By 1946 this had led him into agreements with the Zionists regarding the fate of Palestine. Such decisions may well have been well-intentioned but they also played a part in weakening a united Arab position regarding proposals for the partition of Palestine.

The Palestinian political leadership (still weakened and dispersed as a result of British suppression of the Palestinian revolt ten years earlier) itself refused to meet with the UNSCOP delegation and flatly rejected the proposed partition. The leadership seemed almost paralyzed by the enormity of what was befalling their people as the promise and pledges of the British to respect the rights of the Palestinian Arabs dissolved in chaos and violence. The dawning of a new era was upon the Palestinians. As one native of Jerusalem reflected:

> It was not long before we realized that the country was being rapidly transformed into the repository of Zionism's credo and was becoming an apartheid state. Palestinians lacked an equivalent ideology and had no counter-strategy.
> (Toubbeh, 1998: 23)

Ultimately the Palestinians remained at the mercy of the international community. The international community had decreed the following:

> The primary objectives sought in the foregoing scheme are, in short, political division and economic unity: to confer upon each group, Arab and Jew, in its own territory, the power to make its own laws, while preserving to both, throughout Palestine, a single integrated economy, admittedly essential to the well-being of each, and the same territorial freedom of movement to individuals as is enjoyed today. The former necessitates a territorial partition; the latter, the maintenance of unrestricted commercial relations between the States, together with a common administration of functions in which the interests of both are in fact inextricably bound together.
> (UNSCOP, 1947: n.p.)

The future decided

The major Jewish organizations had responded to the proposal, as we have noted, with acceptance. They continued to lobby at the United Nations and among other influential parties such as the USA to ensure that when the vote took place on 29 November 1947 the partition would become a fait accompli with UN legitimacy to boot. There were some within the ranks of Zionism such as the armed elements of the Irgun and Stern Gang who rejected the partition proposal but they were not sufficient in number to influence the prevailing trend for Jewish support of it. There were other elements, moreover, who were concerned that the proposed state would leave the Jews with a sizeable Arab minority to contend with and that the new state would not enjoy territorial contiguity. The issue of an Arab presence in the Jewish state had of course been debated within Zionist circles before 1947. In those earlier debates transfer of the Arabs had been outlined and discussed by leading luminaries of the movement. Masalha has outlined the various elements within Zionism that grappled, before November 1947, with the transfer issue as a means of achieving Zionist goals of an exclusive Jewish state in Palestine. Of these various plans he notes that some carried more weight within the movement than others:

> those put forward by the mainstream Yishuv leaders ... the Jewish Agency ... the Jewish National Fund, ... as well as the official transfer committees are far more important [and] ... highlight the ideological intent that made the Palestinian refugee exodus of 1948 possible.
>
> (Masalha, 1992: 165)

Palestinian memoirs from the period also begin to record evidence of an increasing tension between the Jews and Arabs and the first violent acts undertaken by the Jewish militias that forced Palestinian Arabs in cities like Jerusalem to flee their homes. As one voice from the period recounts:

> We in Bethany knew trouble was on the way earlier than most people, in 1946 and early 1947. Truck loads of young Jews used to pass through the village to and from the Dead Sea where they received military training. They sang warlike songs and hurled insults at us as they drove through the town. They weren't the Jews of old; they were a new alien group who obviously didn't like us.
>
> (Aburish, 1991: 100)

Other scholars contend that claims of a Zionist plan to transfer the Arab population or engage in ethnic cleansing paint a one-sided picture of the conflict and portrays only the Arabs as victims of violence. Such a picture, it is contended, overlooks the Arab violence in the wake of the partition, in which one scholar claims '1,256 Jews were killed in five months [November 1947–April 1948]' (Frantzman, 2007).

The vote in favour of the Partition Plan presented the Zionist leadership with a fulfilment of some of their dreams but also a formidable challenge in terms of actually achieving statehood as a Jewish state in the midst of Arab neighbours. This was something that was acknowledged by Ben Gurion, who by the following year would be Prime Minister, in a speech in November 1947:

> Political developments have swept us on to a momentous parting of the ways – from Mandate to independence. Today, beyond our ceaseless work in immigration, settlement and campaign, we are set three blazing tasks, whereof fulfilment will condition our perpetuity: defence, a Jewish State and Arab–Jewish Cupertino, in that order of importance and urgency.

... We can stand up to any aggression launched from Palestine or its border, but more in potential than yet in fact. The conversion from potential to actual is now our major, blinding headache. It will mean the swiftest, widest mobilization, here and abroad, of capacity to organize, of our resources in economics and manpower, our science and technology, our civic sense. It must be an all-out effort, sparing no man.

(Ben Gurion, 1947)

Ben Gurion and his colleagues in the Zionist movement began to organize the so-called defence even before statehood was upon them. Whether one end of this defence was the deliberate expulsion or transfer of the Palestinian Arab population is open to fierce debate.

The response of the Arab leadership to the passing of the UN resolution was characterized by their impotence, in contrast to the determination of key international players such as the USA to resolving the Jewish issue after the Holocaust. Arab opposition to the partition was based on the logic of demographics and international rights. They had contended that the vote for partition ignored the wishes and rights of the majority Arab population and moreover that many Palestinian Arabs would also find themselves citizens of a Jewish state that they vehemently opposed. Many ordinary Palestinians still placed their trust in their notable and nationalist leadership believing that in alliance with the Arab leaders of states like Egypt, Iraq and Jordan that the Zionist cause would be headed off easily. Of course many in the Palestinian leadership remained in exile, including the former Mufti of Jerusalem, Hajj Amin al-Husseini. Hajj Amin al-Husseini had made a disastrous alliance with the Axis powers during the war and by the middle to late 1940s remained in exile from Palestine. At the end of the war he had 'disappeared' in the fall of Berlin and reappeared in Cairo in 1946, from whence he sent messages of resistance and defiance to the Palestinian people. His presence in the region symbolized a form of hope (albeit doomed) for the Palestinians: 'Brooding despair gave way to a desire to fight, for the Mufti, with all his colossal faults, embodied Palestinian Arabs' will to resist . . . No one knew what would happen next . . .' (Aburish, 1991: 94).

As Kimmerling and Migdal note, the:

UN vote shattered two illusions shared by Jews and Arabs: that a resolution to the question of Palestine's future would not be quick and that the colonial power would pass its authority on to its successor in an orderly fashion.

(Kimmerling and Migdal, 1993: 140)

If the political future was hard to predict the spectre of violence was not so hard to anticipate. Waves of anti-Jewish violence and attacks followed waves of anti-Arab violence; both were random and increasingly pulled ordinary civilians in a deep undertow of mutual antagonism and hatred. Ordinary Jewish–Arab relationships, friendships, business ventures and partnerships were largely imperilled by the undertow of enmity. As neighbourhoods, districts, streets and shopping areas became increasingly insecure for the conduct of everyday life a small trickle of Palestinians began to move. They moved from one part of a city to another, sharing rooms and property with members of their extended families. Some Arabs sensed the danger and began to move their families away from the towns and cities where the conflict would often spill over into violence. The internal displacement of the Palestinian people had already begun but soon the trickle would turn into a tidal wave of exodus amidst the bloodshed and threat of violence from one side or the other.

The violence in the wake of the UN vote in November 1947 soon turned into riots between and against Jews and Arabs. Local Palestinians began to arm themselves with whatever they could lay their hands on and the local leadership ordered strikes amidst the ensuing hostility and chaos. Arab violence against Jewish targets occurred in Jerusalem and Jaffa and on traffic in the surrounding countryside. The violence was quickly organized by the local Arab leadership. Yet each side tells the story differently. Let us compare the account by the Palestinian author, Aburish, with that of Israeli Benny Morris. They are both writing about the same period – just before and following the passing of the UN resolution for partition. First Morris says of the vote, how it 'triggered haphazard Arab attacks against Jewish traffic . . . Strategically speaking, the period December 1947–March 1948 was marked by Arab initiatives and attacks and Jewish defensiveness, increasingly punctuated by Jewish reprisals' (Morris, 2004: 65). But Aburish contended that: 'Fear filled the land. Armed Jewish gangs raided Arab quarters, terrorized the inhabitants by tossing hand grenades into crowded souks or shooting at innocent passers-by . . . The Palestinians retaliated' (Aburish, 1991: 102). While interpretations differ, Aburish perhaps best sums up the consequence of the descent into violence: 'Both sides were the victims of hysteria and hate, hate of people who until very recently had been their neighbours and friends' (Aburish, 1991: 103).

Britain meanwhile prepared to quit and sought nothing other than to extricate itself from the quagmire. It was prepared to let the Palestinian Arabs and the Jews fight it out between them. The arbiter, the facilitator of the ascent to independence and freedom, excused itself from the theatre of conflict that it had played such a significant role in creating in the first place. Britain announced it was to conclude its Mandate in Palestine on 15 May 1948. The mandate of their imagination in 1920 had become a nightmare for them by the 1940s and was only one part of a wider set of problems that concerned British ambitions in the Middle East at the time.

British blight?

For a little more than 30 years (1917–48) the British struggled to realize its policies in the Promised Land. It had commenced its occupation of Palestine with the promise, made by Balfour, to support in Palestine 'a national home for the Jewish people', while protecting the rights and political status of the indigenous population. 'The British left the country [in 1948] because more and more of them had come to realize that the Balfour Declaration had been a mistake' (Segev, 2001: 489). The mandate structure issued to Britain in the early 1920s by the League of

Nations that was supposed to transform life in Palestine from military occupation to independence was a dream realized for one party only. The mandate structure was useful only to the Zionists when it was employed or utilized in direct service to their cause. The Zionists portrayed themselves as pioneers in a barren land forced to turn against the British as it acted against their interests. Yet the British ultimately facilitated and serviced Jewish immigration, settlement, the formation of militia and other armed elements, and allied with them against the Palestinian Arab population. The British were instrumental in the rise of the state of Israel and the catastrophe that befell the Palestinian people. For Palestinian Arabs the Mandate seemed to conspire to constrain and deter the realization of every aspect of their rights to self-determination and independence in their own land. As some of Israel's current historians of the period highlight, the Palestinians became subjects of a dual project of colonial ambition (Segev, 2001). Firstly the British and secondly the Zionists saw the land through the tinted lens of colonialism. To perceive of the Zionists as engaged in a colonizing project – which ignores the rights of the native population – and the British as the handmaidens to this process leads to a different interpretation of the events during this period.

The irony is that British colonial policy and the devices for controlling the native population proved themselves to be ineffective and ultimately inimical to British interests in the Middle East and India. Moreover, the early appeal of supporting Zionism as a 'solution' to the Jewish problem in Europe (Britain itself had restricted Jewish immigration in 1902 at a time when many were attempting to flee the Russian pogroms against them) soured when the Zionists turned against them during the Mandate period. In Palestine British officials came to realize the extent to which Zionist leaders were better able to influence Ministers in London. As the British High Commissioner in Palestine from 1931–38 opined with regard to the Zionists: 'The thing is I have never met the PM [British] and I don't suppose I ever shall. Weizmann [Zionist leader] can go in there whenever he wants to' (Segev, 2001: 64). Under Britain's aegis the Palestinians worst fears were realized, as British-supported Jewish immigration, land settlement and land sales took place all around them. The dynamic of Zionism underpinned by the promises inherent in the Balfour Declaration appeared increasingly unstoppable. British officials were perceived as doing little to stop this drive towards Jewish statehood (thinly disguised in the rhetoric of a Jewish national home). British officials appointed Zionists into some of the most important positions in the Mandate authority, including High Commissioner. Such a position was one of real power, especially when compared to the façade of religious pomp and circumstance in British-created official Muslim positions, such as the Mufti of Jerusalem or the Supreme Muslim Council. Such power was harnessed in support of the Jewish project, often at the expense of Arab rights and demands.

In the joint memoirs of a husband and wife who served in the British administration of the Mandate in Palestine the authors close their book by asking a question. 'What is the balance sheet of the British Mandate for Palestine,' they ask, 'from the Jewish aspect?' (Bentwich and Bentwich, 1965: 216). The balance sheet looks pretty good:

Broadly the Jewish National Home was established . . . politically, economically and culturally. The combination of Jewish enterprise and British administration brought back Palestine, after 700 years of isolation, to the world highways . . . the new social and economic conditions worked a revolution. The motor car supplanted the donkey; the lorry supplanted the camel. The health services . . . reduced enormously infant mortality and the general death rate . . . Hebrew the language of the Bible and of prayer, became a living tongue for the vast majority of the Jewish population . . . Israel is again a 'people of the Book'.

(Bentwich and Bentwich, 1965: 216, 220)

Of course the greatest omission in the above account is the balance sheet of the British Mandate for Palestine from the Palestinian Arab perspective. It is not too difficult to second guess what that balance sheet might look like and perhaps it is for these reasons that British officials sought to play up their 'successes' and disguise their disgraces. Certainly the perception from the Palestinian side was that the British had failed to live up to their promises or recognize the rights of the Palestinian Arab population in determining its own future.

What came next

We have already outlined some of the events leading up to the United Nations passing the resolution for the Partition Plan and the immediate responses – including Arab and Jewish violence – from both sides. But what came next, according to authors such as Benny Morris and others, was the enacting of a plan to dispossess the Palestinian Arabs of Palestine. Morris outlines five periods or episodes of armed violence organized by the Jews in order to depopulate Palestine of its non-Jewish inhabitants. The evidence provided by Morris is straight from the mouth, so to speak, because he has meticulously researched the Israeli state archives, as well as other sources from the time, to outline the waves of violence orchestrated from December 1947, and including March–April 1948 when the Zionist Haganah activated what became known as Plan D (*Tochnit Dalet*). The objective behind Plan D was to secure Jewish settlements and their inhabitants. Some historians argue that Plan D was ultimately a case, as it prepared for statehood, for the mass transfer of the Palestinian Arab population. The method of expulsion included the option of extreme violence against unarmed civilians (Pappe, 2004: 131). Morris's own work is more ambiguous regarding a central Zionist plan for expulsion. Instead he declares that:

My feeling is that the transfer thinking and near-consensus that emerged in the 1930s and early 1940s was not tantamount to pre-planning and did not issue in the production of a policy or master-plan of expulsion; the Yishuv and its military forces did not enter the 1948 War, which was initiated by the Arab side, with a policy or plan for expulsion. But transfer was inevitable and inbuilt into Zionism – because it sought to transform a land which was 'Arab' into a 'Jewish' state and a Jewish state could not have arisen without a major displacement of Arab population; and because this aim automatically produced resistance among the Arabs which, in turn, persuaded the Yishuv's leaders that a hostile Arab majority or large minority could not remain in place if a Jewish state was to arise or safely endure.

(Morris, 2004: 60)

During the two months from April to May 1948 Plan D was carried out by Jewish forces on Palestinian cities, towns and villages in the Galilee (including Tiberias), the North (including Haifa), around Jerusalem and also the coastal town of Jaffa. The news of the massacre of villagers at Deir Yassin in April 1948 played a part in hastening the exodus with expulsions/transfers, further violence and usurpation by the Jewish forces in Palestinian territories. Jewish operations targeted Palestinian centres of population with the view of seeing an end to the Palestinian presence (as either a threat or not). Hostilities deepened as the Arabs, supported by neighbouring states, began to mobilize for their defence and protection.

By July 1948 a third round of Jewish operations led to over 100,000 Palestinians fleeing their homes into exile under the protection of other Arab states. For Israelis, who had celebrated their independence on 15 May and found themselves at war with the Arab states the following day, antipathies towards the Palestinians had grown to unprecedented levels. The following is the account of one soldier in the wake of the battle for Ramle that left some 200 Palestinians dead:

My jeep made the turn and here at the . . . entrance to the house opposite stands an Arab girl, stands and screams with eyes filled with fear and dread. She is all torn and dripping blood – she is certainly wounded. Around her on the ground lie the corpses of her family . . . And the girl understand nothing . . . Did I fire at her? . . . Everyone is an enemy. Kill! Destroy! Murder! Otherwise you will be murdered and will not conquer the town . . . Yes! . . . I kill everyone who belongs to the enemy camp: man, woman, old person, child. And I am not deterred.

(Morris, 2004: 426)

Further waves of violence led to the flight of hundreds and thousands of Palestinians. The land was literally emptying of its Arab inhabitants as they variously obeyed Arab orders to flee or ran for their lives in the face of violence committed by the Zionist armed elements. Morris actually puts paid to the Israeli claim that the Palestinians fled their homes on Arab orders and demonstrates this to be an Israeli myth or propaganda obscuring the face of events as they truly unfolded. The relentless movement of people flooding from the North of Palestine, the coastal area, Jerusalem corridor, and the Galilee created turmoil throughout the land and exodus for many Palestinians. By the summer of 1948 the Israeli government had also decided on a policy of refusing to allow any of the Palestinians to return.

Whose history? The events of 1947–48

> The Jews ordered all our family to line up against the wall and then they started shooting us. I was hit in the side, but most of us children were saved because we hid behind our parents . . . But all the others with us against the wall were killed: my father, my mother, my grandfather, my uncles and aunts and some of their children.
>
> Fahmi Zeidan, survivor of Deir Yassin (Collins and Lapierre, 1972: 274)

Approximately 700,000 Palestinian Arabs ended up exiled and as refugees between 1947 and the signing of the 1949 armistice. As Jewish refugees from Hitler's Europe had entered the country, Palestinian Arabs found themselves displaced from their home and usurped by the new immigrants. The movement of this population occurred in a series of waves, as we have said already, both before and during the first Arab–Israeli war of 1948. Palestinian Arabs from all sectors of society, both genders, young and old, rich and poor, urban and rural, Christian and Muslim, temporarily ceased to exist as they became stateless and refugees forced to make new homes in foreign countries.

Some Palestinians towns were depopulated en masse with entire families compelled to leave their homes in fear for their lives and livelihoods. The massacre of Palestinians in villages such as Deir Yassin also drove the expulsion process, with Zionist armed elements and the new armed units of the state responsible for generating the human tidal wave of refugees that fled their homes. The issue of whether the exodus of the Palestinians from Palestine was part of a Zionist strategy for transfer or ethnic cleansing has been extensively debated. Masalha has argued that there was a Zionist plan to expel Palestinians from their lands and dispossess them of their heritage. He painstakingly documents the major debates and contributions of Zionists, including figures such as David Ben Gurion who would become the first Prime Minister of Israel, in arguing for the transfer option (Masalha, 1992). Benny Morris, on the other hand, addressing the connection between Zionist thinking on transfer and the actual events of 1947–48, states 'my feeling is that the connection [between the thinking and events] is more subtle and indirect . . . Nothing that I have seen in Israeli archives during the past decade indicates the existence before 1948 of a Zionist master plan to expel the Arabs of Palestine' (Morris, 2001b: 48). Norman Finkelstein, however, contends that in debunking one myth, Morris replaces it with another that speaks instead of events being 'born of war' rather than intention or plan. This, Finkelstein argues, 'exonerate[s] Israel of any real culpability for the catastrophe' (Finkelstein, 2003: 52). Once again the scholars' war over 1948 and the Palestinian exodus continues.

But Palestinians were expelled from their homes by Jewish armed militias before the state was established and by the Israeli Defense Forces (IDF) once the state was founded in May 1948. In early 1948, for example, following the Zionist expulsion of over 60,000 Arabs from the town of Ramleh and Lydda, leading Zionists acknowledged that, 'there is a feeling that *fait accompli* are being created . . . The question is not whether or not the Arabs will return or not return . . . The question is whether the Arabs are [being or have been] expelled or not' (Masalha, 2003: 30).

Clearly there was concern at the time from some Zionist officials that the campaigns against the Palestinians – the retaliatory violence, the massacres, the expulsions 'a very large number . . . at gunpoint', the acts of looting, instances of poor discipline – had moral as well as political consequences. The Zionists were not delighted at the prospect of Arabs remaining in the state proposed to them under the UN Partition Plan and Zionist visioning had always relied on the figment of a land for a people without a land (Palumbo, 1987). In the wake of the war of 1948, the 1949 armistice and the tasks of state-building, official history makers dodged the issue of the expulsions by narrating an alternative version of events in their history books. In this version of events the Arab leadership ordered ordinary Palestinians to flee their homes until it was safe for them to return. Under the proud banners of the Arab armies Palestine would be restored in its entirety to the Palestinian people once the Israelis had been militarily defeated and cowed on the battlefield. In this way Israel was able to absolve itself for any form of responsibility for the creation of the refugee issue and its resolution (Morris, 2004: 286).

Although historians have revealed evidence that there were Zionist figures who were well aware of the events and activities that were taking place in the 1940s, the official version of events that were 'produced' by the state of Israel were different and portrayed events from the Jewish perspective of having to undertake defensive measures against Arab violence. Certainly any moral qualms regarding the violence perpetrated against the Palestinians – which according to some perspectives amounted to ethnic cleansing – and the forcing of expulsion were dampened down with the industry of the official discourse. This discourse, because it went unchallenged for so many decades, was absorbed into the making of the Israeli national identity as a fact rather than a myth, making it difficult, when the time came, to assess any alternative narrative. The challenge of such a narrative, therefore, lay not merely in questioning what had become accepted 'facts' but a pillar of Israeli identity in and of itself.

The challenge to the historical hegemony of Israel regarding the events of 1947–48 came from a generation of Israeli historians that had access to hitherto unopened archives covering the period. They were called the 'new historians' and the furore in Israel surrounding the publication of their work on the 1948 war was an indicator of how deeply such assessments contradicted the accepted wisdom of the time. One of the most controversial contributions came from Israeli historian Benny Morris in his book *The Birth of the Palestinian Refugee Problem, 1947–48*. At the time of its publication the author's contribution not only seemed contentious but turned the stereotype of pro-Israeli Israeli scholarship on its head. It presented a revision of the official Israeli account of events and drew on Israeli sources for evidence. Employing archival and contemporary sources, Morris was arguing that neither the official Israeli nor Arab explanation of events exactly mirrored the reported facts from events at the time. Instead, Morris argued that, 'that war and not design, Jewish or Arab, gave birth to the Palestinian refugee problem'

(Morris, 2004: 588). He conceded, however, that 'the displacement of Arabs from Palestine or the areas of Palestine that would become the Jewish state was inherent in Zionist ideology and, in microcosm, in Zionist praxis from the start of the enterprise' (Morris, 2004: 588). It was Morris's belief, however, that although Israeli actions during the period under study included massacres and rapes of ordinary unarmed Palestinian civilians and could be considered 'war crimes', other actions such as population transfer were 'in certain conditions, . . . not a war crime. I don't think that the expulsions of 1948 were war crimes. You can't make an omelette without breaking eggs. You have to dirty your hands' (Shavit, 2004). Morris, like many Israelis, argued that this form of ethnic cleansing was necessary in the face of the Arab opposition that the Jewish people encountered. He maintained that the 'Jewish state would not have come into being without the uprooting of 700,000 Palestinians. Therefore it was necessary to uproot them. There was no choice but to expel that population' (Shavit, 2004). Not everyone agrees with this assessment. There are those who contend that Morris's work should have been unequivocal in his condemnation rather than excusing them as an expediency of survival in an existential battle for the continued existence of the Jewish people. As one critic opines: 'The bottom line of Morris' reassessment represents the Israeli national consensus: "What happened in 1948 is irreversible." That is to say, there can be no consideration of a Palestinian right to return in any form' (Beinin, 2004).

Such debates continue to rumble on but the contribution of such scholars in assessing Israel's relationship with respect to the Palestinians and vice versa remain a controversial task. From the Palestinian perspective critics opine that there really has been no evidence of the emergence of any revisionist account of this period or any other in recent history where an unexpurgated version of events and decisions taken by Palestinian and other Arab leaders against the Jews has been exposed. This is because the issues to which these scholars address themselves have powerful political and legal ramifications even in the present day. Moreover such issues remain at the heart of the conflict and the difficulties surrounding its resolution. This is often difficult for those external to the conflict to understand. Europeans and North Americans who shape policies towards the Middle East express a different perspective on their own history and that with respect to the Israeli–Palestinian conflict. In seeking resolution to conflict the past may appear less relevant that the pressing issues of present-day violence, terrorism and the political and socio-economic problems that often accompany it. For Palestinians and the Israelis the past is not irrelevant and in many ways sustains the political narratives of the present and explains the absence of peace.

Legacy

If history is cited by the politicians and policy-makers it tends to be used selectively and employed evidentially in support of one position over another. For Palestinians and Israelis, however, history matters much to the present and the ways in which they not only define their conflict with each other but their sense of identity, victimhood and nation cohesiveness too. The Palestinian *nakbah* and the Holocaust of the Jews had remained sacred cows of a sort until the new historians sought to review the past to better understand it as a series of multi-dimensional events in which both good and bad collide within the same communities and nations. Often the goal of such reappraisals of past events has been to promote greater comprehension in the present of the problems that appear so intractable between the two people. Such goals challenge the collective memory at large within the two societies, which work at cross-purposes to each other in teaching generation after generation of Palestinian and Israeli children about the victims and victors of the conflict. Finding dispassionate, accurate and common ground between the two peoples where there is agreement over the historical genesis of the conflict and accountability is rare.

The 'official' versions of history that bind the two nations together and in opposition to each other lead to the negative subjectification of the other. Naturally such historical accounts and their representation – whether in books, films, cultural activities and diplomatic outreach to the international community – are selective and employed in the service of political positions. The new historians have challenged the processes of selectively reproducing history on both sides of the divide. They have in turn been accused of engaging in highly divisive political meddling as a result. Historians such as Avi Shlaim assert that his role is not merely to 'record facts' but to be a 'judge, and above all a hanging judge. And therefore . . . sit in judgment on Israeli leaders' (Shlaim, 2002). Whether such accounts have decisively influenced policy-makers, in particular external powers such as the USA, is questionable. Nor have such works yet been much in evidence in terms of legal accountability of the actors involved in the conflict. Attempts to incorporate revisionist thinking into the teaching of history in Palestinian and Israeli schools have also been limited in scope and more often than not stymied by the breakdown of the peace process and with it the desire to better understanding within the two communities.

The events of 1947 and 1948 are thus commemorated and celebrated but are also firmly accorded a place in the annals of the history of this conflict. The controversy and culpability of the culprit of history during this period will, however, remain open to fierce political challenge until the myriad issues that bedevil the conflict in the present day are resolved.

Further Reading

As I indicated in earlier sections of this chapter historical accounts of this period of the conflict vary greatly in terms of the explanatory motivations of the actors involved. The further reading in this section concentrates on providing a broad range of these accounts, including those that contest the period of the creation of the Palestinian Diaspora and refugee community before the establishment of the state of Israel in May 1948. One controversial starting point is the book by Segev (New York: Free Press, 1986) which forensically dissects the events surrounding the establishment of the state of Israel to expose a chronicle of friction among the

Zionists and between Israel and the Arabs. The debate on the mandate and events in 1948–49 are further explored in Cohen's works of 1978 and 1988, Finkelstein (London: Verso, 2001), Flapan (New York: Pantheon Books, 1987) and Rogan and Shlaim's edited work (Cambridge: Cambridge University Press, 2001). Edward Said presents a searing account of the opening stages of the conflict during this period in his co-edited work (London: Verso, 2001) entitled *Blaming the victims*. Shlaim gives deep insight into the developing Zionist–Jordanian axis in his work of 1998 (Oxford: Clarendon Press).

Some compelling memoirs that reflect on this period from the Palestinian perspective include Ghada Karmi's book (London: Verso, 2001), Aburish (London: Bloomsbury, 1991) and Toubbeh (London: McFarland, 1998). Although the authors of these accounts were quite young children or young teenagers during the period under discussion, their insights into the changing world around them and their subsequent sense of displacement and exile gives an interesting insight into the period. Such memoirs can usefully be be compared with accounts of the same period from Jewish and Israeli sources in Benny Morris's work on the period (Cambridge: Cambridge University Press, 2004), Shlaim's work (London: Penguin, 2000) and Segev (New York: Owl Books, 2000). Masalha's work is a firm rebuttal to the earlier work from Morris (London: Pluto Press, 2003). The refugee issue is further examined in books such as Bowker's work (Boulder, CO: Lynne Rienner, 2003), Fischbach (New York: Columbia University Press, 2003), and Gelber (Brighton: Sussex Academic Press, 2006) – this is a theme that we address further in Chapter 4 of this book.

Aburish, S. (1991) *Children of Bethany, the story of a Palestinian family*, London: Bloomsbury.

Bowker, R. (2003) *Palestinian refugees: Mythology, identity, and the search for peace*, Boulder, CO: Lynne Rienner.

Cohen, M. (1978) *Palestine: Retreat from the Mandate: The making of British policy 1936–45*, London: Paul Elek.

—— (1988) *Palestine to Israel: From Mandate to Independence*, London: Frank Cass.

Finkelstein, N.G. (2001) *The Holocaust industry: reflections on the exploitation of Jewish suffering*, London: Verso.

Fischbach, M.R. (2003) *Records of dispossession: Palestinian refugee property and the Arab–Israeli conflict*, New York: Columbia University Press.

Flapan, S. (1987) *The birth of Israel: Myths and realities*, New York: Pantheon Books.

Gelber, Y. (2006) *Palestine 1948. War, escape and the emergence of the Palestinian refugee problem*, Brighton: Sussex Academic Press.

Karmi, G. (2001) *In search of Fatima, a Palestinian story*, London: Verso.

Masalha, N. (2003) *The politics of denial, Israel and the Palestinian refugee problem*, London: Pluto Press.

Morris, B. (2004) *The birth of the Palestinian refugee problem revisited*, Cambridge: Cambridge University Press.

Rogan, E. and Shlaim, A. (eds) (2001) *The war for Palestine: Rewriting the history of 1948*, Cambridge: Cambridge University Press.

Said, E. and Hitchens, C. (2001) *Blaming the victims: Spurious scholarship and the Palestinian question*, London: Verso.

Segev, T. (1986) *1949, The first Israelis*, New York: Free Press.

—— (2000) *The seventh million: the Israelis and the Holocaust*, New York: Owl Books.

Shlaim, A. (1998) *Collusion across the Jordan: King Abdullah, the Zionismt movement and the parti-tion of Palestine*, Oxford: Clarendon Press.

—— (2000) *The Iron Wall, Israel and the Arab world*, London: Penguin.

Toubbeh, J.I. (1998) *Day of the long night, a Palestinian refugee remembers the Nakba*, London: McFarland.

4   Israel reborn

Chapter outline

- Divine model or democracy by expediency   78
- Political parties and the Israeli–Palestinian conflict   82
- Labour Zionism   83
- Revisionist Zionism   85
- The religious Zionists   87
- Between a rock and a hard place: the Israeli Arabs   90
- Israel's democratic future   94
- Further reading   96

> I adore Hatikva. But it's time it was changed. It's time its words were changed. It's
> time it was replaced by an anthem that all Israelis can sing in good conscience,
> non-Jews as well as Jews.
>
> Bradley Burston (Burston, 2007)

Since independence in 1948 the state of Israel has undergone some significant
changes in its political system, its perspective on the conflict with the Palestinians
and other Arab states, as well as a society, economy and nation. In 2008 as Israelis
celebrated 60 years of statehood it was apparent that while the major political
edifices of the state remained intact the constituent parts of the state, including its
army and legislature, were enduring some of the worst crises in their history. From
a critical perspective, the anniversary of independence and commemoration of the
fortieth anniversary of the 1967 Six-Day War a year earlier was also a reminder of
the price paid for the establishment and maintenance of a Jewish state wrought
from the ashes of Britain's mandate misadventure in Palestine.

Today, some argue that the integrity of the Jewish state – territorial, political,
cultural, religious, economic and social – is characterized more by internal fissure
than unity. This chapter will frame the events of 1947–48 and their consequences
in terms of the emerging Israeli state and its political system. The chapter will then
analyse the institutions of the state, state- and nation-building and the growing

issue of enmity with Israel's Arab neighbours. This evaluation of the new state will delineate the nature of Israeli society, including its secular and religious dimensions as well as the emergence of the Israeli political party system. We will observe the numerous accounts that attempt to explain the processes of state-building and consolidation through visions of Zionism that often pulled Israeli voters and political activists in opposite ideological directions. For Zionism and even post-Zionist discourse has impacted on the direct linkage established through the achievement of independence in 1948, the Jewish nation and the Jewish state.

Some explanations are thus derived from the discourse that addresses Jewish nationhood in terms of the religious or divine claim to the land of Israel in terms of a perpetual covenant to the Jewish people. Thus the modern state reflects this covenant through its institutions, citizens and concept of statehood. There is little by way of contradiction with this view and that of modern Zionism as a form of nationalism that also came to express itself in competition with the rising force of Palestinian nationalism. This nationalism found itself in competition with the Palestinians in terms of the aspiration for territorial self-determination and statehood. Ultimately the development of the state of Israel as a democratic product is linked to these discourses. These discourses have centred on the external security of the state, the means by which to fix the borders of the state and the means by which to define the nation within the state. None of these issues have been easily resolved because they are affected by a range of discourses within the aegis of Zionist and post-Zionist thinking.

After independence and state formation in 1948 some distinct patterns of power distribution were apparent within the political institutions of the new state. The major distinction identified by most authors on the topic lay between the dominant communal character of Western or Ashkenazi Jews, Sephardic or Oriental Jews, and those 160,000 Palestinian Arabs that remained on their lands and in their homes and thus found themselves within the boundaries of the new Israeli state. Within this mix it became apparent that communal tensions would arise over the secular or religious character of the forgoing Zionist project and thus the state. Judaism had been declared 'the established religion of the state', as defined by orthodox Judaic prescription. Thus the Chief Rabbinate represents the institution of the state with respect to all religious matters. This means, for example, that in the modern state of Israel civil marriage is not permitted and until recently the notion of Jewish identity in relation to citizenship was predicated on orthodox dominance.

With a population of more than 6 million, of whom more than 1.3 million are Palestinian Arab, the modern state today is a functioning model of politics with a democratic framework. The state offers universal adult suffrage to all its citizens (Jewish and non-Jewish), it has a multi-party parliamentary system, holds frequent free and fair elections and there is an independent judiciary. It should be noted, however, that in the wake of state formation in 1948 the state was deliberately constructed to provide *the* national impetus for the Jewish people and the organization of the nation as the 'centre for world Jewry.' The state and its institutions were thus the locus of the Israeli economy, its cultural life, education, welfare, immigrant absorption and military structures. Until relatively recently this left little room for non-governmental movements and organizations and when they were initially organized they grew out of forms of opposition to the state that were often seen as a challenge to the very nature of Jewish identity as well.

In the wake of the war of 1948 and the birth of the nation the state of Israel and its political leaders were aware of the challenges inherent to the discourse of enmity that would now dominant relations with their Arab neighbours. In this way it was apparent that the state would forge a unique relationship with its own military. As a former chairman of the Jewish Agency and Speaker of the Israeli parliament (the Knesset), Avraham Burg, acknowledges, 'I think we are a society that in its feelings lives by the sword' (Shavit, 2007: 9). This was a challenge in terms of preserving its democratic credentials and in avoiding the model of military authoritarianism that would emerge in other parts of the Middle East. While it is true that the political landscape in Israel would be shaped by men in (or newly divested of) military uniform, Israelis were convinced by the necessity of the national security argument that democratic culture could still be preserved.

This changed somewhat in the wake of the War of 1967 when Israel's military occupied the Palestinian territories as well as the territories of Egypt (the Sinai) and Syria (the Golan Heights). Israel denies the label of occupation. As Pappe highlights, 'The Israeli government declared from the very onset of its occupation that these areas were "territories under custody" in which military rule would apply' (Pappe, 2004: 199). Some argue that since 1967 the moral and ethical dimensions of this paradox of democracy and occupation have never truly been resolved within Israeli society and have established political tensions and fissures between the state and society (Avner, 1993). These tensions are enduring and they impact on the nature of the domestic political landscape, the identity of Israelis, as well as the way in which Israel projects itself externally. Burg sums up this dilemma by contending that 'there is no Israeli whole. The Israeli is a half-Jew. Judaism always prepared alternatives. The strategic mistake of Zionism was to annul the alternatives. It built an enterprise here [in Israel] whose most important sections are illusions' (Shavit, 2007: 9).

Divine model or democracy by expediency

David Ben Gurion, the first Prime Minister of Israel, and his Zionist colleagues established an architecture for the state that reflected what they had practiced through the agencies and institutions of Zionism in Palestine. This goes some way in explaining the immutable Jewish character of the state as well as its democratic institutions and structures.

The Israeli legislature was established when the provisional government transferred its authority to the 'constituent assembly', which at its first session in February 1949 was declared the Knesset. One of the first tasks of the new legislature – which consisted of a single chamber, a single constituency, and 120 members – was to address the task of writing a constitution. This was abandoned, however, when it became clear that it would not be possible to reconcile the religious character of Zionism with the secular nature of the state; as Garfinkle notes:

> no way could be found to integrate Jewish religious law into a document expressing its relationship to the state. The secularists would not agree that *halakha* should hold any privileged position in Israeli law overall, which would have ceded substantive authority to rabbis over a vast legal arena, and religious Zionists would not agree to a constitution that did not so privilege *halakha* at least in principle.
>
> (Garfinkle, 2002: 158)

The electoral system, with its single constituency, and principle of proportional representation has meant that the party with the most votes is asked to form a government through negotiation with other political parties or blocs. A multiplicity of political parties emerged in Israel – seeking to take advantage of the electoral system that permitted low thresholds in order to gain a seat in the Knesset. This system has allowed a more representative picture of the Israeli polity to emerge: from across the political, ethnic, and religious spectrum. It has also been argued though that this allows some political elements to punch above their political weight in governments of coalition. This point has been made with respect to religious parties who have enjoyed:

> [a] political leverage incongruent with the actual size of their support base, particularly when bargaining for positions within a coalition cabinet. Accordingly, the portfolios of education, religious affairs, and the interior ministry came to be prized cabinet positions among religious parties, since they allowed the propagation and inculcation of their particular values throughout Israeli society.
>
> (Jones, 1999: 161)

Until more recent times, this, however, did not make it difficult for any one party to be dominant in a coalition government. In fact from 1949–77 the Israeli Labour Party always polled enough votes to form the government and its main partner in coalition was the National Religious Party (NRP). Under this arrangement certain spheres of power or influence between the secular socialists and the National Religious were largely maintained: Labour mostly enjoyed a free rein with respect to government portfolios such as foreign affairs or national defence and the NRP held sway over religious affairs. Thus it needs to be remembered that in Israel power-sharing as a result of proportional representation has meant that the Westminster system of one-party dominance in the legislature is simply not on the agenda.

The politics of the legislature are vulnerable to the vagaries of both internal pressures as well as external factors, particularly as they relate to the conflict or peace process with the Palestinians. Coalition partners, thus, have the capacity to make or break processes that are inextricably tied to the Palestinian issue and how the government of the day deals with it. On the contentious topics of territorial compromise or negotiation with the Palestinians, peace deals, or refugees, coalition governments have been made and broken.

As commendable as proportional representation is as a device for optimizing democracy through mechanisms of power-sharing in diverse societies, it appears to work against the unitary impulse of Israel as a Jewish state. In practice then the Knesset has been described as 'little more than a talking shop with the opposition parties unable to wield much influence over the scope and pace of legislation' (Jones and Murphy, 2002: 33). Political power in practice is vested in the elected executive – the Prime Minister – with the President acting as the symbolic Head of State. Unfortunately this has not prevented the President from becoming mired in public controversy. In 2006, for example, President Katsav, mired in allegations of sexual misconduct, was forced to take a Knesset-approved 'leave of absence' while he dealt with the accusations.

Until 1996 the leader of the winning party in general elections was asked to form the government and become Prime Minister. In 1996, however the Knesset passed legislation providing for direct election to the post of Prime Minister. The move was designed to strengthen the executive and leave him/her less vulnerable to coalition pressures. In the elections of 1996, 1999 and 2001 voters directly elected Benjamin Netanyahu of the Likud Party, promoting himself on an anti-peace agenda, Ehud Barak of the Labour Party, who promised a pro-peace agenda and an Israeli withdrawal from south Lebanon, and finally Ariel Sharon, who declared that there was no Palestinian negotiating partner and took a unilateralist approach to the Palestinian issue. On 7 March 2001, the Knesset voted to change the system of direct prime-ministerial elections and restore the one-vote parliamentary system of government that had operated until 1996. Some believed this to be a retrogressive step that would once again allow smaller coalition parties to determine who should lead the government of the day. The benefits of the direct-election system were lost:

> The ability to bridge between conflicts of interest in the two-ballot system was much greater. It is a fact that the government which was formed in 1999 included almost everyone and offered an incredible opportunity to integrate immigrants, ultra-Orthodox, the right, and the secular – an opportunity that was lost due to poor management.
>
> (Ramon, 2002)

Hence the system of direct election did not appear to empower the Knesset in relation to the Executive. Some argued that in fact it promoted opportunities for an even greater monopoly of power by the Prime Minister as 'producer and director of the entire show' (Arian, 1997: 243). This has continued to allow room for personality politics to skew the task of governance. In respect of the Israeli–Palestinian conflict there is plenty of evidence to demonstrate that the politics of personality or leadership has played both a powerfully positive as well as negative role either in terms of exacerbating or resolving the conflict. Crick has identified this issue of leadership as an obstacle to peace and it is certainly the case that with respect to relations with the Palestinians the office of the Prime Minister has had some considerable impact on the way in which issues are handled and developed and vice versa in terms of the Palestinian counterpart (Crick, 1990).

Coalition government, however, has resulted in some rather unusual political bedfellows and have also led to left–right, secular–religious alliances that have in turn resulted in internal political crisis and government collapse. Larger parties have become the hostage of smaller parties that often represent the extreme end of the Israeli political/religious spectrum. These governments, however, have been the wellspring of Israeli legislation, with the Knesset itself doing little by way of bringing new legislation on to the Israeli national agenda. As mentioned previously there was some hope that the legislation allowing direct election to Prime Minister would release some of the pressures felt within the coalition system on larger parties by the smaller groups but it proved unsuccessful and Israelis returned to the status quo ante.

In the absence of a written constitution Israel has outlined its fundamental character as a state in the Basic Laws. The 'Right of Return' law is one of the most important of these laws and it is commonly cited as defining Israel as a modern nation state. In 1950 the Knesset established the principle of citizenship of the state for every Jew no matter where in the world they resided. Through this legislation every Jew that immigrates to Israel has the right to citizenship and thus all the benefits that citizenship derives. Hence Elliott who is Jewish, who was born in Scotland in the late 1960s and came to live and work in Israel in the 1990s, has the automatic right to citizenship of the state. Musa, who is Palestinian, who was born in Jerusalem in the late 1950s and went to study in the United Kingdom but returned in the 1980s, does not have the right to citizenship or residency and is fighting the Israeli authorities against deportation. The enactment of this legislation was inspired by both the imperative of Israel's state-builders to ensure that the Jewish character of the state was enshrined in law but also expediency as the new state engaged in a process of state-building through immigrant absorption.

Since 1948 millions of Jews from all over the world have exercised their 'right of return'. Thousands of Holocaust survivors, more than half a million Jewish immigrants from the Maghreb and other countries in the Middle East, such as Iraq and Yemen, and more than a million Jews from Russia and the former Soviet Union states have availed themselves of a 'right of return' to the state of Israel and citizenship. The 'Law of Return', passed on 5 July 1950, declares that 'Every Jew has the right to come to this country as an *oleh* [immigrant]'. In 1970 an amendment to the law made provision for the 'return' of non-Jews who are the spouse, children or grandchildren of Jews. In principle the Israeli 'Law of Return' does not exclude non-Jews from immigrating to Israel but in practice naturalization for non-Jews is an extremely difficult process, particularly for any Arabs.

The 'right of return' with respect to Palestinian Arabs is, for example, a politically contentious issue for the Israeli state. Palestinian refugees, from the conflicts of 1948 and 1967, believe that they and their descendents have the 'right of return' to Israel/Palestine. A UN resolution passed in 1949 recommended that refugees who wished to return to their homes and live at peace with their neighbours should be allowed to do so, and that compensation should be paid for the property of those choosing not to return and for loss of or damage to property. Yet Israel's politicians and policy-makers understand that if it were to comply with the UN resolution and Palestinian refugees and their descendants were allowed to return, then the demographic change would terminate Israel's status as a Jewish majority state. The ethos of the nation and the state itself would be terminally undermined. Some argue that this logic explains why Israel refuses to address the 'return' of Palestinian refugees (see Chapter 5). Others contend that the Arab demand for a Palestinian return to Israel/Palestine is nothing more than another tactic for the destruction of the state of Israel but this time through demographic warfare. Yet others, such as Avraham Burg, contend that the 'Jewish state' has become unworkable. He says:

> It can't work anymore. To define the state of Israel as a Jewish state is the key to its end. A Jewish state is explosive. Its dynamite . . . The Law of Return is an apologetic law. It is the mirror image of Hitler. I don't want Hitler to define my identity . . . Our confrontational Zionism vis-à-vis the world is disastrous.
>
> (Shavit, 2007: 8)

Burg's perspective reflects a minority view that in acknowledging a 'right of return' for Palestinian and Jew alike the possibility of peace, prosperity and stability is increased.

Political parties and the Israeli–Palestinian conflict

There are a number of ways in which to delineate or explain the party system in Israel. Some address the party system in terms of Zionism and its manifestation along the lines of Labour Zionism, Revisionist Zionism and Religious Zionism. Others address the issue in terms of a play on Israel's tribes – referring to the Ashkenazi, Sephardim, Haredi and Arab 'tribes' in terms of traditional party affiliations and voting patterns. Suffice to say they all, in some way, represent a system that is rooted in the early Zionist community that settled in Palestine during the mandate and most closely align to the ideologies of Labour Zionism and Revisionist Zionism (Garfinkle 2002). The ethnic base of party affiliation or support grew first from the impact of the immigration of the Sephardic Jews of the 1950s, and later from the million or so Jews who emigrated from the former Soviet Union. Thus, in the 2006 elections the Israel Beytanu 'Israel our home' party, which is mainly composed of and supported by Russian immigrants, won 11 seats in the Knesset, and their leader, Avigdor Liberman, entered into coalition with the Kadima-led government, becoming Deputy Prime Minister and Minister for Strategic Affairs. To be fair, the 'victory' of the party was publicly perceived to be less about immigrant politics and more about the right-wing anti-Arab sentiments of Liberman and its implications in terms of the peace process. This was an election during which not only parties from Israel's right, such as Likud and Kadima, but also Labour presented a hawkish position vis-à-vis the Palestinians, leaving only small leftist parties such as Meretz and the Arab parties to promote a less unilateralist approach to conflict settlement.

Thus, although it is fair to argue that there is an ethnic pattern to the emergence of political parties in Israel – Ashkenazi, Sephardim, Russian immigrant, and Arab – the ideological impulse behind the emergence of the Israeli party system simply cannot be discounted or perceived as irrelevant to explaining the system, its evolution and its importance in electing governments that hold a particular ideological position when it comes to the conflict. The proliferation of political parties – even within broad ideological coalitions – is one other way in which the diversity and frictions within Israeli society are manifested. It is argued, for example, that the Israeli political system has been affected by the Israeli occupation of 1967. Wahrman contends that occupation has played its part in corrupting the political system: 'It was only a matter of time, inevitably, before the lawlessness of the occupied territories – and their support networks throughout the Israeli state apparatus – began infecting Israel proper' (Wahrman, 2007). He complains that Israel's political system and its democratic character have been eroded as a result of what he contends is ethically and morally questionable behaviour in relation to the Palestinians, first in 1948 and second in 1967. The legacy, he argues, is manifest in the political crisis, scandal and corruption that dog almost every aspect of the Israeli political system today. Opponents of this view contend that Israel, despite being surrounded by enemy states intent on its destruction and motivated by ideologies of authoritarianism, has nevertheless managed to build the only functioning democracy in the Middle East. Its security issues in terms of the Palestinians are centred on defence not occupation.

Labour Zionism

During the mandate period the wellspring of Zionist politics burst forth and from this, one element eventually emerged dominant: Labour Zionism. From this early struggle against the revisionists for dominance Labour Zionism represented the steering force of the project to establish an independent state for the Jewish people. Segev describes the relationship between the forces of Labour Zionism, represented by David Ben Gurion, and Revisionist Zionism, represented by Ze'ev Jabotinsky, as one of 'competition and animosity', which 'grew far more intense' (Segev, 2001: 332).

After independence the dominance of Labour Zionism was also apparent in the key institutions of the new state, including the defence force, the labour movement, the party system and the *kibbutz* movement. In essence, the core structures established by the Labour movement during the mandate period (*Yishuv*) were converted, as a result of its dominance, post-independence into key institutions of Israel as an independent nation state. This hold on the state and wider Israeli polity would only be broken in 1977 when the old enemies of Labour Zionism in the guise of the Revisionist Zionists would gain electoral advantage and lead the government.

In 1949, however, all that was ahead of David Ben Gurion and his followers who established the Mapai Party and led the transition to a full-functioning democratic state and party system. The consolidation or expansion of Labour Zionism was also apparent in 1968 when Mapai merged with Achdut Ha'Avoda, the core of which was drawn from the kibbutz movement, to form the Israeli Labour Party (Avoda). Under successive Prime Ministers that included Ben Gurion, Sharett, Eshkol, Golda Meir and Yitzhak Rabin, the Labour alliance not only dominated the domestic political agenda but determined the nature of Israel's relationship with the Palestinians and neighbouring Arab states. Throughout this period, while it was possible to discern the extent to which the principles of Labour Zionism – including an ideological commitment to socialist politics – were shaping the state of Israel, it is argued that there was little, as we shall see in the following chapters, to distinguish it in terms of the relationship with their own Palestinian citizens, or those of the territories that they occupied after the war of 1967.

After 1967 it was difficult to discern how Israel's Labour-dominated governments reconciled socialist-leftist thinking with what its critics argued was the subordination of the Palestinian people. Indeed as Arian acknowledges, since 1967, Israeli governments (irrespective of their political hue) have 'had two underlying themes: (1) to avoid changing the legal status of most of the territories taken in 1967, and (2) to support Jewish settlements in the territories' (Arian, 1989: 27). It was only in the 1990s, when Labour won elections on a specifically pro-peace platform and was able to form a coalition government that was not dependent on the religious or rightist parties, that the true import of such politics was translated successfully into the domain of politics with the Palestinians. This was the government, led by the 'old general', Yitzhak Rabin, that initiated the dialogue with the PLO that led to the 1993 Declaration of Principles (Oslo Accords), and recognition of the PLO as the sole legitimate representative of the Palestinian people. This was the manifestation of Labour Zionism that felt secure enough in a government coalition to manoeuvre for a 'land for peace' deal that would preserve national security and bring prosperity to Israel.

Today Labour Zionism has been caught up in the domestic and external crisis linked to the collapse of the peace process, the collapse of the main pillars of the socialist project in Israel, and a growing apathy within Israel's polity for the formal politics of the party system and the state. Under the Labour-aligned government led by Ehud Barak, in 1999 Israel came closer to peace with the Palestinians than ever before. But, as Chapter 9 outlines, a collapse in confidence during the process also concluded with the outbreak of the al-Aqsa armed Intifada and the decision by the electorate to place power in the hands of the centre-right. Avishai, in a defence of Labour Zionism and its past achievements, however, contends that without change traditional Labour Zionism will wither the longer the democratic project in Israel continues to decline (Avishai, 2002).

Revisionist Zionism

Like Labour Zionism the Revisionist movement is a product of the mandate period and the internal tensions and fissures that affected the Zionist movement as it struggled to build a state and achieve independence. It should be noted that the founder of the Revisionist movement enjoyed close relations with the leading luminaries of Labour Zionism until the split of the 1920s. The split lay not in the fundamental objectives of the Zionist movement but the pace or means by which the goal of statehood could be achieved. Ze'ev Jabotinsky, the father of Revisionism, quarrelled with David Ben Gurion over issues such as immigration, Jewish self-defence and land settlement. For Jabotinsky, moreover, the territorial scope of the Zionist project was broader than that which the leaders of Labour Zionism were prepared to accept. As such the revisionists were vehement critics of the 1947 UN Partition Plan considering it a compromise too far (Segev, 2001: 496). Jabotinsky also believed that the transfer idea, as it pertained to the Palestinian Arabs, may have been acceptable if it meant that Jewish statehood could be realized in all of Eretz Israel (Greater Israel). By Greater Israel the Revisionists often refer to a geographic entity for the Jewish 'commonwealth' that would today extend beyond the boundaries of the current state.

In terms of the political parties of Israel the Revisionist Zionist strand was reflected in a number of spheres. These included the Herut and Liberal parties, which during the 1970s, after a merger with the former Labour La'am group, formed the Likud Party. The Likud Party itself fissured again in 2005–06 over the controversial plan by party leader, Ariel Sharon, to proceed with a plan for disengagement from the Gaza Strip. From Likud emerged the centre-right party of Kadima, which contested and won the right to form the coalition government in 2006.

Revisionist Zionists have eschewed the socialist roots of the early Zionist movement, preferring to focus on the economic and ethnic imperatives for Zionist settlement and statehood. They became clearly distinguishable, post-1948, from the other expressions of Zionism within the foundation institutions of the state. In this respect the Revisionists spent many years in opposition to the hegemony of Labour Zionism and its projects enacted through the structures of the state. In the election of 1977, however, that hegemony was broken by Likud in a victory at the polls that shook Labour Zionism to its core. Jabotinsky's close associate and political heir, and believer in the philosophy of territorial redemption of Israel through force, Menachim Begin, was now the head of the Likud-led government.

Begin scored another electoral victory in 1981 and during his tenure led the country into peace with Egypt in 1979, including the dismantlement of Israeli settlements in the Sinai, and to war in Lebanon in 1982. In Lebanon Begin's Defence Minister, Ariel Sharon, was accused of complicity in the massacre of Palestinian civilians at the refugee camps of Sabra and Shatilla. Compelled to leave the centre stage of politics due to ill-health in 1983 Begin was succeeded by Likud hardliner, Yitzhak Shamir. Ariel Sharon personally lauds Begin for the:

way he had held his party together for twenty-nine years, building it step by step until his great personal victory in [the election of] 1977. The historic achievement of peace with Egypt . . . second election victory in 1981 . . . The great settlement projects in Samaria, Judea, Gaza and the Galilee. The decision to eliminate the PLO's kingdom in Lebanon . . . All there were remarkable achievements, done under his leadership.

(Sharon with Chanoff, 2001: 528)

Shamir then won the 1988 election over Labour and headed a Likud-led coalition with Labour until 1990.

Under the leadership of Yitzhak Shamir, Likud and the Revisionist bloc in general embarked on a period of intense infighting as a series of powerful personalities attempted to displace Shamir. In time, of course, they were successful. Shamir was first replaced by Benjamin Netanyahu who brought victory to Likud in the 1996 election. After Netanyahu lost the 1999 election he was replaced by the hardliner, Ariel Sharon. As was previously mentioned, Likud infighting in 2005 over the issue of disengagement led Sharon to split from the party and for Netanyahu to re-emerge as party leader. In the 2006 election Likud were badly beaten at the polls, losing votes not only to Sharon's new Kadima Party but to other electoral players under the Revisionist umbrella, such as Israel Beytanu. Likud barely scraped into third place in the Knesset and have thus found their ability to influence government formation severely restricted. By this point it was also clear that Likud has lost its former appeal to ethnic elements such as Israel's Sephardic community or Russian immigrant groups.

The issue where Likud will now have to fight to retain its identity and support is, of course, the key revisionist principle of territoriality and territorial expansion of the state of Israel as defined by the Greater Israel principle. Linked to this, of course, are the settlements and settler movement as they epitomize this principle, the question of the indigenous Palestinian population and its future as well as the identity of Israel as a Jewish state. Under Begin settlement expansion, as detailed in Chapter 6, occurred at an unprecedented rate and was closely tied to the national security agenda.

But Likud does not enjoy a monopoly on the principle of territorial integrity and other small Revisionist parties such as *Tehiya* (Revival), *Tsomet* (Crossroads) and *Moledet* (Motherland) also consider this to be an important part of their political platform. *Tehiya*, for example, was formed in the wake of opposition to Begin's peace deal with Egypt, which included the dismantlement of the Sinai settlements and a commitment to grant the Palestinians some form of limited autonomy in the West Bank and Gaza Strip. None of these parties has been prepared to consider 'land for peace' deals with the Palestinians and in fact argue strongly for the retention of such territories as Israel's right. The Motherland Party, along with the newly formed Israel Beytanu and extreme right-wing parties such as Kach (which was eventually banned) also advocate the 'transfer' of the Palestinians. The fortunes of these parties have risen and fallen in line with the extent to which a negotiated solution to the conflict with the Palestinians, according to some territorial formula, has proved popular with Israelis.

The religious Zionists

The distinction between religious Zionists and secular Zionists is as important as the one between religious non-Zionists and secular non-Zionists, reflecting once again the core tensions within Jewry over state, nation, religious prophecy and modern politics in Israel and the Middle East. The prominent role that religious Zionists, and more specifically Haredi parties, have played in determining the policies of the state in Israel have impacted on society and modern democracy as well as with the Diaspora community. Hence there are elements that fear that the religious Zionists seek to remove the secular dimension of the Israeli political system altogether. They point to the impact, at the level of local or municipal politics that the Haredi parties have had in Jerusalem – as compared to other Israeli cities like Tel Aviv – where the tenor of the city is shaped by the religious Haredi parties. The truth is that over the decades since independence the Haredi parties have gained power through their participation in the democratic system, thus making it harder to deny them a voice.

The impact of the religious Zionists on Israeli politics also raises the issue of the extent to which the modern state in Israel can accommodate the religion of Judaism and the degree to which it should be allowed to define the state. Nevertheless it is also important to remember that some religious Jewish groups eschew the Israeli state. Some Haredim (religious Jews) traditionally shunned the Zionist enterprise and settlement that took place during the late nineteenth and early twentieth century. Indeed there were elements of the Haredim that contended that the establishment of the state of Israel, before the return of the Messiah and the redemption of the Jewish people, was tantamount to apostasy. Today there are some elements of the Haredim, such as *Neturei Karta*, who have refused to compromise their religious beliefs by supporting Zionism or the state of Israel.

Others within the religious community of Haredim have debated the importance of political action as a means to achieve the return of the Messiah and the unity again of the Jewish people. One such group is the National Religious Party (*Mafdal*) which was formed by religious Jewish Zionists who believed that the principles of Zionism should be shaped by the Jewish faith itself and not the secular socialist ideals of the leftists. In this way the aspirations of the Zionists who held faith to be the centre of the political project gained a foothold in the system of politics that evolved first in the Zionist project and later within the political system that evolved after statehood was achieved in 1948. In this way Judaism as a faith system would shape the evolution of the state system that would unite Jews of the world through citizenship and territoriality. The elements of Zionism that came to be represented by the NRP wanted to ensure that the nature of the state would be shaped by Judaism.

Within a decade of Israel's independence in 1948 the NRP emerged as a formal political party contesting elections on a religious-political platform and had won a place in national government. Following the war of 1967 and the Israeli occupation of the West Bank and Gaza Strip the NRP opposed any 'land for peace' deal formula that would entail relinquishing their lands, which they considered covenanted from God. In this way the NRP also supported and in turn drew support in elections from the settler movement and more generally those who occupied the right-wing of the Israeli political spectrum.

The party enjoyed power in many national unity governments but its biggest challenge came between 2003 and 2005 when it was a member of the coalition government, led by Ariel Sharon, that pursued the plan for disengagement from the Gaza Strip. The NRP, traditionally enjoying support from the settler community, vehemently opposed the disengagement and with elements of Likud they tried to prevent the withdrawal from Gaza occurring. The NRP split over whether to oppose the plan from within or outside government. The party called for a national referendum on the disengagement but failed to sway the government or Knesset. In November 2004 the party resigned from the coalition and the government in protest. But in February 2005 elements within the NRP split again to form a new party, which contested the 2006 elections. In the 2006 poll the NRP managed to poll only enough votes in alliance with National Union (*Moledet* and *Tkuma*) to gain three out of nine seats in the Knesset.

A large number of disputes and splits have occurred among the religious Zionist parties but nevertheless they have proved their longevity and their determination to make the Israeli political system more rather than less religious. Many of these parties, in the absence of a constitution that enshrines religion at the heart of the political project, portray themselves as the guardians of Israel's Jewish character. They believe that Judaism should be at the heart of the Jewish state. They thus exist in uneasy coexistence with the secular parties of the Israeli political system.

In the Israeli elections of 2006 the three major religious parties or coalitions – Shas, NU/NRP and United Torah Judaism – gained 27 out of 120 seats in the Israeli Knesset. Shas joined the coalition government and gained four cabinet posts but none of them in areas of governance where a religious Zionist agenda might be influential in terms of determining the identity or character of the state and its citizens. This should be compared, for example, to the elections of 1999 when Labour Prime Minister, Ehud Barak, was careful not to antagonize the religious groups by offering them cabinet positions that gave them influence over welfare/social affairs, including housing and religion. This was part of a well-known practice in terms of handling the demands of the religious Zionists and their coalition clout. The religious Zionists have always wanted to shape the Jewish character of the state from within the centre of power and they have traditionally enjoyed a degree of religious sway over many issues relating to civil, social and religious life in Israel.

Voter apathy had meant that unprecedented numbers of Israelis failed to participate in the 2006 election but this did not appear to affect the religious Zionist parties too greatly – the damage or weakening had, of course, occurred within NRP during its tenure in the government led by Ariel Sharon. The influence of these parties has remained constant and their leaders and representatives have weathered many of the recent political storms and their accompanying scandals, mostly without being at the centre of the allegations and claims. The power of the secular Israeli political parties has been weakened by such claims and the religious parties have gone some way in benefiting. This is illustrated in terms of the emergence of Shas which is essentially an orthodox religious party without pretensions to Zionism. Shas was established in 1984, by Rabbi Ovadia Yosef, the outcome of yet another Israeli party split, and has grown in popularity ever since. Contesting its first election in 1984 the party won four seats in the Knesset, in 1999 it had succeeded in winning 17 but by 2006 its number of seats was down to 12. The policies of the parties are formulated through a consultation process presided over by the Council of Torah Sages. The party opposes an attempt to remove faith from the Israeli state, arguing that it undermines the Jewish identity of the citizens. Shas is socially conservative in outlook and with respect to the conflict with the Palestinians it advocates the principle of Eretz Israel (Greater Israel) but from a non-Zionist perspective. They are against territorial concession in terms of 'land for peace'. In 2005 the party's leader, Rabbi Ovadia Yousef, ordered all 11 Shas members of the Knesset (MKs) to vote against Sharon's Gaza disengagement plan. And although they failed, in September 2005 Rabbi Ovadia Yousef caused some controversy when he stated that Hurricane Katrina was God's punishment for US President George Bush's support for Israel's disengagement from Gaza. Shas has often enjoyed the balance of power in coalition governments between Likud and Labour. It has been argued that the majority of its supporters and voters are not Haredim but are drawn from Israel's modern orthodox community. It is difficult to determine whether the non-Zionist principles of Shas also mean that it is of relevance to debates about politics in the post-Zionist age (Usher, 1998: 36).

One indicator with respect to this dimension of the debate is the extent to which the Haredim community embraces democracy or rejects it. In early November 2006 the usually quiet, conservative religious neighbourhoods of Mea Shearim in Jerusalem were transformed after Haredim men sporting their peyote and black hats rioted against a proposed Gay Parade planned for the city. For a number of nights, under cover of darkness, the Haredim rioted and battled with Israel's police force. Posters in Mea Shearim defamed the District Commander of Police in Jerusalem as a 'Nazi'. Israel's newspapers, television and radio stations buzzed with the debate about who had the right to parade and who had the right to stop the parade in a democratic state. The Mayor of Jerusalem pleaded for calm and well-known commentators entered the fray. Some commentators stated that they feared that if the Haredim were allowed their way this would be a death-knell for democracy in Israel. At the end of fraught days of violence the Gay Parade was cancelled altogether and replaced by a rally – well away from the religious neighbourhoods of Jerusalem – which thousands of Israelis and others attended. Indeed the event became a rallying point for Israel's secularists and leftists, one of whom, Rabbi Gilad Kariv, a leader of Israeli Reform Judaism and associate director of the Israel Religious Action Centre, declared:

I think that it was quite clear that the main issue is not gay and lesbian rights in Israel . . . From a very early point in the battle, it was about democracy, human rights, and the character of our society as a liberal and Western society.

(Kariv, 2006)

Suffice to say, not all Haredim or Israel's ultra-orthodox community feel so strongly about their rights to the exclusion of others. Though there are many who believe that Israel would be better constituted as a theocracy that represents authentic Jewish identity and belonging.

There is not always a clear line between such views and the boundary of democracy and theocracy is constantly being tested by a variety of actors within the Israeli political system. Ambiguity about the boundary between Judaism and politics does, however, prevail. This set of relations had created a layer of tension with respect to inter-communal relations that pits the observant and the non-observant, the religious and the secular against each other and the ways in which they perceive Israel to be their state and the political repository of their aspirations. Secular Israelis fear the growing demographic threat that they believe high birth rates in Haredi society pose to them. They object to a culture which largely absolves Haredi sons and daughters from national service in the IDF and instead compels their young to study in Yeshivas dependent on charitable donations. Secularists have also chafed under the social restrictions that have been imposed on them and resent the Haredim for what they believe to be intolerable power over the political mainstream.

Between a rock and a hard place: the Israeli Arabs

If Israel had never conquered the West Bank (Judea and Samaria) and Gaza Strip, if it were an island in the Mediterranean Sea, it would still face an Arab demographic threat . . . That's because Israel's own Arab minority has been growing as a percentage of the country's total population, and continuing a process of 'Palestinianization'.

(Rozenman, 2007)

Israel's Arab population finds itself between a rock and a hard place and their presence, as the quote above illustrates, poses a problem for those Zionists whose vision of the state and its political system is exclusive in nature. Not only is the presence of this ethnically different population an issue but many Jewish Israelis view this as a threat. They argue that the threat is principally demographic but within it are the seeds of a politically existential danger as well. Fears abound that within the first two decades of the twenty-first century the Palestinian population between the Mediterranean Sea and the Dead Sea will have reached a point of parity with the Jewish population. Awareness of this issue partly explains the Jewish immigration (*aliyah*) imperative that has impacted so heavily on Israel's political agenda – particularly in the last 20 years.

Even the notion of Israel's Arabs is contentious, conferring as it does a label on the indigenous Palestinian Arab population of Mandate Palestine who after 1948 found themselves living in Israel. Today Israel's Arab/Palestinian citizens account for 20 per cent of the population and include Muslims, Christians and the Druze. These are the Palestinians who remained but whose identity has been defined by a political system with a hegemonic Zionist foundation.

From 1949 to 1966 Israel's Arabs were compelled to live according to a discrete set of laws that some argued were tantamount to martial law. In theory Arab citizens of the state were supposed to enjoy the same rights as Jewish citizens. In practice, it is contended, the Israeli measures, which included checkpoints, travel permits, land and property confiscations, identity checks and the practice of IDF-imposed 'closed areas' in Arab towns and villages, were tantamount to prejudice. In this respect the early state and its institutions set up a series of measures which discriminated against its Arab citizens. The land confiscation policies had a major impact on diminishing the economic power and associated status that this community had previously enjoyed. On the grounds of security and the legal codes of the Absentee Property law Palestinian land inside the borders of the state of Israel was confiscated. Through these means hundreds of thousands of acres of land were expropriated.

Arabs were clearly treated with suspicion and their loyalty and identity within the new state was called into question. This made the task of promoting a multi-cultural state founded on the principle of good inter-communal relations almost impossible. These approaches by the state to its Arab population also limited their economic opportunities and altered their economic status – losing land, for example, increased urbanization and patterns of migration by the Arab communities to Israel's city – thus undermining their traditional social status as well. A weakening of traditional power structures within a community already fractured by war eventually dislocated power from traditional clan and family structures dissipating, to some extent, political power as well. Israel, it is argued, was looking for a subordinate passive Arab community that would not seek to stir the political pot on the basis of their national identity and representation (Tessler and Grant, 1998).

In the late 1960s and early 1970s incipient political and community activism was regarded with degrees of hostility by many within Israel's political elite. Rights-based associations that sought to highlight the ways in which the community were discriminated against did experience a high degree of scrutiny from state intelligence and security agencies as well as forms of harassment. In March 1976 a demonstration organized by Arabs against land confiscations led to clashes in which the Israelis police killed six of the Arab demonstrators. The annual commemoration of 'Land Day' has become a protest against the state's treatment of Israel's Arab/Palestinian minority as second-class citizens. This was underscored again in 2000 when Arabs in Israel protested at Sharon's controversial visit to al-Aqsa that led to the outbreak of the second Intifada. In the demonstrations that ensued Israeli police killed 13 and the state was ordered to investigate the unprecedented level of violence perpetrated by its officers (Usher, 2000). There was also a lingering fear that the Palestinians of Israel were part of a fifth column that would undermine the Jewish state and bring about its destruction from within. These Palestinians were clearly conflicted in their loyalties – so many had retained deep-rooted family links with that part of the Palestinian population that now found itself stateless. As Rouhana remarks:

> As Israeli citizens, they [Palestinian Israelis] have failed to influence Israeli policy vis-à-vis the conflict and they have shied away from significantly shaping the nature of the state of Israel. As Palestinians, they are increasingly showing signs of support for the Palestinian cause, but have made only a limited political contribution.
>
> (Rouhana, 1989: 38)

There is no doubt that the failure to resolve the Israeli–Palestinian conflict has left the Palestinian citizens of Israel between a rock and a hard place.

Since 1966, when Palestinians of Israeli citizenship were permitted to play a full and legitimate role in the political system, they have formed political parties that represent their ethnic minority interests or joined centre-left parties that tend to promote a multi-ethnic approach and a 'land for peace' deal with the Palestinians. But during the late 1980s and 1990s support for such parties went into decline and other political forces achieved Arab electoral and political support. There has, since the late 1980s, also been the growing phenomenon of Israel's Islamic fundamentalists and their impact on the political system. Their leaders and spokesmen have claimed much public attention for their protests and demonstrations. The Islamist movement in Israel also reflects the growing importance of local Islamist elements in the West Bank and Gaza Strip, such as the Palestinian Islamic Jihad (PIJ) and Hamas. It became a potent actor on Israel's local political stage. By the early 1990s it had won control of Arab municipalities and it appeared that the national stage – through party formation and contesting Knesset elections – was inevitable. This was problematic though in terms of a desire to marry the demand for democratic representation with the wider Islamist issue of recognition of the state of Israel. Many in the more militant wings of the Islamist movement in Israel have explicitly ruled against this kind of relationship with the state of Israel.

In the 2006 elections the United Arab List electioneered on an openly Islamist platform. One of the major leaders of this faction, Ibrahim Sarsur, was quoted as saying:

> Voting for the Zionist parties is supporting those who spilled our blood, robbed our land and violated our holy places . . . If you give your vote to them, a Jew will enter and an Arab will not . . . Islam has opened our hearts – this is our message.
>
> (Wilson, 2006)

In this way the Islamists competed for and won many votes from the socially conservative classes of Israel's Arab population.

In terms of voting patterns traditional allegiances have reflected developments both as they affect the Arab/Palestinian citizens of Israel and as a result of Israel's policies in the occupied territories. In the late 1970s and early 1980s, for example, many voted for Israel's Labour Party and the leftist parties because they believed these would best serve their interests and those of the occupied Palestinians. Support for the right with its pro-settlement polices was virtually unheard of. By the late 1980s and early 1990s and the waning of communism and communist parties globally, electoral allegiance for Rakah – the Israeli Communist Party that many had previously supported – also went into decline. Support for Arab political parties and organizations has continued to grow and in some respects is said to reflect alienation with the record of Labour governments in respect of the Palestinians. Arab parties include the Arab Democratic Party and Balad, as well as the United Arab List, all of which contested the 2006 elections. There are as a result a number of Arab/Palestinian citizens of Israel who now represent their constituencies in the Knesset. Such MKs have been investigated by their own state for visiting Arab states of the region such as Syria (with which Israel remains at war). In April 2007 Arab/Palestinian MK and former Balad Party chairman, Azmi Bishara, fled Israel amidst public claims and state investigations of 'consorting with the enemy, treason and passing secrets'. Bishara, an outspoken critic of Israel's policy towards the Arabs had gone on trips to Syria and other Arab countries during the 2006 Israeli war on Lebanon. The Israeli press has accused Bishara of disloyalty. 'Each of his tirades only further serves to stigmatise Israel's Arab citizens as fifth columnists', declared an editorial in the leading English language *Jerusalem Post* newspaper on 11 April 2007.

In February 2007 a prominent group of Arab citizens of Israel issued a public call on Israel to stop defining itself as a 'Jewish state and become a consensual democracy for both Arabs and Jews' reflecting polls that had revealed that 57 per cent of Israel's Arab population 'wanted a change in the character and definition of the state' irrespective of whether this state was a consensual democracy or a binational product (Kershner, 2007). Once again these views hinted at the uneasy nature of democracy in the present configuration of the Jewish state and a desire for greater consideration of a post-Zionist vision of statehood that would be inclusive of the Arab population.

Authors such as Rouhana (1989) contend that the Palestinian citizens of Israel still face forms of discrimination from the state. Such discrimination, in terms of opportunities to grow as equal citizens in the state, has continued to dog Israel's claim to democratic credentials. The usual official or unofficial riposte tends to point to the status of Arab citizens elsewhere in the region. Israeli officials and pundits point out that Israel's Arab population enjoys better economic opportunities and standards of living, rights and responsibilities when compared to neighbouring states such as Egypt or Syria. This is a truism that fails to shine the light on Israel itself. The political activism of Israel's Palestinian citizens has led to some fateful episodes of state violence perpetrated against them as the cost for making their voices heard. In March 2007 when Israel's first Arab Muslim cabinet member admitted he would not sing the Israeli national anthem, Hatikva, his prime-time tussle with an Israeli news anchorman exposed again the unpalatable side of a nation state with such an exclusive ethnic base. The MK and Labour Party member declared he would not sing such an exclusivist anthem:

> Of course I would not sing the anthem in its current form. But before we talk about symbols, I want to talk about equal education for my children. It's more important that my son would be able to buy a house, live with dignity . . . the Arabs are not in a mood to sing right now . . . I fail to understand how an enlightened, sane Jew allows himself to ask a Muslim person with a different language and culture, to sing an anthem that was written for Jews.
>
> (Meranda, 2007)

Resolving these identity issues and their impact on the political arena has enormous consequences not only for the internal character of the state but in terms of its relations with its Arab neighbours.

Israel's democratic future

It has been argued that Israel is the most democratic country in the Middle East. Studies that work on indicators of democracy regularly demonstrate that compared to Arab neighbours such as Egypt, Jordan, Syria and Lebanon the state of Israel exhibits a democratic character. Israel's citizens enjoy the right to vote in free and fair elections and there is a multiplicity of political parties. Israel's citizens enjoy many of the same democratic rights as those in Western rather than Middle Eastern states.

Some theorists and critics, however, have contended that two major features or factors with respect to present-day Israel now inhibit and make problematic its own claim to democratic credentials. The first factor centres on the nature of the state and more specifically its Jewish character. The second questions the extent to which the democratic character of any state is weakened or undermined by engaging in occupation. Amidst the rhetoric of critique and counter-critique on this topic a number of important points emerge.

With respect to the first factor, when the Israeli state was founded in 1948 it was established as a Jewish state but the reality of the state some 60 years later is that Israel is a multi-ethnic and multi-cultural society with a political system that, some argue, does not accommodate these features in a democratic fashion. The continuing absence of a written constitution to protect the rights of all Israel's citizens, for example, is identified as problematic (Lerner, 2004). Kimmerling, on the other hand, has argued that because 'the main characteristic of the Israeli society is Zionist hegemony . . . expressed in the taken-for-grantedness of the equivalence between the Jewish religion and nation', that Israel cannot be strictly defined as a secular democratic state (Kimmerling, 1999: 339). So Israel's political system, which is largely Western in structure reflecting consociational approaches to democratic politics, is still bedevilled, according to its critics, by its Jewish character. Some scholars have argued that it would in fact be more appropriate to refer to Israel as an 'ethnic democracy', an 'ethnorepublic' or even an 'ethnocracy'. Such labels tend to denote a political system of rule by one dominant ethnic group 'within the state and beyond its borders' (Yiftachel, 1999: 5). In response to such critiques Israel's democratic defenders highlight the fact that despite attempts from its many regional enemies to destroy the state and undermine its security to the extent that Israel becomes untenable the country has survived and maintained a fully functioning democratic system.

The other issue that some contend has a detrimental effect on Israel's democratic credentials is the 40-year occupation of Palestinian territories. In 1967 Israel, as a result of the Six-Day War, became responsible, according to the terms of the Fourth Geneva Convention, for the population of the territories it now occupied. Israel, however, contended that the West Bank and Gaza Strip did not qualify as 'occupied territories'. Many of Israel's legal scholars do not define the West Bank and Gaza Strip as 'occupied territories'; as the former Chief of the Israeli supreme court argues there is no de jure applicability of the Fourth Geneva Convention since in the case of the West Bank and Gaza Strip there had not been a legitimate authority that had been ousted as a result of the war.

Avnery contends, however, that Israel is an occupying power and that:

> the occupation causes rot, which penetrates all the pores of the national organism . . . At the end of the Six-Day War, the entire world saluted us. Little, brave David had won against Golaith. Now it is we who are seen as a heartless, brutal Goliath.
>
> (Avnery, 2007)

Many opine that the democratic credentials of the Jewish state have been compromised internally with respect to how it manages the ethnic identity of the state with citizens who are not Jewish and externally in terms of the extent to which occupation has corrupted the political system. They point to the resignation of army generals, the prosecution of the President and government ministers, the allegations of fraud and corruption that is rampant among Israel's political classes, the assassination of Premier Yitzhak Rabin by extreme religious nationalists, the accusations of apartheid modelling in the Palestinian territories, the illegality of settlements and walls, and the allegations of human rights abuses and inequitable treatment of the occupied population. They wonder whether the democratic edifice of the Israeli state and its political system has become so fractured that it is on the point of collapse. Defenders of the democratic project in Israel remind the critics that the Jewish tradition is inherently democratic but that only in a post-Zionist age can Israel come to terms with its past and its Palestinian neighbours. For such figures only a multi-cultural Israel instead of the ethnic-particularity of the Jewish state can provide the solution to Israel's security and the recovery of its institutions as democratic beacons (Nimni, 2003). The birth of the Jewish state in 1948, the development of its political institutions and its relationship with the Palestinian people has been shaped by the prevailing forces of Zionism and military occupation leading to a polity that has been divided over its destiny. Others robustly contend that Israel has only acted in legitimate self-defence against a persistent Arab onslaught, which seeks the termination of a Jewish state and presence. Political leaders like Ariel Sharon contend that the future of the Palestinian people lay in a:

> Palestinian state [that] has existed since 1922 . . . where most of the popula-
> tion is Palestinian, most members of parliament are Palestinian, and most of
> the prime ministers have been Palestinian. Jordan is in fact if not in name a
> Palestinian state with which we should be discussing the future of the inhabit-
> ants of the Samaria and Judea.
>
> (Sharon with Chanoff, 2001: 545)

For figures like Ariel Sharon the future of the state of Israel is resolved by moving the Palestinians to Jordan. For others the future of the state of Israel and the main-tenance of its democratic political systems lies in either a two-state or one-state solution to the conflict with the Palestinians that preserves the state through requiring that its enemies recognize its right to exist.

Further reading

There is some very worthwhile material to engage with on Israel and its political system. A good starting place would be Jones and Murphy (London: Routledge, 2002), Garfinkle (New York: M.E. Sharpe, 2002) and Barari (London: Routledge, 2004). Evaluating issues such as Zionism and the development of the political system, the books by Kimmerling (Berkeley, CA: University of California Press, 2001), Shafir and Peled (Cambridge: Cambridge University Press, 2002), Cook (London: Pluto, 2006) and Sternhell (Princeton, NJ: Princeton University Press, 1998) make for provocative reading. Arian's book (Chatham, NJ: Chatham House Publishers, 1997), *The Second Republic: Politics in Israel,* and recently updated, is a very good overview and outline of the political system in Israel and its institutional setup.

On developments within Zionism and the state since 1948 the books by Avishai (New York: Farrar, Straus and Giroux, 1985), Beilin – a former government minister and one of the architects of the peace process with the Palestinians – (New York: St. Martin's Press, 1992) and Ellis (London: Pluto Press, 2002) provide historical oversight plus a critical secularist discourse on the nature of Israel, the democratic political project and the conflict with the Palestinians in the post-1948 period. Debates that focus on Judaism and Israel as a modern nation state include those authored by Beit-Hallahmi (Concord, MA: Pluto Press, 1992), Evron (Bloomington, IN: Indiana University Press, 1995) and Hazony (New York: Basic Books, 2000). Sacher (New York: Knopf, 1996) and Segev (New York: Free Press, 1986) examine developments within Zionism as statehood and independence were achieved in the post-1948 era. Dimensions of diverse political being and expres-sion in Israel and its broad political spectrum are examined in books such as that by Roane and Shainin (New York: The New Press, 2002), which presents dissenting voices against Israel's occupation and its moral impact on the soul of the nation. Friedman (New York: Random House, 1992), Lustick (New York: CFR, 1988) and March (Louisville, KY: Westminister/John Knox Press, 1994) overview

Israel's settlers, their political project, territorial and religious discourse and impact on right-wing politics in Israel. In the past Israel's Arab citizens were often overlooked in studies of Israeli politics but the following book provides a very comprehensive analysis: Louer (New York: Columbia University Press, 2007). Finally the accounts by Israeli authors David Grossman (New York: Farrar, Straus and Giroux, 2003) and Amos Oz (London: Hogarth Press, 1983) offer intimate portraits of Israel, its citizens and its conflicts.

Arian, A. (1997) *The Second Republic: Politics in Israel*, Chatham, NJ: Chatham House Publishers.

Avishai, B. (1985) *The tragedy of Zionism: Revolution and democracy in the land of Israel*, New York: Farrar, Straus and Giroux.

Barari, A.H. (2004) *Israeli politics and the Middle East Peace Process 1988–2002*, London: Routledge.

Beilin, Y. (1992) *Israel: A concise political history*, New York: St. Martin's Press.

Beit-Hallahmi, B. (1992) *Original sins: Reflections on the history of Zionism and Israel*, Concord, MA: Pluto Press; reprint, New York: Olive Branch Press, 1993.

Cook, J. (2006) *Blood and religion: The unmasking of the Jewish and democratic state*, London: Pluto.

Ellis, M. (2002) *Israel and Palestine out of the ashes: The search for Jewish identity in the twenty-first century*, London: Pluto Press.

Evron, B. (1995) *Jewish state or Israeli nation?* Bloomington, IN: Indiana University Press.

Friedman, Robert (1992) *Zealots for Zion: Inside Israel's West Bank settlement movement*, New York: Random House.

Garfinkle, A. (2002) *Politics and society in modern Israel: Myths and realities*, New York: M.E. Sharpe.

Grossman, D. (2003) *Death as a way of life: Israel ten years after Oslo*. Translated by Haim Watzman. New York: Farrar, Straus and Giroux.

Hazony, Y. (2000) *The Jewish state: The struggle for Israel's soul*, New York: Basic Books.

Jones, C. and Murphy, E. (2002) *Israel: Challenges to identity, democracy and the state*, London: Routledge.

Kimmerling, B. (2001) *The invention and the decline of Israeliness, state, society and the military*, Berkeley, CA: University of California Press.

Louer, L. (2007) *To be an Arab in Israel*, New York: Columbia University Press.

Lustick, I. (1988) *For the land and the lord: Jewish fundamentalism in Israel*, New York: CFR.

March, W. Eugene (1994) *Israel and the politics of land: A theological case study*, Louisville, KY: Westminster/John Knox Press.

Oz, Amos (1983) *In the land of Israel*. Translated by Maurie Goldberg-Bartura. London: Hogarth Press; reprint, New York: Vintage Books, 1984.

Roane, C. and Shanin, J. (eds) (2002) *The other Israel: Voices of refusal and dissent*, New York: The New Press.

Sacher H.M. (1996) *A history of Israel: From the rise of Zionism to our time*, 2nd edn, New York: Knopf.

Segev, T. (1986) *1949, The first Israelis*, New York: Free Press.

Shafir, G. and Peled, Y. (2002) *Being Israeli: The dynamics of multiple citizenship*, Cambridge: Cambridge University Press.

Sternhell, Z. (1998) *The founding myths of Israel: Nationalism, socialism, and the making of the Jewish State*. Translated by David Maisel. Princeton, NJ: Princeton University Press.

5 The dispossessed

Chapter outline

- Becoming refugees: origins of an issue   99
- We who are refugees   101
- Refugees: the key to peace?   108
- Compensation   111
- Talking about refugees   113
- Further reading   117

> This is all that I am. I live in a room that leaks in an overcrowded camp where as a refugee I have no rights, no state and no future. This is all that I am but I still have Palestine in my heart.
>
> (Umm Mohammed, 78 years old, Bourj al Barajneh refugee camp Lebanon)

In today's world of spiralling ethnic conflict, war, famine and poverty, refugees have become a familiar sight in news reports from across the globe. The UN agency tasked with addressing the safety and rights of refugees estimates that there are more than 25 million refugees from around the world. It is estimated that there are over 8 million Palestinian refugees making them the largest single group. These Palestinians lost their homes in 1948 and 1967 and they and their descendents have remained scattered across the world ever since. They form a Palestinian Diaspora – stateless and in exile from their homeland. The stories of these refugees are epitomized by symbols of belonging; they cling to the keys and property deeds of their lost homes. Their memories and the imagined sense of belonging of their descendents are as tenuous as the scent of orange blossom in the spring or the whisper of the wind through the branches of an olive tree. And yet such a sense of identity and belonging also sustains a national movement for self-determination and independence and calls for an end to Israel's occupation of the Palestinian territories.

The struggle of the Palestinian people to express the 'right of return' to the land they consider their own has become a major political issue, motivating the demand not only for statehood but a need to have dispossession recognized by Israel in terms of all its consequences. In essence it is argued that this territorial dispute between Israel and the Palestinians will never be resolved if the issue of the refugees does not come first. This chapter, then, examines the birth of the refugee issue in 1948 and its escalation in 1967, as well as responses to it by a variety of actors. The chapter will outline the effective dismemberment of Mandate Palestine in a territorial carve up that left Palestinians without a state. It will look at the impact in terms of the regional nature of the conflict, and the political disempowerment of the Palestinians themselves as refugees. The chapter will also focus on themes such as human rights, citizenship and the 'right of return', and will examine the response of the international community. This means that theories of nations – as imagined communities that embrace culture as well as politics – will be explored in this chapter (Anderson, 1991).

Becoming refugees: origins of an issue

In one sense the origin of the Palestinian refugee issue begins with the settlement movement of Zionists in Palestine. The Zionist movement was organized around the idea of a homeland for the Jewish people. In practice the attraction of Palestine lay in the opportunity for some Jews in Europe to flee persecution, pogroms and extermination. Jewish refugees flooded Palestine's shores in the 1930s and 1940s and they all wanted a home. Yet it is estimated that between 1947 and 1948 some 750,000 Palestinians fled their homes and constituted a refugee problem that remains unresolved. Relative sanctuary from conflict and war was found in the neighbouring Arab countries of Egypt, Jordan, Syria and Lebanon, and further abroad in Europe and North and South America. Families, clans, communities, villagers and townspeople moved en masse leaving their past lives behind them.

The reasons for the flight from 1947–48 and the controversy surrounding the issue of Palestinian refugees ever since has been endlessly debated by a variety of parties with an interest in the conflict and its resolution. Israel, for its part, has asserted in very bald terms that Palestinians are refugees of their own making – they left through their own choice or because they obeyed the orders of Arab commanders at the time. Many an Israeli officially and unofficially has opined that the 'refugee problem' was an Arab creation and that if Palestinians just accepted citizenship in the Arab states in which they reside the whole issue would be resolved anyway. They speak of the futility of continuously portraying the tattered torn image of the refugee in his shanty shelter when a better life has always beckoned. From this perspective the Palestinians should 'own the problem' of becoming refugees and thus solve it themselves 'through absorption' into the states that have hosted them as refugees.

Palestinians, for their part, maintain that they were forcibly dispossessed as part of strategic decisions and policies within the Zionist movement to expel them. They believe that the Zionists wanted to empty the new state of Israel of its Arab population. The dispossession (*nakbah*) is a defining element of national consciousness and the subsequent movement for resistance and liberation. Palestinians claim that they watched helplessly as their lands were grabbed by Israel and Israelis, their homes turned over to new Israeli immigrants, while at the same time the majority of them were denied the 'right of return'. From the Palestinian perspective Israel is the source of the refugee problem and the reason why it remains unresolved. Also from the viewpoint of many in the international community Israel has defied international norms and laws on this issue and through 'acts of violence' engendered flight, seized Palestinian land and stole Palestinian homes in the wake of 1948.

The controversy over the genesis of the refugee issue matters in terms of assessing levels of responsibility for the 'problem' and its solution. There are real political and practical dimensions to this issue. These include the applicability and thus leverage of particular UN resolutions on the issue, whether the 'right of return' can take place in practice, and to what extent the issue of compensation becomes relevant and applicable.

Clearly, in 1949, the newly formed United Nations recognized that the war of 1948 had resulted in the dispossession of the Palestinians and that as such they possessed certain rights which should be respected. A UN (non-binding) resolution on the issue promoted the idea of refugee return for the Palestinians along with compensation for those choosing not to return.

In this case the government responsible was Israel. Israel made it clear that it did not wish to have hundreds of thousands of Palestinians returning to settle within the boundaries of the new Jewish state. These boundaries had, through their territorial gains in war, far expanded beyond what was originally outlined by the United Nations in the 1947 Partition Plan. The Palestinian presence, although a number had remained and were made Arab citizens of the Israeli state, was portrayed as representing both a strategic and demographic threat to the infant Jewish state. Successive Israeli governments have maintained a solid line on this issue. Each has broadly declared that the return or 'entry into Israel' of Arab refugees would undermine the security of the state and the Jewish character of society. The demographic argument about the threat posed by a return of Palestinian refugees has also been cited decade after decade as another reason why they should be kept out of Israel. Such a view is not simply something expressed on the Israeli streets but has been at the foundation of official state policy on the issue of the Palestinian refugees. In the meantime Israel has 'welcomed home' millions of Jewish 'refugees' from the Arab world (1950s) and the former Soviet Union (1990s) in an attempt to always keep the demographic balance sheet in their favour. Jews across the globe enjoy the 'right to return' to the state of Israel with entitlements to citizenship even if they have been born and bred elsewhere.

The Palestinians have interpreted such actions as hostile and a denial of their rights. As one such declares: 'Who will compensate me and my family for all the suffering we went through? Financial compensation cannot replace the right of return. . . . The main thing is to go back to where I belong' (Shavit and Bana, 2001). Palestinians have continued to assert their 'right of return' to their home-land irrespective of Israeli objections. Palestinians do not wish to be 'resettled' in host or third countries. Their very existence in some of these countries has, in fact, been perceived as a major problem by host states and Palestinians there have been forced to endure a marginal existence (Sayigh, 2001). In the Palestinian refugee camps of Lebanon, for example, it would be fair to say that the majority of the community has, since 1948, existed in a state of suspended animation; they are neither allowed to be part of Lebanon nor to return to their homes in Palestine.

Attempts by the international community to push for a resolution of the refugee issue have faltered and failed in the face of Israeli intransigence and non-cooperation. Success was only measurable in terms of establishing some form of relief to those who found themselves stranded in the tented refugee camps of the Middle East. In 1950 the UN Relief and Works Agency (UNRWA) was founded to provide some temporary assistance to the refugees. By 1951 UNRWA had compiled a list of 950,000 registered refugees. UNRWA has subsequently fed, housed and provided healthcare and education and other forms of assistance for 'tens of thousands of fleeing refugees' and their descendents. Their work continues to the present day. In 2006, for example, when fears of a humanitarian crisis abounded following the international boycott of the Hamas government in the Gaza Strip, UNRWA was distributing emergency food rations to some 800,000 out of 1.5 million Gazans.

We who are refugees

With the absence of a resolution of the refugee issue on the diplomatic and political front it was only natural that the number of refugees would continue to grow. In 1967 the Six-Day War contributed to a further growth in refugee numbers, although most of these people did not end up on the official UNRWA registration list. By March 2006 UNRWA was reporting that there were 4,375,050 refugees. This, however, was half the story. For according to a variety of statistics and classifications, as they relate to international law, a further 4 million Palestinians are also refugees. Kanaana, for example, contends that in 1948 about 70 per cent of the Palestinian population became refugees (Kanaana, 1998). Many Palestinians were 'displaced' internally and externally as refugees; leaving their homes to live with family members elsewhere. As one Jerusalemite notes:

> my mother's family were from Jerusalem and her father worked for the lands authority under the British occupiers but they went to family in Jordan after the war. My mother came back as a bride to my father here in Jerusalem.
>
> (Taha, 2007)

Of course those that had left of their free will were not permitted by Israel to return to their old homes and businesses. There were also those who were out of Palestine in 1948 or 1967 and by dint of bad luck were subsequently excluded.

The number of refugees remains open to fierce debate and interpretation with contesting arguments pitted by one side against the other. Israel is accused of using a variety of means to prevent Palestinians from reaching their historic lands and birthright. The Israelis for their part claim that Palestinians constantly inflate their numbers; that Arab states conspire against Israel to keep the refugee issue alive, and will do anything to aid and abet the Palestinians in their false claims to a 'right of return' and compensation. Those who are refugees, however, feel the stigma of their status on a daily basis.

The way of life for refugees varies considerably and much of their subsequent existence has depended on where they 'ended up' after the turmoil of war and displacement in 1948 and 1967 (Brand, 1998). In the Gaza Strip the majority of Palestinian residents live in or are from the refugee camps. There are nearly 1 million Palestinian refugees registered with UNRWA. Almost all of this number is squeezed into one of the most densely populated areas of the world, living in camps that consist of breeze-block shelters with the most basic amenities. Families that fled particular villages and districts in Palestine in 1948 ended up living alongside each other in the packed camps of the Gaza Strip. UNRWA runs eight camps, from Rafah in the south, with a camp population of over 95,000, to Jabalia in the north, with a population of over 106,000 residents. In the case of all the camps, you smell and hear them before you see them. In the late 1940s and early 1950s camp shelters were constructed from tents but today the 'camp' is simply a mass of tightly packed shanty dwellings and narrow alleyways that teem with human life. The displacement of 1948 created a reaction of resistance among some of the refugees. One elderly refugee from Nusseirat in the Gaza Strip recollects how in the early 1950s he joined the resistance organized by the Muslim Brotherhood in his camp:

> I was from the village of al-Jura near Ashkelon and when I was a pupil in elementary school I was always thinking about my village and getting back there . . . a man in the school told me about the Muslim Brothers and when I became involved in their units they enabled me to be like a strong tower to be involved in a war to restore and return to my village . . . we were all refugees . . . discharged from our land . . . I swore to be a good Muslim defending Islam and our lost land. Putting my hand on the Koran I swore to be a good example to our community . . . I was not afraid because I was armed with Allah's blessing.
>
> (Abu Mohammad, 1993)

Some 50 years later the grandchildren and great-grandchildren of the original refugees, like the old man of Nusseirat camp, devoted themselves to the same struggle:

> My great-grandfather and all my family were dispossessed of their homes and denied their rights . . . We in this camp, in the factions and the youth groups are fighting to win recognition of our rights . . . we will not let Israel deny us the future that they denied my parents and grandparents . . . but the rest of the world has to also give us our rights . . . we will never forget that we are the sons of the land of Palestine and not children of the refugee camps and the hopeless future.
>
> (Abu Mohammad, 1993)

In large part refugee aspirations and resistance are located in the wider political discourses that surround the Palestinian movement for liberation and self-deter-mination, as well as the conflict with Israel and international discourses on rights and recognition. Such rights have often been stymied by the powerful asymmetry that characterizes the way in which Israel and the Palestinians have been perceived by the outside world and, in particular, by the foreign policy-makers of powerful national governments.

From 1948–67 (with a six-month interruption only) Gazan refugees were subject to Egyptian political administration. From 1967 onwards Gazans experienced Israeli occupation in the form of military and civilian rule, plus the establishment of illegal settlements and developments. Since 1994 Gazan refugees have come to experience the experiment in limited autonomy under the Palestinian Authority. And although the peace negotiations outlined the refugee issue as fundamental to any final settlement between Israel and the Palestinians, by 2006 the tenuous plight of Palestinian refugees in Gaza had only worsened. Gazan refugees experience high rates of unemployment and an economic status that often sees families subsisting on rations of flour, rice and oil from UNRWA distribution centres. Many refugee groups have, past and present, engaged in direct forms of politics and protest in an attempt to play a part in determining their political future.

In the West Bank UNRWA run 19 refugee camps for some 185,000 residents out of a total registered refugee population of 705,207. The total Palestinian popu-lation of the West Bank is 2.5 million. The camps are similar in terms of basic provisions and amenities to those in the Gaza Strip. Balata camp in the city of Nablus, for example, is part of a huge squalid squeezed-in urban space. Down dark alleys one makes one's way to refugee shelters where families often live in tiny homes seven to ten to a room, often dependent on UNRWA food rations because any opportunity for work is lost because of Israeli closures, walls, checkpoints and barriers. Israel remains in occupation of the West Bank and any sense of autonomy for the camp dwellers and wider refugee community is circumscribed by the secu-rity arrangements imposed by Israel.

For many of the residents of the camp political action to promote the wider cause of Palestinian self-determination and liberation becomes their primary preoccupation. As one Fatah activist states:

> My whole family are giving their life to Fatah, to the *tanzim* [armed militia], to serving the people in our parliament and on the council, we have to reach resolution so that we can leave life in the camp behind and return to our homes.
>
> (Tirawi, 2006)

Other camp residents engage in more direct forms of confrontation with the Israeli occupation authorities. Groups such as the Fatah-affiliated al-Aqsa Martyrs Brigades (AMB) have acquired guns from the black market and have used their weapons in armed engagements with the IDF. At night gun-fights shatter the silence of the camp as special IDF units send in their men to engage the AMB fighters. As one fighter declares: 'we are here to protect our people from the occupation . . . we have to fight because they [Israel] have destroyed our police . . . we bring law and order, will end the chaos and fight the occupation until victory.'

Elsewhere in the Arab world the fate of Palestinian refugees has been dependent on the response of specific regimes to the Palestinian presence in their midst, as well as on the often torrid relationships that have evolved between these states and Palestinian political organizations such as the PLO and latterly Hamas and Islamic Jihad. Those who are refugees are subject to forms of discrimination and hostility, as well as being used as pawns in a political battle that plays out on a wider regional stage. Palestinian refugees remain in camps – often under guard or closely scrutinized by Arab internal intelligence agencies such as the *mukhabarat* – while they await their fate as part of the wider settlement of the Palestinian–Israeli and Israeli–Arab conflict.

In Lebanon, for example, even a hint of a Palestinian accent is likely to evoke tension and hostility from some sections of Lebanese society, who blame the Palestinians for much of the tortuous civil conflict that gripped the country from 1975–90. Palestinian armed groups, under the command of Yasser Arafat and other PLO leaders in Lebanon became embroiled in the civil conflict, siding with various factions and at the same time launching attacks against Israel from Lebanon's southern regions. Israel responded by invading Lebanon on two occasions (1978 and 1982), and occupying the southern area of the country until 2000. Many Lebanese blamed the Palestinians for bringing Israel into their country as occupiers (Fisk, 1990).

In August 1982 the PLO leadership and its fighters were forced to leave Lebanon but they left behind many thousands of their fellow Palestinians in the refugee camps. The remaining population, mostly the old, women and children, were vulnerable to Lebanese and Israeli ire. This vulnerability was fully exposed in September 1982 when Israeli soldiers surrounded the Palestinian refugee camps of Sabra and Shatilla in West Beirut and provided cover for Phalangist Lebanese forces to conduct a massacre of the Palestinian residents – between 800 and 2,000 died. The massacre ignited worldwide controversy and outrage. The UN General Assembly condemned the events at Sabra and Shatilla as an act of genocide. Robert Fisk, one of the few Western journalists to witness the immediate aftermath of the massacre wrote:

> At first, we did not use the word massacre . . . They were everywhere, in the road, in laneways, in back yards and broken rooms, beneath crumpled masonry and across the top of garbage tips. The murderers – the Christian militiamen whom Israel had let into the camps to 'flush out terrorists' – had only just left . . . these people, hundreds of them had been shot down unarmed. This was a mass killing . . . that was also an atrocity . . . It was a war crime.
>
> (Fisk, 1990: 359–60)

More than 25 years later Shatilla camp is little changed from those days in September 1982, when so many of their own defenceless residents were killed.

Today the camp is a squalid, overcrowded and impoverished memorial to the refugees who still dream of a return to Palestine. Their poorly constructed shelters, where families live in extreme poverty, are often decorated with posters of their political leaders and historic landmarks such as the Dome of the Rock in Jerusalem.

The fate of Palestinian refugees in Lebanon is thus a precarious one. Few have the opportunity to acquire citizenship – otherwise the delicate sectarian balance may be imperilled – they are excluded from countless professions and job opportunities, they are not permitted to own land nor enjoy state services such as health or education. In the camps the Palestinian armed militias are an active element:

> Lebanon's worries stem also from the continued presence of these armed Palestinians in the camps, because they represent a potential for instability, threatening to re-enact the civil war days unless a solution for the Palestinians is found: 'If Palestinian refugees in Lebanon were not given the right to return home, they will become a time bomb'.
>
> (Haddad, 2000: 1)

In 2007 the infiltration of radical Islamist elements in the Nahr al-Barid refugee camp and the subsequent government-led campaign to oust them once again left the Palestinian refugee residents of the camp caught up in the middle of terrible conflict.

It is clear that Lebanon will never accept the settlement of the Palestinian refugee community in their country as part of a wider peace settlement package between Israel and the Palestinians. Successive Lebanese governments, usually fractious over many issues, are unusually united in respect of the Palestinian refugees and their tenuous future in Lebanon. Though by 2007, when sectarian pressures among Lebanon's Muslim population re-emerged, the Palestinians were courted once again. Preliminary surveys have revealed the depth of Lebanese opposition to Palestinian resettlement in the country. And even if the reasons for opposing Palestinian resettlement differ, Lebanese opinion transcends the usual sectarian divisions on this issue (Khashan, 1994).

In Jordan the majority of Palestinian refugees do enjoy Jordanian citizenship and because of the size of Palestinian presence in the Hashemite kingdom they are assimilated into the country in ways which differ radically from their counterparts in Lebanon. Although to all intents and purposes Palestinian refugees in Jordan may be indistinguishable from their Jordanian compatriots there have been major political and historic differences and this has meant that there are important degrees of exclusion that Palestinians face from the real centres of power in the Jordanian state and monarchy (Milton-Edwards and Hinchcliffe, 2001). Native or 'East Bank' Jordanians have feared the political weight of the PLO and its influence in Jordan. Much of this fear stems from the memory of the internal fighting that took place between the PLO and Jordanian forces in September 1970. These events are referred to as Black September and resulted in King Hussein of Jordan expelling the PLO from the country.

In the wake of the 1967 war Jordan had had to give refuge to thousands of Palestinian refugees who had fled the West Bank as Israel and the armies of Jordan, Egypt and Syria battled it out. Among their number were the fedayeen fighters of the PLO led by Fatah's Yasser Arafat. From their base in Jordan the Palestinian fedayeen launched attacks on Israel. The PLO, moreover, established administrative, military and other structures that were an obvious challenge to King Hussein. In 1968 the IDF launched an assault on PLO forces in the Jordan village of Karameh close to Jordan's border with Israel. The PLO fighters, (assisted by the Jordanian army), however, emerged as victors from the skirmish with the IDF. The 'battle of Karameh' became a legend that was exploited by the PLO in their propaganda. In the wake of the attack the PLO enjoyed unprecedented popularity in almost every Arab capital except Amman. The ranks of the PLO were swelled with new recruits from the refugee camps who had been inspired by the stories of the heroism of Yasser Arafat and his comrades. In the end Karameh had only exacerbated King Hussein's problem with the PLO. In September 1970 an emboldened PLO attempted, several times, to assassinate King Hussein. They also engaged in a major hijacking in the kingdom and used the media spotlight on them to confront the King.

King Hussein's response was draconian; on 16 September 1970 he declared martial law and the following day he ordered his troops to attack PLO positions throughout the country. Jordan was soon embroiled in a civil war. Inevitably, outside parties intervened; Syria and Palestinian armed elements on one side and the USA and Israel on the other side. But it was in Cairo that King Hussein and Yasser Arafat were compelled to meet and reach an agreement to end the hostilities. There was no immediate end to the fighting and subsequent skirmishes between PLO fighters and the Jordanian army continued for some months. By April 1971 the Jordanian army was able to get the Palestinian fedayeen out of Amman but Fatah called for the overthrow of the state. King Hussein told his troops to finish off the fedayeen. To all intents and purposes it looked and sounded like the PLO were going to take the throne from Hussein.

Nevertheless, when the fighting did end the PLO leadership were forced to disarm and dismantle PLO armed forces and to recognize the authority of King Hussein. The notion of the PLO forming a state within a state in Jordan had come to an abrupt and violent end. Although some radical PLO factions rejected Jordanian terms for peace, they found themselves bereft of an internal backer and thus left the country for more politically amenable locations. The fighting during 1970 and 1971 created thousands of casualties and in the aftermath a long lingering distrust of the Palestinians remained. For decades afterwards the specific enmity between the PLO's Yasser Arafat and Jordan's King Hussein remained. For the Palestinian refugees of Jordan this enmity often meant that any form of political organization was suppressed or prohibited. Palestinian political activists were subject to the scrutiny of the state secret services and many landed up in prison or had their lives severely circumscribed. The stability of King Hussein's regime, after Black September, thus came to depend on a hostile and suspicious stance with respect to the Palestinian political agenda.

As the country recovered from the internal strife of the 1970s, King Hussein's regime also came to have serious concerns that the demographic balance in the country may have, already, tipped in favour of Jordanian citizens of Palestinian origin. Although there are no accurate figures for the number of Jordanian citizens of Palestinian descent, there is a widespread belief that by the twenty-first century they account for some 60 per cent of the population. Palestinian refugees and their descendants have, however, sought to maintain their sense of identity through a variety of activities. In the camps one Palestinian woman described how lectures, outings, games, cooking and traditional crafts helped Palestinian women explore their origins and maintain their distinctiveness: 'I think these activities are important because they keep Palestinian crafts and identity alive', stated one woman (Abdallah, 1995: 63). In 2002 Hussein's successor, the Jordanian monarch King Abdullah II, launched a national campaign that clearly addressed the issue of Palestinian identity in Jordan and, indirectly, addressed future options for the refugees. The campaign, 'Jordan First', has been designed to consolidate national identity in a way that is driven and orchestrated by the state rather than separate national groups within the kingdom. Without the resolution of the Palestinian refugee issue as part of a package of peace between Israel and the Palestinians, however, the issue remains very much a live one in host states like Jordan, Syria and Lebanon. Refugee resettlement thus has important implications for Jordan politically, economically and socially.

In Syria the Palestinian refugee community are not citizens but do enjoy access to state services and employment. Nearly 50 per cent of Syria's Palestinian refugees live on or below the poverty line. The majority of Palestinian refugees believe in their 'right of return', though were sceptical that the Oslo peace process would deliver a just settlement to their case (Said, 2000). However, for as long as the Syrian state remains in enmity with Israel the fate of the Palestinian refugees there also remains tied to that of the Syrian–Israel track in any peace negotiations. Syria is commonly perceived as the last 'withholding' state when it comes to resolving the Arab–Israeli conflict.

Palestinian refugees in Syria, as with others formerly in places like Kuwait, Iraq, Libya and Egypt, cannot enjoy the freedom to always air their political viewpoints. Ultimately all of these refugees remain vulnerable because of their statelessness and the vagaries of a region buffeted by the impacts of the wider Israeli–Arab conflict. This became glaringly apparent with respect to the Palestinian refugee community of Iraq after the fall of Saddam Hussein's regime in 2003. Before that time some 35,000 officially registered Palestinian refugees, plus another 90,000 Palestinian refugees from elsewhere in the Arab world, had made their home in Iraq. Although they did not enjoy citizenship or the right to own property, the Palestinian refugees received free housing and other services from the regime. Saddam Hussein had often used the Palestinian issue to bolster his own standing. Since 2003, however, the fate of the Palestinian refugees in Iraq has become increasingly precarious. They have been subject to attacks and persecution and many thousands of them have fled the country or become internally displaced. Their presence, whether in Ein el-Helweh camp in Lebanon, the

Baladiyat compound in Baghdad, Wihdat camp in Jordan or Aida camp in the West Bank is a constant reminder of the failure, to date, to resolve the Israeli–Palestinian conflict and its enduring legacy for literally millions of people.

Refugees: the key to peace?

> We promise that we will not rest until the right of return of our people is achieved and the tragedy of our Diaspora ends.
>
> Palestinian President, Mahmoud Abbas (UNISPAL, 2004)

Irrespective of the reasons for the renewed efforts to revive the Palestinian–Israeli peace process in the 1990s it became clear to all those involved that without addressing the issue of the refugees a peace settlement would be unobtainable. The key to peace lies in the interrelated factors of the principle of the 'right of return' and the question of reparations and compensation to Palestinians for the lands, properties and possessions lost in wars with Israel.

The 'right of return' is a powerful concept for Palestinian refugees and is often posited or countered against the 'right of return' principle that any Jew enjoys in respect of Israel and citizenship. As previously outlined in Chapter 4 of this book the Jewish 'Law of Return' allows Jews and those of Jewish descent to settle in Israel and acquire citizenship. This right – given under Israeli law – to Jews world-wide is exercised at the same time that Palestinians (and their descendents) are not permitted by Israel to return to their homes and their lands over the pre-1948 borders with Israel. Palestinians believe that their 'right of return' lies in the foundation of international laws on refugees and rests in the hope and belief that the refugees of 1948 and 1967 will be allowed to return to their homes in the present-day state of Israel. Palestinians and their descendents literally dream of returning to their 'home'. Here are some Palestinian narratives of Jaffa:

> One of the saddest moments was our visit to [Jaffa] the Harbour where Rima narrated how her father, Hassan Hammami, a teenage boy then, embarked a boat with his family, as did hundreds of families on May 10th 1948 and left Jaffa for the last time in the direction of the ship that took them to Beirut and permanent exile. As they embarked, gun shells were exploding all around them, spreading panic and mayhem.
>
> Liza was crying all the way in anticipation of the encounter with her lost city. Later, she told me that she was crying because her father died without having the chance to visit Jaffa.
>
> (Tamari, 2000)

Irrespective of the viability of such aspirations, more than 60 years after Palestinians experienced dispossession and statelessness all the parties to the conflict have had to address this thorny issue. It is said that: 'With rare consensus, the bulk of the Israeli left and right argue that the right of return [for Palestinian refugees] would spell the eventual end of the Jewish state' (Haaretz, 2007). Hence, for the majority of Israelis they see in the assertion of the Palestinian 'right of return' their own extinction. Israel, moreover, as pointed out in earlier sections of this chapter, refuses to acknowledge any responsibility for the creation of the refugee problem in 1948 in the first place. Hence, for them, there is no logic in Israel being compelled to be part of the solution for a problem they claim they did not make. As Gazit contends:

> Israel denies the legality of the Palestinian claim. If it recognizes the 'right' of return it would also be admitting responsibility, and perhaps even culpability for creating the problem. But Israel categorically denies any responsibility for the War of 1948.
>
> (Gazit, 1995: 7)

The PLO and subsequently the PA has always been outspoken on the issue of the 'right of return'. They are the standard bearers for a generation of refugees who dream of 'return'. The symbol and concept of 'return' has been assiduously cultivated and deployed by the PLO as part of the wider struggle for self-determination and independence. The internal debate among Palestinian intellectuals, some of whom have been officials in the Palestinian Authority, over the exercise of the actual 'right of return' to those lands that after 1948 were designated as Israeli, however, has not been without controversy. Some have opened a public debate on a re-interpretation of the 'right of return' that says less about a physical return to the Palestinian lands and homes of 1948 and more about tying 'return' to citizenship in a Palestinian state in the West Bank and Gaza Strip, with East Jerusalem as its capital. Such figures acknowledged that a distinction must be drawn to the 'right of return in principle' as possibly part of a political settlement with Israel and the literal exercise of return as an obstacle that will never be overcome if peace is to be achieved (Abu Zayyad, 1994: 77). In 2001 the PA Information Minister, Yasser Abed Rabbo, addressed a meeting in the USA, saying:

> We asked for the principle of the right of return, but the implementation of it, it should be discussed in a very practical and even pragmatic way, without affecting – yes, without affecting – the Jewish nature of the state of Israel. We said it. This was our position.
>
> (Hamzeh, 2003)

Abed Rabbo has been described as a 'traitor' by others in the Palestinian national movement. In 2003 a prominent Palestinian figure of the national movement, Sari Nusseibeh, also argued that Palestinians should relinquish the 'right of return' to the lands of 1948. He declared:

> We have two rights. We have the right of return, in my opinion. But we also have the right to live in freedom and independence. And very often in life one has to forego the implementation of one right in order to be able to implement the other rights. In this case it is very clear to me that we would have to

forego the implementation of the right to return in order that we are able to create the possibility of fulfilling our right to live in freedom. . . . It is not full justice, but it is practical justice, this is what is possible.

(Nusseibeh, 2003)

Many others within the PLO and the Islamist national organization of Hamas vehemently oppose any form of Palestinian concession over the 'right of return'. The late PLO leader, Yasser Arafat, had consistently maintained that the conflict could not be resolved without resolution of the 'right of return' for refugees. Addressing the topic of resistance and when it would come to an end, Hamas leader, Dr Abdel Aziz Rantissi, clearly outlined the 'right of return' as a prerequisite: 'Hamas refuses to concede any part of Palestine. When the Palestinian state is to be established on the whole of the land of Palestine and our people have returned to their homes, then the resistance will end' (Rantissi, 2002). The election of the Hamas government in January 2006 meant that the refugee affairs portfolio inevitably fell into Hamas hands as well. Dr Atef Adwan, the Hamas Minister for Refugee Affairs, argued for the 'right of return' according to both international legal norms and the moral right of Palestinians to their homes:

> According to international law, the Right of Return is a remaining fact for all of those who have been deported by force from their own land. So the Israelis should not be allowed to steal this absolute right. The Palestinians at this moment who are immigrants even inside their homeland and outside are determined to keep this right alive, and this is what convinces them to fight on in the Intifada.
>
> Fighting for your right is not being unpragmatic [sic]. . . . I don't think that the Palestinian refugees will benefit anything from the present Road Map. This project is not just a time winning attempt, it actually doesn't give the refugees any hope to return to their homes. The Israelis believe that the Road Map gives the Israelis the right to abolish the Right of Return and because of this Sharon declared that he will not allow any Palestinian refugee to enter Palestine in the future.
>
> (Adwan, 2003)

The position of Hamas as opposed to elements of the PLO and the PA, however, was the one more broadly shared among Palestinians polled on issues related to the 'right of return' and compensation. Polling refugees in overcrowded refugee camps about whether they *really* wanted to carry on clinging to a dream of a return has proved to be a bit like asking children if they like cakes and sweets! It's a political no-brainer debate. Hamas's opponents accuse them of pandering to popular sentiment, while pointing out that they are the ones truly grasping the political nettle in order to move everyone – Palestinian and Israeli – to some form of realistic permanent political settlement over the issue of the refugees. The challenge for those less intimately connected with the debate has been to push the two sides towards something that looks like a fair and equitable solution to the issue.

Compensation

> All people live in their lands except for Palestinians; their land lives in them . . . in their hearts.
>
> (Adwan, 2003)

There can be little doubt that if it has been difficult to get Israeli and Palestinian politicians and representatives to agree that the Palestinian refugee issue exists and needs to be addressed as part of the efforts to resolve the conflict, then the same will hold for the issue of refugee compensation and reparation. The issue, of course, is historically rooted in legal precedent about war and its outcome – especially for civilian victims of conflict such as refugees or the internally displaced. In one sense then the issue is also intimately linked to the debate about victims and the means by which they can access justice. In the UN resolution that was passed in 1948 on the issue of the Palestinian refugees it addressed compensation in the following ways:

> compensation should be paid for the property of those choosing not to return and for loss of or damage to property which, under principles of international law or in equity, should be made good by the governments or authorities responsible.
>
> (UN GAR 194 (III) of 11 December 1948)

With respect to the Palestinian–Israeli conflict the first obstacle to overcome is one of recognizing responsibility and owning the issue of the refugees in relation to compensation. Once this has been achieved then the next area that becomes open for negotiation is the size, source, procedure and definition of eligibility for compensation. Estimates, as they relate to the Palestinian refugees and their descendents, range widely and sources proposed do not just include Israel but other states as well. Literally billions of dollars would have to be dispersed to refugees in compensation for their losses and, perhaps, a decision not to return to their historic lands.

Since the early 1990s, scholars, diplomats, legal experts and others have negotiated, conducted studies, formed multi-party working groups, and benefited from external mediation and support to devise a series of criteria with respect to compensation, those who should get it and how they can get it. Proposals – inspired as a means to overcome obstacles to peace – have often foundered not because they are not viable, or unrealistic or too complicated, but because the political will has been lacking in the negotiations between Israel and the Palestinians on this issue. One reason why difficulties have been encountered is that a dimension of the compensation debate necessarily deems the state responsible for dealing with compensation.

There is no doubt, as the above sections have illustrated, that there are many Palestinian refugees and their descendents who dream of returning to their homes and land. Whilst it is true that there are also many who would prefer to return to their cherished homeland there are others for whom this is not a choice. The question of their official resettlement thus becomes all the more pressing. Resettlement could mean that many refugees choose to stay in their host states, become citizens of an independent Palestinian state or accept citizenship elsewhere.

In 2006, for example, the issue of Palestinian resettlement hit local news headlines in the West Bank and Gaza Strip when the Refugee Affairs Minister for the Palestinian Authority complained that Jordan was allowing Palestinian refugees, who were subsequently refugees again from Iraq, to settle in Canada! These Palestinian refugees from Iraq had been stranded in a camp near Rweished on the Jordanian–Iraqi border for up to three years. The Canadian government had offered to ease their plight by resettling them in Canada. It was reported that the Refugee Affairs Minister had complained to Jordan on the grounds that Jordan could easily have absorbed this number of refugees themselves and that 'the issue [of Canadian resettlement] could be the end of the refugees cause and cancel their right of return to Palestine'. Thus, what on first glance may appear to have been mean-spirited disapproval of an opportunity for Palestinian refugees to enjoy a better life for themselves was clearly interpreted by the Hamas-dominated government of the PA as an affront to the principle of the 'right of return'.

If such 'resettlement' initiatives gain momentum, then, many Palestinians ask, when will they actually result in transfer and thus in an end to refugee claims for a right to return or compensation? Transfer of the Palestinians, from Israel, the West Bank and Gaza Strip, and East Jerusalem, is the objective of many Israeli right-wing politicians. One of the most significant advocates of this 'option' for the settlement of the Palestinian–Israeli conflict became deputy Prime Minister of Israel in 2006. Avigdor Liberman caused a furore shortly after his appointment in 2006 when he advocated the transfer of Palestinian Arabs. In such an environment the sensitivities around the issue of resettlement are clearly apparent. In this respect this is but one reason why Palestinian political leaders opt to keep the refugee issue alive by talking about the 'camp dwellers' rather than the new citizens of such and such a state who were originally Palestinian.

Of course, should a settlement of the Palestinian–Israeli conflict be satisfactorily negotiated then it is to be expected that there will be some Palestinians who will not seek to assert their 'right of return', opting for permanent absorption into their host or other countries. The aspiration, however, may not be politically acceptable to all the host countries. In Lebanon, for example, there is little evidence of a willingness by this state – held together under the delicate framework of power-sharing among ethnic and sectarian elements – to allow Palestinian refugees to become citizens who might then destabilize the state. Here the principal concern is not with the economic impact of resettlement on the host state but on the nature of the state itself. As Salam as highlighted: Palestinian 'resettlement [in Lebanon] could . . . undermine the national reconciliation forged by the Lebanese through the Taif agreement of 1989 . . . ' (Salam, 1994: 24). The political consequences of the resettlement of over 400,000 Palestinians in Lebanon, thus constituting 10 per cent of the population, has meant little acceptance within the state for such a solution. Lebanese politicians, moreover, are unlikely to put up with a resident Palestinian population if Palestinian statehood is achieved in the West Bank, Gaza Strip and East Jerusalem. In such circumstances they may well choose to act as the Kuwaitis did in 1991 when it expelled most of its resident Palestinian population of 400,000 for supporting Saddam Hussein during the invasion and occupation of their country. Alternatively with the deployment of more subtle means the Lebanese state could still achieve the same ends: getting Palestinians out of Lebanon and denying them citizenship rights. Of course, this is a worst case scenario and more pragmatic solutions have been proposed (Salam, 1994). Such solutions focus on issues of identity, a right to citizenship even if not resident in a state and residency even if not a citizen of a state. Yet devising such scenarios was increasingly perceived as an exercise in futility as the peace negotiations of the 1990s foundered and stalled.

Talking about refugees

Palestinian national organizations such as the PLO, as well as specific groups and projects, sought, over the decades that followed the war of 1948, to keep the refugee issue alive and to assert the rights of Palestinian refugees. Yet without evidence of substantive negotiation or conclusion of negotiations between the PLO – as the 'sole legitimate representative of the Palestinian people' – and the government of Israel the fate of the Palestinian refugees remained largely undetermined for many years. Older refugees would reminisce about their lives before the *nakbah*, while their children and grandchildren were engaged in the struggle to gain their state and independence.

In 1991, as a result of the inception of the Madrid Peace Process, the refugees were identified as a significant issue in the negotiations for the resolution of the conflict between Israel and the Palestinians. The Madrid Peace Process, initiated at the historic conference between Israel, the Arab states of Syria, Lebanon and Jordan, as well as representatives of the Palestinians, led to subsequent negotiations. The negotiation process took place on a number of 'tracks', bilaterally or multilaterally. The refugee issue came up on the multilateral track of negotiations. The Refugee Working Group (RWG), as it was formally entitled, was tasked to work on seven themes:

- Family reunification
- Child welfare
- Human resource development
- Job creation and vocational training
- Public health
- Economic and social infrastructure
- Data bases

In an inauspicious start to the RWG process Israel boycotted the first meeting, and haggled over the nature of Palestinian representation and other issues in some subsequent sessions. By 1997 the Arabs had also called for a boycott of the RWG and in September 2000 and the outbreak of the second Intifada the work of the RWG went into suspension mode.

Under the Oslo framework that had been agreed in 1993 some of the issues that had been pertinent to the work of the RWG were carried forward while others were abandoned and replaced with new concerns. The Declaration of Principles (Oslo Accords) had recognized and agreed on the need for negotiations on 'final status issues', which included refugees. A timetable for the negotiations and their conclusions was outlined but, like so many other efforts associated with the Oslo process, the work of the RWG was systematically stymied by the wider effects of a breakdown in the Oslo process and events on the ground. By 2000, when Israel and the Palestinians entered what many had hoped were final status negotiations at Camp David and Taba, a number of difficulties were encountered over the refugee negotiations. According to the official Israeli narrative the refugee issue was 'the most difficult issue to be resolved'. Some aspects of the refugee issue, however, engendered a spirit of cooperation and a practical strategic approach emerged between the two sides.

It appeared that, although Israel would not recognize the Palestinian 'right of return', an alternative form of words expressing 'regret' rather than complicity might have been acceptable within a narrative about the events of 1948. The leaking of a 'non-paper' by the EU Special Envoy to the Middle East Peace Process gave a representative account of what was agreed upon by Palestinian and Israeli negotiators with respect to the refugees:

Refugees

Non-papers were exchanged, which were regarded as a good basis for the talks. Both sides stated that the issue of the Palestinian refugees is central to the Israeli–Palestinian relations and that a comprehensive and just solution is essential to creating a lasting and morally scrupulous peace. Both sides agreed to adopt the principles and references which could facilitate the adoption of an agreement.

Both sides suggested, as a basis, that the parties should agree that a just settlement of the refugee problem in accordance with the UN Security Council Resolution 242 must lead to the implementation of UN General Assembly Resolution 194.

3.1 Narrative

The Israeli side put forward a suggested joint narrative for the tragedy of the Palestinian refugees. The Palestinian side discussed the proposed narrative and there was much progress, although no agreement was reached in an attempt to develop an historical narrative in the general text.

3.2 Return, repatriation and relocation and rehabilitation

Both sides engaged in a discussion of the practicalities of resolving the refugee issue. The Palestinian side reiterated that the Palestinian refugees should have the right of return to their homes in accordance with the interpretation of UNGAR 194. The Israeli side expressed its understanding that the wish to return as per wording of UNGAR 194 shall be implemented within the framework of one of the following programs:

A Return and repatriation

    1 to Israel
    2 to Israel swapped territory
    3 to the Palestine state.

B Rehabilitation and relocation

    1 Rehabilitation in host country.
    2 Relocation to third country.

Preference in all these programs shall be accorded to the Palestinian refugee population in Lebanon. The Palestinian side stressed that the above shall be subject to the individual free choice of the refugees, and shall not prejudice their right to their homes in accordance with its interpretation of UNGAR 194.

The Israeli side, informally, suggested a three-track 15-year absorption program, which was discussed but not agreed upon. The first track referred to the absorption to Israel. No numbers were agreed upon, but with a non-paper referring to 25,000 in the first three years of this program (40,000 in the first five years of this program did not appear in the non-paper but was raised verbally). The second track referred to the absorption of Palestinian refugees into the Israeli territory that shall be transferred to Palestinian sovereignty, and the third track referring to the absorption of refugees in the context of family reunification scheme.

The Palestinian side did not present a number, but stated that the negotiations could not start without an Israeli opening position. It maintained that Israel's acceptance of the return of refugees should not prejudice existing programs within Israel such as family reunification.

3.3 Compensation

Both sides agreed to the establishment of an International Commission and an International Fund as a mechanism for dealing with compensation in all its aspects. Both sides agreed that 'small-sum' compensation shall be paid to the refugees in the 'fast-track' procedure, claims of compensation for property losses below certain amount shall be subject to 'fast-track' procedures.

There was also progress on Israeli compensation for material losses, land and assets expropriated, including agreement on a payment from an Israeli lump sum or proper amount to be agreed upon that would feed into the International Fund. According to the Israeli side the calculation of this payment would be based on a macro-economic survey to evaluate the assets in order to reach a fair value. The Palestinian side, however, said that this sum would be calculated on the records of the UNCCP, the Custodian for Absentee Property and other relevant data with a multiplier to reach a fair value.

3.4 UNRWA

Both sides agreed that UNRWA should be phased out in accordance with an agreed timetable of five years, as a targeted period. The Palestinian side added a possible adjustment of that period to make sure that this will be subject to the implementation of the other aspects of the agreement dealing with refugees, and with termination of Palestinian refugee status in the various locations.

3.5 Former Jewish refugees

The Israeli side requested that the issue of compensation to former Jewish refugees from Arab countries be recognized, while accepting that it was not a Palestinian responsibility or a bilateral issue. The Palestinian side maintained that this is not a subject for a bilateral Palestinian–Israeli agreement.

3.6 Restitution

The Palestinian side raised the issue of restitution of refugee property. The Israeli side rejected this.

3.7 End of claims

The issue of the end of claims was discussed, and it was suggested that the implementation of the agreement shall constitute a complete and final implementation of UNGAR 194 and therefore ends all claims.

(Moratinos, 2002)

The failure to conclude a peace treaty in 2000 and early 2001 combined with a progressive breakdown of the peace process and the outbreak of the al-Aqsa Intifada meant that the refugee issue, along with others, went into abeyance. What many had hoped to be a turning point on the path to peace proved instead to be a dead end.

The political successors of Clinton, Barak, and Arafat have not been able to recover the momentum and the sense of being close to final agreement that occurred in 2000 and early 2001. Indeed, although President Bush as successor to Clinton promoted the concept of a two-state solution, he ruled out American support for the exercise of the 'right of return' for Palestinian refugees to Israel. In a statement that he issued in 2004 he declared:

> The goal of two independent states has repeatedly been recognized in inter-national resolutions and agreements, and it remains a key to resolving this conflict. The United States is strongly committed to Israel's security and well-being as a Jewish state. It seems clear that an agreed, just, fair and realistic framework for a solution to the Palestinian refugee issue as part of any final status agreement will need to be found through the establishment of a Palestinian state, and the settling of Palestinian refugees there, rather than in Israel.
>
> (Bush, 2004)

The realists on the Palestinian side of the debate about the fate of the dispossessed accept that Israel will never agree to the 'right of return' or the physical return of anything more than a handful of Palestinians who fled their lands in 1948 within the borders of what Bush referred to as the 'Jewish state'. They understand that by tying concessions from Israel over the definitive nature of a Palestinian state in the West Bank, Gaza Strip and East Jerusalem to the return of refugees as the solution to the issue that they will not succeed. Yet there remain many Palestinians who are firmly wedded to the ideological, moral and ethical claim that Palestinians have 'inalienable' human rights and that this should include the 'right of return'. Such 'inalienable' rights are enshrined in the ideology and rhetoric of powerful political movements, such as Hamas, who contend that no Palestinian political leader has the right to negotiate away or bargain with Israel over such a fundamental principle.

At the first Israeli–Palestinian peace talks in over seven years, held in the US town of Annapolis in November 2007, it was notable that in the joint declaration issued by the two sides the refugee issue was conspicuous by its absence. For the millions of Palestinians that want to return to properties their families lost after Israel's 1948 creation this was a bitter blow. Israel continues to oppose any return of the refugees, saying it would mean the end of the country as a Jewish state. A spokesman for the Israeli Foreign Ministry stated at Annapolis that Israel would only agree to a return of the Palestine refugees within the borders of a future Palestinian state established as a result of negotiations with Israel. Today these victims of war and conflict also remain central to the resolution of the ongoing conflict that scars Israel and the Palestinians.

Further reading

There is a wealth of further reading to access on the topics raised by this chapter. Good starting points are Gelber (Brighton: Sussex Academic Press, 2006), Morris (Cambridge: Cambridge University Press, 2004) and Palumbo's (London: Faber and Faber, 1987) account of the creation of the Palestinian refugees. Masalha's work (Washington, DC: Institute of Palestine Studies, 1992 and London: Pluto, 2003) analyzes the extent to which Zionism and Israel promote the concept of Arab transfer. Accounts of the Diaspora experience vary; the memoirs of Edward Said (London: Granta Books, 2000) and Ghada Karmi (London: Verso, 2001) tell the same story of dispossession but not of exile. Other more general accounts include studies such as that by Peteet (Philadelphia, PA: University of Pennsylvania Press, 2005) on the refugee camps in Lebanon, Grandahl (Cairo: AUC Press, 2003) with some stirring photographic portrayals and Chatty and Hundt (London: Berghann Books, 2005). Life in exile is also documented in the classic studies by Rosemary Sayigh (London: Zed Books, 1984 and 1994). Schulz (London: Routledge, 2003), Artz (New York: Council on Foreign Relations, 1997) and Bowker (Boulder, CO: Lynne Rienner, 2003) outline contrasting perspectives and analysis of the resolution of the refugee issue in the wider context of the Palestinian–Israeli conflict and the Middle East Peace Process.

Arzt, Donna E. (1997) *Refugees into citizens: Palestinians and the end of the Arab–Israeli conflict*, New York: Council on Foreign Relations.

Bowker, R. (2003) *Palestinian refugees: Mythology, identity, and the search for peace*, Boulder, CO: Lynne Rienner.

Chatty, D. and Hundt, G.L. (eds) (2005) *Children of Palestine: Experiencing forced migration in the Middle East*, London: Berghann Books.

Gelber, Y. (2006) *Palestine 1948. War, escape and the emergence of the Palestinian refugee problem*, Brighton: Sussex Academic Press.

Grandahl, M. (2003) *In hope and despair: Life in the Palestinian refugee camps*, Cairo: AUC Press.

Karmi, G. (2001) *In search of Fatima, a Palestinian story*, London: Verso.

Masalha, N. (1992) *Expulsion of the Palestinians, the concept of 'transfer' in Zionist political thought, 1882–1948*, Washington, DC: Institute of Palestine Studies.

—— (2003) *The politics of denial, Israel and the Palestinian refugee problem*, London: Pluto Press.

Morris, B. (2004) *The birth of the Palestinian refugee problem revisited*, Cambridge: Cambridge University Press.

Palumbo, M. (1987) *The Palestinian catastrophe: The 1948 expulsion of a people from their homeland*, London: Faber and Faber.

Peteet, J.M. (2005) *Landscape of hope and despair: Palestinian refugee camps*, Philadelphia, PA: University of Pennsylvania Press.

Said, E. (2000) *Out of place: a memoir*, London: Granta Books.

Sayigh, R. (1984) *Palestinians from peasants to revolutionaries*, London: Zed Books.

—— (1994), *Too many enemies: Palestinian experiences in Lebanon*, London: Zed Books.

Schulz, Helena L. (2003) *The Palestinian Diaspora*, London: Routledge.

6 The occupation generation

Chapter outline

- The Six-Day War   119
- Spoils of war   121
- A framework for control   123
- Facts on the ground: Israel's settlements   125
- Resistance under occupation   131
- Liberating Palestine through an organization   132
- Occupation and employment   136
- The pressure cooker   137
- Further reading   139

It was not only the events of the 1967 Six-Day War that changed the dynamic of the Israeli–Palestinian conflict but the consequent process of Israeli occupation, Israeli settlement, Arab crisis, Palestinian dispossession again and the emergence of a Palestinian resistance force and the state-like entity of the PLO. Hence themes such as occupation, settlement policies, terrorism and the continuing internationalization of the conflict – either through peace settlement (with Israel and Egypt in 1978) or Israeli military adventure (in Lebanon in 1978 and again in 1982) – and the subsequent expulsion of the PLO and its factionalism will be explored in this chapter. By looking at, for example, settlement policy and the establishment of 'facts on the ground' the economic and geographic dimensions of the conflict will also be revealed.

Human rights debates will be examined through the growing intimacy between these enemies that became constructed around the institutions and mechanisms of occupation. In this way I will demonstrate the effects that occupation had on the dynamics of both Israeli and Palestinian society.

The Six-Day War

Although an armistice agreement had been reached between Israel and its Arab neighbours after the war of 1948, the prospect of another conflict was never far from the horizon. In 1956 Israel had sided with the British and the French against the Egyptians during the Suez crisis, and border raids and skirmishes were a frequent occurrence between Israel and the Arab states. Moreover, the move to popular Arab nationalism in countries such as Egypt and Syria in the late 1950s and early 1960s also garnered official support and a rallying call to the plight of the Palestinian people. The likelihood of further conflagration increased through the acceleration of the arms race between Israel and the Arab states, each supported against the other by the superpowers. By the early 1960s the region had become a theatre of Cold War rivalry as the Soviet Union and the USA vied with each other for global dominance (Milton-Edwards and Hinchcliffe, 2007).

In the spring of 1967, as a result of Soviet misinformation to the Syrians about the possibility of an Israeli attack, the tension between the two states intensified. Syria turned to its ally Egypt for support and President Nasser was forthcoming – seeing this as an opportunity to ratchet up the hostility with Israel. President Nasser ordered Egyptian troop movements in areas bordering Israel and advised UN forces to evacuate the area before blockading the Israeli port of Eilat. Nasser also utilized his considerable popular support not just in Egypt but across much of the Arab world to whip up backing for a showdown with Israel. He understood that popular pressure could play its part in compelling the leaders of more conservative regimes, such as that of Jordan, to side with Egypt.

Popular support for the Egyptian move was voiced across the Arab world and, much as Nasser had calculated, a reluctant Jordan also joined the new Arab alliance against Israel. Israel, seeking to act decisively to end the tension, undertook a pre-emptive strike against Syria and Egypt on 6 June 1967 destroying their jet fighters. Within six days Israel would defeat the Jordanian forces on its eastern flank, the Egyptians on its southern and western flank and Syria to the north. Jordan was forced to relinquish its control of Jerusalem and the West Bank; its King, Hussein, had effectively lost the Hashemite grip on the third most holy site in Islam. President Nasser of Egypt was utterly humiliated and offered to resign while hundreds of thousands took to the streets begging him to remain in power. Syria also endured defeat and occupation of its territory in the Golan Heights at Israeli hands. The whole of the Arab world was shaken by the defeat and this has been marked as a watershed in the politics of the region ever since.

In six days Israel had become the foremost regional military power. The speed and efficacy of Israel's victory discredited the Arab regimes as liberators of the Palestinian people. In the wake of the war the mantle of resistance would emerge from the Palestinian national movement and the era of total dependence declared at an end. From this point forth Palestinians would raise their arms against Israel and no longer wait for their Arab brethren to fight the war on their behalf. Yasser Arafat, who would emerge as leader of the PLO and become President of the Palestinian Authority, vowed that the resolution of the 'national question' would never against rest solely in the hands of his Arab comrades.

Spoils of war

War has been but one feature of the conflict between Israel, the Palestinians and a variety of Arab states, such as Egypt, Syria and Jordan, who have supported the Palestinian cause. With war acting as a form of decisive military engagement between opposing armies and the prospect of decisive defeat or victory achieved, the acquisition or loss of territory can be highly important. The loss or gain of territory may be important for strategic reasons; it may give an advantage over the enemy in terms of defence because that territory has a height advantage. The loss or gain of territory may also be important in terms of resources such as oil or water, or there may even be strong ideological (including religious or political) motivations for wishing to hold on to or gain a piece of land or territory (Lustick, 1993). In the modern age, of course, where sovereignty lies within the borders of territorial units known as nation states, loss of such lands may be cause for international intervention. Sometimes, war over territory may give rise to a combination of the aforementioned factors but with some dimensions assuming more importance than others. In other words the territorial dimension of war should never be underestimated in the context of the larger conflict between Israel and the Palestinians.

One significant, if not the most important, outcome of the Six-Day War between Israel and the Arab states in June 1967 was the territorial gains that Israel made in the region of historic Palestine: East Jerusalem including the old city, the West Bank and Gaza Strip. The Egyptian territory of the Sinai Peninsula and the Syrian lands of the Golan Heights also came under Israeli control at the end of the war. With the exception of East Jerusalem, including the holy places of Islam, Judaism and Christianity, which was annexed by Israel, the other territories that came under its direct control became subject to military occupation. The status of Jerusalem and Israeli sovereignty was particularly contentious. In the immediate wake of the war the Israeli authorities succeeded in expanding the municipal boundaries of Jerusalem by an additional 70 square kilometres from the surrounding areas of the West Bank. The Israeli government had already made Jerusalem its capital in 1950 but post-war the de facto inclusion of East Jerusalem was seen as further evidence of encroaching Israeli sovereignty. In 1980 the Basic Law of Israel declared Jerusalem a 'complete and united' capital of the Israeli state, but the majority of the international community had recognized a UN resolution that declares such an act 'null and void'. The Palestinians of Jerusalem were offered the status of permanent residents in the state of Israel. Most declined the opportunity to acquire Israeli citizenship, understanding full well that their 'cousins' who had remained in the state since 1948 were nothing more than poorly treated second-class citizens. The political point in refusing Israeli citizenship was also apparent: maintaining the right to be citizens in the state of Palestine with Jerusalem its capital.

Now, in becoming an occupier of the Palestinian population of the West Bank and Gaza Strip, many believed that Israel was obliged to act according to the international laws and norms set out as binding in the Fourth Geneva Convention.

This meant that Israel had certain duties and responsibilities to the Palestinian population over which it ruled. Israel, however, rejected the label and declared that as far as they were concerned they were not in military occupation of the territories and that these territories were instead 'disputed'. As Dore Gold remarks: 'It would be far more accurate to describe the West Bank and Gaza Strip as "disputed territories" to which both Israelis and Palestinians have claims' (Gold, 2002). From Israel's perspective, if the territories are 'disputed' rather than 'occupied', this also undermines the Palestinian claim to legitimate resistance against the occupation and the sympathy that this has engendered in the international community and its forums.

Since 1967 Israel has relinquished some of the territories it occupied – to Egypt in the peace treaty of 1980 and to Jordan in 1994. They have also changed the status of East Jerusalem, which we have discussed above. The Golan Heights were also annexed in 1981 and Israeli laws, jurisdiction and administration applied to the resident population. In August 2005 Israel engaged in an evacuation of its settlers and military forces from the Gaza Strip, but while it remained in effective control of Gaza's borders there was a lack of consensus over whether this constituted an end to Israel's occupation of the area. As one Palestinian pointed out almost a year after the Israeli evacuation:

> In that strict and limited sense, the 'physical' Israeli occupation of Gaza has ended, but Israeli control over Gaza remains almost total and has become even more restrictive since the disengagement. In fact, Gaza's economic situation has steadily worsened since disengagement with a solid majority of the population unemployed, living under the poverty level of $2 per day.
>
> (Dajani, 2006)

Irrespective of such subsequent territorial 'right-sizing', Israel gained control of the territories of the West Bank, Gaza Strip and East Jerusalem in 1967. Through its policies it has systemically altered the ways in which Palestinians live their daily lives and has caused their demands for self-determination and independence in these territories to be effectively stymied. The Palestinians have had to live life under a harsh Israeli-imposed military regime that has denied them citizenship (with the exception of East Jerusalem Palestinians) while at the same time extending the privileges and favours of citizenship to the Israeli occupants of the West Bank and Gaza Strip who have played a major part in establishing and maintaining the hundreds of illegal settlements that now epitomize much of these territories. Israel also attempts to validate its position in the Palestinian territories on the grounds of security. Successive Israeli governments have, moreover, given extensive support to the religio-ideological movement of settlement as a form of realizing Eretz Israel (Land of Israel).

Such settlements have been declared illegal by the United Nations and the International Court of Justice. The settlements are also recognized as a key factor in terms of resolving the conflict and were placed on the agenda of final status issues in the Oslo Accords of 1993. It was decided that settlements could not be dealt with under the interim arrangements that the Accords enshrined but that they had to form a pillar of the final status negotiations in terms of achieving a final resolution to the conflict between the Palestinians and Israelis. Such positions were seen by many elements within the settler community as antagonistic and they were furious at their Prime Minister, Yitzhak Rabin, for agreeing to such arrangements. In this respect Rabin was made to pay for his 'concessions' when he was assassinated by an extremist pro-settler Israeli at a peace rally in 1995 (Aronson, 1995). The shockwaves experienced throughout Israeli society in the wake of the assassination were palpable and many turned against the settler movement and its political backers on Israel's right-wing who had engendered such responses at the peace overtures agreed to by Rabin.

Has the acquisition of control of such territory been treated as a spoil of war by Israel? As with most aspects of the conflict there is much divided opinion on this topic and there is no definitive position to be determined. Israel has argued that it merely obtained the territories in defence of itself from the onslaught of the Arab armies. It has contended that it retained these territories for security reasons. Others maintain that, through 'facts on the ground' and the varying ideological motives of many actors across the Israeli political spectrum, the occupation established Israel in near permanent enmity with the Palestinians. In purely economic terms Israel has exploited the territories and derived natural resources such as water from it. There has been a cost as well: this includes the subsidy of mortgages for the thousands of housing units that have been built in the settlements, plus the expenses incurred in terms of the military expenditure of the last 40 years associated with the 'costs of occupying' the Palestinians of the West Bank and Gaza Strip. Before the outbreak of the Palestinian Intifada in 1987, however, it was popularly asserted that the occupation was self-financing as a result of the arduous Israeli-imposed scheme of taxation on the Palestinians themselves. Each permit that the Israelis issued, and there were thousands of such permits covering every aspect of Palestinian life, came with a financial levy that many Palestinians believed meant that they paid for the occupation out of their own pockets.

A framework for control

What does an occupation by a foreign army mean for those who come under its control and what does it mean for those that run the occupation and the society from which it draws its occupiers? For occupation is no simple matter. It implies an imposed order by a governing authority over a defeated people. Of course there are plenty of examples of military occupation: the German occupation of France during the Second World War, the Indonesian occupation of East Timor from 1975 to 2002 and the occupation of the Western Sahara by Morocco. Taking a more regional and contemporary perspective it is common to see the citation of the USA's occupation of Iraq, Israel's occupation of Lebanon and Iraq's occupation of Kuwait as examples of the deleterious effects of occupation – whatever the reason for occupation in the first place. Once again Israelis would aver that there are many other contemporary contexts in which territorial disputes over territory – such as Kashmir, Nagorno-Karabakh and Western Sahara – where the term 'occupied territory' is not employed. In Israel and the Palestinian territories, of course, locals joke that this land without occupation would be like cornflakes without milk. They cite the simple fact that since the periods of both the Persian (539 BCE) and Roman (63 BCE) occupations of Palestine the land has been subject to almost continuous contest, conquest and 'occupation' by those which one side or another considers to be a foreign usurper. A glance around the architecture of the old city in Jerusalem provides ample evidence of the truth in such assertions. Examples of Persian, Hellenistic, Roman, Muslim, Crusader, British and Israeli occupation architecture jostle for prominence – forts, walls, governors' buildings, watchtowers, sentry posts, administrative offices. Under each occupation the legal system, economic system, political order, cultural and societal codes of society have been altered and affected by the dominant mores and values of the military occupiers. Under each occupation local resistance has been generated in defiance of those who seek to impose an alternative order through the iron fist of the army. Occupation, like so many other terms associated with description and analysis of the conflict, becomes subject to the politics of semantics. In a newspaper article, published in the English language press in Israel reflecting on the Israeli commemoration of the bombing of King David Hotel by IZL Jewish militia fighters in 1946, the British presence in Palestine as the Mandate authority designated to assist the Jewish people in the establishment of their 'homeland' was continuously referred to as an 'occupation': 'The former fighters [IZL] sought recognition for their role in the establishment of the State of Israel, legitimization of their bombing . . . and vindication for their war against the British occupation' (Prince-Gibson, 2006: 13). In 2004 Israel's then Attorney General also publicly admitted that Israel was in 'occupation' of the West Bank and Gaza Strip, amidst a flurry of condemnation from across the Israeli political spectrum objecting to the use of the term. Ordinary Palestinians who have experienced life under Israel's administration are hard pushed to distinguish their experiences as anything other than occupation. As one points out:

> there are Israeli controlled checkpoints out there whenever I want to travel from one place to another, when I look around I see their settlements and the land eaten up by their settler roads. In the past they have taken the trouble to put us under the microscope of occupation even telling us what time to set our clocks and when and if we can live with or without curfew, with or without arrest, with or without work, even if we have permission from them to bury our dead in the full light of the day . . . what else would you call this except occupation?
>
> (Umm Rajah, 2005)

The establishment and subsequent growth of Israel's settlements in the West Bank, Gaza Strip and Palestinian East Jerusalem was one of the most potent signs of Israel's intentions for the territories.

Facts on the ground: Israel's settlements

As earlier chapters in this book have demonstrated the early Zionist community was very much shaped by the notion, as European settlers in other parts of the world were, of settling land; exploiting it for economic gain, political power and sovereignty (Lustick, 1993). In addition there was always a religious element within the Zionist movement that perceived settlement as part of fulfilling God's Covenant to give the land to the Jewish people. In the wake of the 1967 war and Israel's control of the West Bank and Gaza Strip, elements of this strand of Zionism moved to settle the Palestinian territories under Israel's control. Since 1967 to the present, irrespective of their political hue, successive Israeli governments have supported the settler movement, including the expropriation of Palestinian lands. These governments have variously cited their support in terms of arguments relating to the security of the state or for ideological reasons. Let us look at these two perspectives in turn:

The security of the state of Israel has become a major preoccupation of the state since its founding in 1948. Because the political and military elite of the state are convinced that Israel is imperilled by its Arab neighbours it has also been perceived as seeking a strategic march on these neighbours. Over the decades there have been many ways in which this strategic march was manifest. Israel has developed its weapons technology – including missile systems and nuclear capacity – that is the rival of any other state in the region. Israel has also identified and seen as important geographic high ground and territories that give it a strategic height over its neighbours. This security-related strategic depth became of particular concern in the wake of the 1967 war and the territories to the east of Jerusalem, the Jordan Valley and neighbouring Jordan itself. Proximity of such Arab enemies led various Israeli governments to endorse the settlement activities of its citizens. Jerusalem, after all, is less than 45 miles from the Jordanian capital of Amman, but hostility in the wake of the wars of 1948 and 1967 established a chasm between the two states that Israel started to fill with its burgeoning settlements. Settlement activity in the Jordan Valley began as early as 1967 (Gorenberg, 2006) and has continued to the present day in not only providing Israel with a strategic height over a former enemy (Jordan–Israel peace treaty 1994) but in pushing Palestinians off their lands throughout the area. The argument that the settlement areas provide Israel with a genuine security buffer was further diminished in the wake of the scud missile attacks launched from Iraq on Tel Aviv during the 1990–91 Gulf War, as well as Hizbullah missiles that bombarded Israel during the war of 2006. While some settlements are located close to IDF military positions or outposts it is difficult to discern the security value of housing schemes that would not look out of place in Wisteria Avenue *Desperate Housewives* style. These well-fortified and gated communities offer their residents spacious housing, and enough water (much of which is siphoned off from aquifers in the Palestinian territories) to literally make the grass greener than could normally be imagined in such arid landscapes. Nevertheless, the important point here is that Israel's most important ally, the USA, has always bought the 'settlements as security' argument, with the consequence that not only have such settlements remained (despite international censure) but settlement expansion in such areas has continued and proved to be a major stumbling block in peace negotiations between Israel and the Palestinians during the Camp David process (Gorenberg, 2006). In September 2006, for example, after Israel's international image had taken a battering during the Lebanon war and the Israeli public was expressing anger and discontent at the government led by Prime Minister Ehud Olmert, tenders were issued for the building of nearly 700 apartments in Israeli settlements in the West Bank. In the wake of the announcement an Israeli director of Peace Now declared:

> Instead of evacuating illegal outposts and suspending construction in the settlements, the government is building hundreds of housing units in the territories, and planning to legitimize dozens of illegal outposts. These acts violate Israel's commitment to the Road Map and Labour and Kadima's undertakings to their voters.
>
> (Shragai, 2006)

Whilst it is also true that the IDF have used strategic highpoints within the West Bank for military posts, the same arguments that have been parried with respect to settlements are relevant here. It is difficult in the modern day to imagine how much traction can be gained from a military argument to secure such strategic vantage points.

Let us now examine the ideological perspective motivating the settlements issue. How has an ideological impulse been translated into a movement for settlement that has transformed the landscape of the Palestinian territories and to what extent do events like the end of settlements in Gaza in 2005 demonstrate that there is ideological flexibility or pragmatism on this issue? The religio-ideological impulse, endorsed by Israeli political parties such as Likud, has its genesis in the Eretz Israel and Jewish sovereignty argument. The impulse to settlement was overwhelming in the wake of the 1967 war and was led by a group of settlers associated with Gush Etzion. This movement resulted in the growing expansion of settlements, to the extent that by 2005 over 250,000 settlers lived in 125 West Bank communities, 16,000 in the Israeli-annexed territories of the Syrian Golan Heights and over 180,000 in the illegally annexed territories of East Jerusalem. Today the ideologues of Israeli settlements are a minority but it was their religious and political fervour in the late 1960s and early 1970s that persuaded successive Israeli governments to support them in their plans. These ideologues are sought out by numerous journalists keen to demonstrate the ferocity and tenacity of such individuals as symbolic of the settlement story itself. In towns like Hebron in the West Bank such ideologues were responsible for the first settlers arriving in the wake of the 1967 war and establishing a presence in defiance of the government of the time. In Hebron the settler community has established itself in the heart of the old city, cheek by jowl alongside the Palestinian inhabitants. Such familiarity has merely bred contempt. Jewish settlers to Hebron were led by a Rabbi called Moshe Levinger. Through the subterfuge of posing as Swiss tourists this group of zealots set out to claim Hebron as a Jewish city and re-populate it. Levinger and his supporters were offered succour and weapons from other settlers associated with the Gush Emmunim movement. Since that time hardline settlers have made Hebron a symbol of their cause. and Jewish–Arab relations in the town have deteriorated into enmity and mutual violence. Palestinians attack and kill Jewish settlers and Jewish settlers, including some of their leaders, have attacked and killed Arabs. The IDF has complained that it is caught in the middle as they seek to protect the Jewish settlers. These settlers are infamous for their hardline ideological position against the Palestinians whom they perceive as an unnatural presence in the land promised to them in Covenant by God:

> 'Hebron is a Jewish city,' says Orit Strock, a settler and mother of 11. 'A people who come and live in a place 10 or 20 or even 100 years, it doesn't become their country. A country belongs to the people who lived in that country for thousands of years'.
>
> (O'Loughlin, 2002)

The settlers have drawn battle-lines that have seen them in confrontation with their own state when it perceives its position being undermined by state policies. In Hebron the settlers have attacked Israeli soldiers and police, calling them Nazis, during confrontations to clear illegally settled and Palestinian-owned properties.

In 2005 after Israeli Prime Minister Ariel Sharon announced the evacuation of all the 8,500 settlers from 21 settlements in the Gaza Strip, such sentiments were in evidence in the anti-evacuation campaign organized by the settlers. They tried to mobilize Israeli public opinion against Sharon's plan. Their orange banners and ribbons appeared on cars, on streets, on the balconies of apartments and at rallies, public meetings, settler marches and solidarity vigils. They threatened confrontation, peaceful and otherwise, with the forces of the state ordered to clear them out of Gaza. But it was not enough to dissuade the Sharon government to abandon the plan. In August 2005 Israeli settlers and soldiers shed tears alike as the process of quitting Gaza commenced amidst the glare of the media spotlight. The tears and torah quotes, however, did not deter the Sharon government from its chosen path.

In the wake of the evacuation Israeli public opinion remained divided on its efficacy in terms of Israeli security. The ideologues of the settler movement had, of course, opposed the evacuation on the grounds that it undermined the divinely gifted covenant of Eretz Israel to the Jewish people. Whilst the settlers ultimately acquiesced to the thousands of soldiers and other state personnel who were sent to organize and execute the evacuation they remain determined to pursue settlement expansion either with or without state sanction. In June 2006 extremist settlers distributed leaflets calling for attacks, which were designed to ignite further violence over the issue (Weiss, 2006). These elements have remained implacably opposed to any further efforts by the Israeli government to halt settlement expansion, dismantle settlement outposts or evacuate pre existing settlements. Hence the short-lived 'convergence plan' for settlement evacuation of some areas of the

West Bank announced by the government of Ehud Olmert in the spring of 2006 met with vehement opposition from parts of the settler community.

The settlements have become a series of facts on the ground (Aronson, 1987) that some believe may never be dismantled even if it brings peace between the Palestinian and Israeli people. The settlements have changed the landscape of the West Bank and Gaza Strip. Their physical presence along with their inhabitants have further circumscribed the lives of ordinary Palestinian people, underscoring the possibility that occupation may become annexation, transfer and the end of the aspiration for Palestinian statehood in the West Bank, East Jerusalem and the Gaza Strip.

Even if for many Israeli settlers such 'land theft' and 'colonization', as the Palestinians and others refer to it, is far more prosaically rooted in the reduced mortgages and convenient commuter distances, the remaining hardcore and those that support them within the Israeli political establishment remain significant. State-sponsored settlement, moreover, has contributed to the expansion of a formidable infrastructure that makes Israel complicit in action deemed illegal by the international community. These settlements are evidence of a violation of the Fourth Geneva Convention that Israel, as an occupying power, should abide by. According to the Convention an occupying power should not move any of its own civilian population into the territory that it occupies. In other words the state of Israel should not move Israeli citizens into settlements in the West Bank or the Gaza Strip. In the case of the Gaza Strip, Israel did not remove its settlers from there until August 2005. The law also states that an occupying power such as Israel should not make changes within the occupied territory on a permanent basis that deprive the local population – the Palestinians – of benefits. In the case of the West Bank and Gaza Strip, Israel has been accused on a number of counts of violating these conventions with settlement-building, expropriation of Palestinian land and building infrastructure (and thus making permanent changes) for the use of Israeli settlers and not the local Palestinian population.

Palestinian resistance against the settlement activities by Israeli settlers or the Israeli state of their lands in the West Bank, Gaza Strip and in East Jerusalem were initiated as Israel sought to settle. Many times Palestinian landowners, many of whom were farmers, sought redress through legal avenues, placing their faith in petitions, affidavits and lawyers making their case to the Israeli courts. Legal redress and resistance, however, mostly resulted in the Israeli case being upheld by the Israeli courts. Palestinians went away empty handed, with huge legal bills and their lands settled on by the settlers from Israel. Other resistance measures including calling for boycotts by Palestinian labour in the building of settlements or their infrastructure. Also, settlements were often subject to armed attacks and hostile relations characterized local contacts between settlers and the local Palestinian communities.

In Hebron, for example, coexistence between Palestinian residents and the Israeli settler community that established itself there became impossible. In a place like Hebron the consequence of the Six-Day War of 1967 not only meant that Israeli soldiers were on Palestinian land but that the settler movement, led by

figures like Rabbi Levinger, who then went on to play a founding role in the political movement of Gush Emmunim, would, with or without government support,
have a drastic effect on their lives. The challenge inherent in the first act of Jewish
settlement in 1968 in Hebron lay in whether the government of the day would
allow the Jews to return to a place where they had fled some 40 years earlier.
Rabbi Dr Chaim Simons, one of the early advocates of building a settlement in
Hebron, perceived the plan for such a community as symbolic of the wider conflict
between Palestinians and Israel. The settlement would demonstrate the balance of
power:

> It is not at all surprising that Sheikh Ali Ja'abari, the Arab Mayor of Hebron,
> was strongly opposed to the building of a Kirya for Jews in the Hebron area.
> In addition, in the summer of 1969, the Israeli Government put off the expro-
> priating of land in the Gush Etzion – the reason, Ja'abari's opposition. It
> was at that period that Menachem Liebman wrote a letter to 'Ma'ariv' and
> he asked my permission to sign it with my name, which I readily gave. This
> letter concluded, 'The residents of Judea and Samaria need to know who in
> fact rules in Judea and Samaria – the Government of Israel or Sheikh Ali
> Ja'abari – in order to know to know to whom to apply for a license to build a
> Kirya. . . . '.
>
> In the March 1970 we received the answer to this question – it was the
> Government of Israel – when they decided on the building of Kiryat Arba
> and the construction of 250 dwellings.
>
> (Simons, 2003)

Gush Emmunim sought to garner its support through a mass-based political
appeal for their efforts to bring a religious vision to the whole of what they considered to be biblical Israel and society as a whole. In one sense Gush Emmunim was
also part of an internal critique after the 1973 war in which Israel's military confidence was shaken by the Arab armies. This dimension of the critique had a decid-
edly religious character to it and was indeed part of a wider regional religious
resurgence and growth of fundamentalist movements. Gush Emmunim, in
common with many of these other movements, constructed an internal critique
based on a theological argument. Their proposed solution was politico-religious
and settlement based. These religious fundamentalists organized themselves as a
coalition with the express political goal of organizing opposition against the
Labour government of the day. They not only established settlements in the West
Bank – which they refer to as Judea and Samaria – but in the Gaza Strip and
Golan Heights as well. Israeli settlements were also established in the Israeli-occu-
pied Sinai. When Israel signed a peace treaty with Egypt in 1979 they had to evacuate 7,000 Israeli settlers. The Israeli leader Ariel Sharon boasts of establishing 64
settlements over a four-year period in the territory he refers to as 'Samaria and
Judea'. He adds that he was motivated by two principles, 'to protect our population centres and to insure the right of the Jews to live in historical Israel' (Sharon
with Chanoff, 2001: 368).

Gush Emmunim mobilized on a number of fronts to make it increasingly harder for the Labour government of the day to consider a 'land for peace' deal over the territories occupied in 1967. Ariel Sharon admired their energies: 'I was acutely aware that without the sudden flow of pioneering nationalism this movement represented, the need to achieve a Jewish presence in Samaria and Judea might well have remained unfulfilled' (Sharon with Chanoff, 2001: 364). By the time of the Israeli general election of 1977, where the Israeli voters replaced Labour with a right-wing religious coalition government led by Likud, Gush Emmunim were confident of support for their settlement projects. Their confidence was not misplaced. The new right-wing political administration officially sanctioned a number of settlements established by the movement. Further evidence of government support for the settlers came in September 1977 when the head of the Israel Lands Administration, Ariel Sharon, who his critics now dubbed 'patron of the settlers' announced that the government would encourage and support the settlement of 1 million Jews in the West Bank. It is claimed that in this alliance lay a joint vision that, 'saw in the depth of the West Bank a sacred territory and a defensible frontier, a border without a line, across whose depth a matrix of settlement could be constructed' (Weizman, 2003). These settlements would not only sit on the 'border' lines of the Jordan valley but, Sharon hoped, could be constructed in strategic high places that would promote depth of 'defence' as well as fulfil the messianic promises inherent to the Gush movement and other religious settlers.

The Likud government did not tarry in its task of settlement-building in the West Bank and Gaza. From 1977 to 1981 hundreds of millions of dollars were dispersed in supporting settlement construction projects, leading to an influx of thousands of new settlers. Settlements meant that land had to be made available and it was clear that by the time that Likud were returned to power in 1981 sizeable areas of land in the West Bank and Gaza would be taken from Palestinian hands to make way for the settlements and necessary infrastructure. By the mid-1980s more than 100 new settlements had been constructed in the West Bank and nearly 50,000 settlers had made their homes there. The Likud government had sanctioned settlement and, in alliance with the settler movement, substantially altered not only the physical but political landscape of the Palestinian territories.

Movements like Gush Emmunim did not always enjoy a fruitful coalescence between themselves and the Israeli government of the day. There were issues of difference such as the Egypt–Israeli peace treaty of 1979 that required the dismantlement of Israeli settlements in the Sinai desert. There were also times when the settlers bemoaned an apparent unwillingness by the Israeli army to act without bias towards their activities in the Palestinian territories. This has led to a historically strained relationship between the IDF and some elements of the settler movement.

Palestinians have abhorred the settlers and all that they have brought with them in terms of what they perceive to be an agenda of racially based hatred and colonization of a land. From such sentiments has grown a major political and social movement that has challenged Israel and its governance of the Palestinian people. This movement has been bound by competing ideologies of emancipation and self-determination in the name of the Palestinian people. It has symbolized much of the politics of Third World populism and revolutionary change that marked the 1970s and 1980s, and by the 1990s was increasingly characterized by an Islamic hue.

Resistance under occupation

For Palestinians the realities of further territorial loss, dispossession and the military occupation by a foreign power of the lands and livelihoods of those who remained in the West Bank, Gaza Strip and East Jerusalem brought about a transformation of nationalist politics, leading to the prominence of the PLO, led by Yasser Arafat, as the major Palestinian resistance movement in the two decades before the outbreak of the Intifada in 1987. It was no mean feat to build a Palestinian leadership capable of leading a diverse resistance movement both inside and outside the West Bank and Gaza Strip against Israel. For decades the PLO were shunned by much of the international community as terrorists and membership of the movement was criminalized by Israel until the signing of the Oslo Agreement in 1993. But in that time, from the founding of the PLO in 1964 through the benevolence of the Arab states to the signing of the Oslo Accords in 1993, the structures of the PLO grew to accommodate many (though not all) dimensions of Palestinian political identity.

As a result of the soul searching among many Arab nationalists in the wake of the defeat in 1967 there emerged a growing conviction among Palestinian nationalists that dependence on Arab regimes for the liberation of their lands from Israel would not automatically work. They felt abandoned by the international community and its forums such as the United Nations, which seemed incapable of getting Israel to abide by resolutions that called for the 'right of return' of refugees and a trading of land for peace. Despite the fact that the UN Security Council and General Assembly had passed resolutions calling for justice in the case of the Palestinians, they had been unable to flex their muscles when Israel simply chose to ignore such resolutions. Although UN agencies, such as UNRWA, were established to provide some basic care and assistance to the refugees, there was little evidence of tangible diplomatic efforts to give the Palestinians much hope.

There was a sense also that their cause had been used by some Arab leaders as a foil to their own domestic concerns and issues and that Palestinians themselves must act to take control of the situation. While it was true that until 1967 the Arab states had supported their Palestinian brethren, rallying their forces in the war of 1948, administering the West Bank and Gaza Strip, and sheltering the hundreds of thousands of dispossessed Palestinians, they had proved themselves unable to inflict a decisive military defeat over Israel and thus provide a solution to the demand for self-determination and independence. The rhetoric of support was in effect not enough to win the war against Israel. Arab infighting over the Palestinian issue also proved to be detrimental to the wider cause of their liberation. Inter-Arab squabbles over who would best represent the interest of the Palestinians and who would not often lost sight of those who, in the wake of 1967, now found them-selves living under Israel's rules but denied citizenship of the state of Israel. Palestinians themselves did find succour from the region but it was not in the pan-Arab posturing of Gamal Abdel Nasser or the claims of King Hussein of Hashemite Jordan. In 1962 the Algerian people had succeeded through popular revolution in throwing off the yoke of French colonial rule and the narrative of this revolution proved inspirational for the Palestinians. If armed resistance could deliver the Algerians from France, figured many in the Palestinian camps, then it was time to organize a guerrilla movement to deal with the Israeli occupation.

Liberating Palestine through an organization

The Palestine Liberation Organization itself had originally been formed as part of an initiative coming out of the Arab Summit of 1964 and was the brainchild of President Nasser. When the PLO was convened in Cairo for the first time it brought together several hundred Palestinians in a forum to call for the right to self-determination and the upholding of the rights of the Palestinian nation. That the PLO came to serve as an organization for liberation and the maintenance of Palestinian national identity meant that it was to serve a dual purpose. Some may well question the notion of nation when there is no state but this issue is core to understanding Palestinian identity not just under occupation but in exile as well. The PLO and its constituent organizations would play a major role in the years to come in defining, and sustaining, that dynamic sense of identity and its place in the global consciousness. For the task of achieving self-determination an army of Palestinian liberation was also deemed essential. Thus the Palestine Liberation Army (PLA) was established and supported by the Arab states.

During this time of radical and populist turmoil in the Middle East, not everyone in the Palestinian camp regarded the formation of the PLO as the key to their own salvation. They were suspicious of Arab motives in establishing and basically supporting the creation of the PLO and PLA, seeing it perhaps as a proxy tool which they alone could control. Others believed that the PLO was too elitist and, amidst the revolutionary fever that had gripped the region, elitism and the notable classes of the ancien régime were definitely considered passé by leftist and other elements. Such elements argued that the younger generation were better able to deliver a revolution in the Palestinian camp and that the older generation had already proved themselves incapable of protecting the Palestinian people from British and Zionist aggression. And it was true that the first leader of the PLO, Ahmad Shuquairi, was unpopular, and following the military defeat of 1967 he was forced to resign.

In his wake came a new generation of Palestinian leaders – younger and many of whom had imbibed the revolutionary ideals of nationalist socialism and Marxism. The individual that came to the fore of the leadership of the PLO, amal-gamating it as an umbrella organization of many factions, was Yasser Arafat. Yasser Arafat was head of the Fatah guerrilla organization and by 1969 became leader of the PLO and its Executive Committee and other administrative bodies.

From this point onwards the PLO would advocate armed struggle against Israel, as well as setting up administrative structures within the Arab world that would provide a series of services for the Palestinian population in exile. As Arafat declared, 'in those days anyone of us could have been a leader, leading our people to liberation from occupation and exile forced upon us by Israel' (Arafat, 2004). Although the Fatah organization that Arafat headed would become the dominant faction of the PLO, other groups included the Popular Front for the Liberation of Palestine (PFLP), the Democratic Front for the Liberation of Palestine (DFLP) and, in the occupied territories, the Palestine Peoples Party (PPP, formerly the Communist Party). When compared with elements of Fatah's socially conservative leadership, these other factions constituted a broad leftist alliance within the PLO. Factional differences, however, have always characterized, and on occasion, marred the organization. Factional splits have erupted at various stages of the PLO's development, leading to intense and long-standing rivalries, fissures, tensions, and occasional bloodletting. In some respects this was because elite bodies within the internal structure of the PLO were not reflective in terms of demands for power-sharing that persist from the past to the present.

The PLO was structured to serve the Palestinians not merely as a guerrilla movement with its guerrilla forces consisting of the PLA and other armed elements, but also as a government-in-exile, model of democratic decision-making, advocate in international forums for Palestinian rights, locus of Palestinian national identity, and provider of services to the people through health, education, training, welfare, culture and media. The Palestine National Council (PNC) was composed of representatives from all the factions as well as other important constituencies in Palestinian society; their job was to convene and 'legislate' on Palestinian affairs. The PNC issued 'guidelines' to the Executive Committee of the PLO and they were assisted in their task by a Central Council. In principle the organization should have had enough checks and balances to ensure the maintenance of democracy, plurality and power-sharing amongst the various constituent factions of the organization (Sayigh, 1997). In practice the organization was manipulated by those with authoritarian tendencies or with ambitions to defraud the PLO of its financial resources. Yasser Arafat's eventual assumption of absolute power and the corrupt cabal that came to surround him also weakened the ability of the movement to mobilize the masses. Sayigh refers to this process as the 'politics of patronage or neopatrimonal bureacratization'; locally Palestinians summed this up with one short Arabic term: *wasta* (Sayigh, 1997: 454). Loosely interpreted *wasta* means having power to affect outcomes through money, influence or both. Through the development of 'a highly personalized system of patronage' Arafat became the locus of allocating resources within the PLO (Sayigh, 1997: 458). In person Arafat was careful to portray himself to Westerners as a reluctant leader among many within Palestinian society but his relations with his own senior people betrayed the reality of power. In the wake of Yasser Arafat's death in 2004 the delicate internal 'unity' of the PLO began to crumble. The failure of Fatah to win in legislative elections in 2006, the failure to proceed with a process of internal reform that would satisfy democratic indicators, the unwillingness to allow Hamas a role in the PLO, the decision to politicize the Palestinian security sector through tightening the grip of Fatah all led to a series of inter-factional confrontations throughout 2006–07 and culminated in Hamas's victory over Fatah after six days of fighting in Gaza in June 2007.

Most historical accounts of the PLO cite the events of 'Black' September 1970 when the organization found itself in armed confrontation with the forces of Jordan's King Hussein as indicative of how quickly it had grown and come to rival other actors in the political arena. King Hussein, believing that his very throne was under threat from the PLO, moved harshly against the Palestinians. In the ensuing violence many were killed in what was virtually a civil war. According to Sayigh: 'unfettered access to the [refugee] camps allowed the construction of a mass base, in which the primary impetus to mobilization was provided by military activities' (Sayigh, 1997: 183). This in turn made possible the emergence of a 'state-within-the-state' (ibid.:184).

By July 1971 the PLO had been expelled to Lebanon and, despite the fact that Palestinians constitute the majority population in Jordan, relations were forever soured (Milton-Edwards and Hinchcliffe, 2001). In Lebanon the PLO became embroiled in the civil war that broke out in 1975. Lebanon became a base from which factions could launch assaults against Israel. PLO attacks against Israel by this point had also included the infamous strike against Israeli athletes at the Munich Olympics in 1972. This attack along with a series of Palestinian-orchestrated plane hijackings and assassinations solidified the image of the Palestinians as terrorists in the minds of many across the globe. The Israelis countered such violence with their own raids, assassinations and the eventual invasions of Lebanon in both 1978 and 1982. In 1982 the primary purpose of the invasion was to oust the PLO from its power base. By the time that the PLO leadership left on 30 August, however, Israel had occupied south Lebanon and Beirut. Less than a month later Israel was implicated in the Sabra and Shatilla massacres where hundreds of defenceless Palestinians were killed in these Beirut refugee camps. Israeli Defence Minister, Ariel Sharon, denied Israeli involvement in the massacre maintaining that, 'it was clear that not a single Israeli officer or solider was involved in what happened' (Sharon with Chanoff, 2001: 508). Sharon argues that the 'tragedy' was used as a 'political cause celebre against the government' with public ire in Israel centred on himself and the Prime Minister. An official Israeli commission of inquiry into the Sabra and Shatilla massacres, however, held Sharon responsible for what had happened and this is turn led to his resignation as Defence Minister early the following year. Following the PLO's ousting from Lebanon the leadership spent the following decade in exile in Tunis, while various elements of the PLA were stationed in Algeria, Sudan and the Yemen. From this great distance it was now almost impossible for the PLO to wage its guerrilla offensive against Israel.

In the wake of the Lebanon debacle there were many internal tensions within the PLO (Sayigh, 1997). In some respects this tension, coupled with the loss of geographic proximity to Israel and wider regional events, robbed the PLO in exile of its energy for armed struggle. Energies were further dissipated in the internal rounds of bloodletting, as the real fallout from the PLO's role in the Lebanese civil war plus the Israeli rout spread through the movement. As one Fatah loyalist who had been released in the 1985 PFLP-General Command (PFLP-GC) prisoner exchange with Israel remarked:

> we felt loyal to the leadership still but we also knew that among those on the outside there was too much going on internally to really keep their focus on the struggle that we were all prepared to sacrifice ourselves for . . . I had been sentenced by the Israelis to over 100 hundred years in prison for my part in the struggle and I was relieved to be released but there were dark doubts among some during this time too.
>
> (Abu Seif, 1994)

Certainly there was an incipient sense that the PLO leadership in Tunis was becoming increasingly disconnected with the Palestinians in the West Bank and Gaza Strip and their lives under the increasingly heavy burden of Israeli occupation. And although the PLO continued to support the families of prisoners and martyrs, to organize campaigns of steadfastness, campaign in solidarity with labour groups and workers, and spread propaganda through its own magazines and newspapers, there were signs that it too was as unprepared for the turn of events in revolt against the occupation in December 1987 as the Israelis themselves were.

Where the PLO mattered, nevertheless, was in the forums of international solidarity for the Palestinian people, whether these were within the non-aligned movement, among the international labour organizations, or at the forums, assemblies and committees of the United Nations, where the PLO, as sole representative of the Palestinian people, lobbied to maintain UN resolutions against Israel and to resolve the conflict peaceably. In 1974, for example, the PLO was considered to have achieved a victory when Yasser Arafat was invited to address the UN General Assembly. At this historic event Arafat declared to his international audience:

> The difference between the revolutionary and the terrorist lies in the reason for which each fights. Whoever stands by a just cause and fights for liberation from invaders and colonialists cannot be called terrorist. Those who wage war to occupy, colonize and oppress other people are the terrorists. . . . The Palestinian people had to resort to armed struggle when they lost faith in the international community, which ignored their rights, and when it became clear that not one inch of Palestine could be regained through exclusively political means. . . .
>
> The PLO dreams and hopes for one democratic state where Christian, Jew and Muslim live in justice, equality, fraternity and progress. The chairman of the PLO and leader of the Palestinian revolution appeals to the General Assembly to accompany the Palestinian people in its struggle to attain its right of self-determination. . . . I have come bearing an olive branch and a freedom fighter's gun. Do not let the olive branch fall from my hand.
>
> (United Nations, 1974)

A year later the US government publicly acknowledged, for the first time, that the Palestinian issue was at the heart of the resolution of the Arab–Israeli conflict. Yet the PLO did not choose the diplomatic path alone and throughout the 1970s and 1980s they continued to wage their 'war' against Israeli and Jewish targets.

There were elements within the PLO who argued that, far from energies for armed struggle dissipating, the events of 1982 had only strengthened a belief that Israel had to be militarily defeated through the Palestinian strategy of armed resistance. To this end alliances were formed internally among radical elements as well as externally with Arab regimes that Western countries such as the USA described as 'rogue states' and 'supporters of terror.' This reflected a tendency within the PLO to be alternatively buoyed or bounced by the political vagaries of Arab politics both at a national and regional level. Hence inter-Arab alliances have formed an important dimension of the PLO both in terms of it being seen as a threat to some Arab regimes such as Jordan and an ally and rallying point for other Arab regimes – often in competition with each other regionally – such as Syria, Iraq or Egypt. By the late 1980s the greatest challenge for the PLO would lay in its ability to win the political prize of statehood by itself and not merely as an adjunct to its Arab supporters.

Occupation and employment

After 1967 and until the outbreak of the Palestinian uprising in December 1987 one dynamic of the relationship between Israel and the Palestinians that emerged was related to the realm of economy and employment. For many Israelis the Palestinian territories became a territorial expansion of Israel in terms of markets for their goods, a place where they could buy and sell and a locus of the import of daily migrant labour. After 1967 Israelis travelled freely throughout the West Bank and Gaza Strip and visited Palestinian towns and villages, shopped in their local markets and enjoyed meals in Palestinian restaurants. For Palestinians the division was more apparent. They became unwillingly tied into economic relationships of dependency with the Israeli business sector with thousands travelling daily to and from their refugee shelters and homes in the West Bank and Gaza Strip.

Such workers were not allowed to stay in Israel overnight; the method of absorption was solely focused on the contribution that Palestinians could make to the burgeoning Israeli economy. They became the underclass of Israel's economy doing menial jobs and tasks for the kind of pay and hours that Israelis themselves would never accept. Palestinians worked in the fields of Israeli kibbutzim and farming communities known as moshav, bringing in the harvests of tomatoes, grapes, cucumbers, avocados, dates, melons and cotton. They worked on the building sites of Israeli cities and even built their settlements for them. They cleaned streets, worked as waiters in restaurants, caretakers in public buildings and institutions, gardeners and dishwashers. Their labour was cheap because Israeli employers were not obliged to offer the entitlements that were bestowed on Israeli workers.

Many Palestinians also worked illegally, meaning that employers exploited them by making them work longer hours with poor pay and conditions. The phenomenon of the 'slave market' where in most Israeli towns and cities there would be a district where Palestinian workers would congregate in the hope of being offered a day's work here and there epitomized the way in which Palestinians were asymmetrically absorbed by occupation into Israel's economy. The poignancy of the 'slave markets', which in the early mornings were thronged with hundreds of men smoking cigarettes and clutching plastic bags with their daily food supplies, was lost on the hard-headed contractors and sub-contractors who were looking for the best deal from Palestinian labour that they could find. At its peak some 200,000 Palestinians were making their living from Israel in this way. They were a part of Israeli society only in terms of its margins, its underclass, its backrooms and building sites.

Economic dependence not only made Palestinians compliant in the workplace in Israel but also in terms of their relationship with the occupation authorities themselves. Irrespective of the context, defiance was rarely expressed by Palestinians in the face of the occupation (Amiry, 2005). As a result of this compliance Israel came to believe it could enforce its occupation with minimum manpower inputs and could get the Palestinians to pay for the occupation itself through the levy of various administration taxes and permit systems.

Palestinian resistance to the occupation during this period was coloured by sporadic and violent attacks and momentary flashes of defiance. These included PLO-organized rallies, protests, national guidance committees and campaigns such as the one for the 1976 municipal council elections when the PLO replaced pro-Jordanian mayors. By the early 1980s the Israelis had retaliated at this evidence of PLO influence and deported the mayors, replaced them with their own appointees, stopped the flow of funds for PLO organized projects and encouraged the growth of an Islamic movement in Gaza as a rival to the nationalist movement and its supporters. Israel became adept at a policy of divide and rule and this was easy to promote in a society as rife with fissure as the Palestinian one. What remained unchanged, however, was a growing sense of Palestinian identity that was founded in insubordination of Israeli occupation hegemony and the myriad laws denying nation to the Palestinian people.

The pressure cooker

To the generation of Palestinians born since 1967, being Palestinian became an act of political defiance to occupation itself. Being Palestinian took many subversive and counter-cultural forms: they were usually associated with the colours of the Palestinian flag. These colours were flown on kites, or shown on coloured enamel dangling from key-rings, or displayed on the flags, hand-sown by a female relative, hidden under mattresses and brought out at night or in private for furtive national enjoyment. Before the outbreak of the first Palestinian Intifada in 1987 when such symbols were displayed in open defiance of the occupation, the mere possession of a flag or a poster bearing the image of PLO Chairman Yasser Arafat, an olive tree (symbol of rootedness) or the image of Handala (the small Palestinian boy penned by cartoonist Naji al-Ali epitomizing resistance and identity) was an act of political subversion.

The image of Handala appeared everywhere – a silent witness to Israel's power over the Palestinian people. Subversion was to be found in the Palestinian dance troupes, the poetry and art that spoke of or symbolized Palestinian identity and the longing for freedom and independence. None of this was enough, eventually, to sustain a community enduring occupation for 20 years. The weight of occupation and absence of either liberation through armed struggle or diplomatic movement in the Middle East arena led to a growing sense of despair among the Palestinians and a form of modus operandi among the Israelis that seemed to convince them that their policies of occupation, settlement and containment in the Palestinian territories could go on forever. By the middle to late 1980s breakaway factions of the PLO, such as the PFLP-GC and the newly emergent Islamic Jihad group, were mounting attacks against Israeli targets. No one, however, anticipated the events that took place in December 1987, which would alter, forever, the dynamic of the conflict between Israel and the Palestinians.

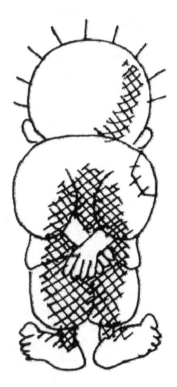

Figure 6.1 Image of subversion: Handala, the small Palestinian boy penned by cartoonist Naji al-Ali.

From 1967 to 1987 Israel remained in occupation of the Palestinian territories of the West Bank and Gaza and East Jerusalem. During that time various governments and citizen movements pursued what Nasser Aruri refers to as a calculated process in terms of reshaping the region. He maintains that the Israeli occupation is a form of:

> politicide – to ensure that the Palestinians will not be able to exercise any sort of self-determination on any of the territory that lies between the river Jordan and the Mediterranean Sea . . . Politicide as a process that has as its ultimate goal the dissolution of the Palestinian people's existence as a legitimate national, social, and economic entity, which may also include partial or total ethnic cleansing.
>
> (Aruri, 2007)

Many Israelis maintain, however, that Israel is in control of 'disputed territories' and that if they do not seek a solution to their own security then the Arabs will continue to wage a jihad against them that will only end when Israel ceases to exist. This is why Israel has consistently demanded recognition and hence legitimacy from its Arab and Muslim enemies. They have demanded that the state of Israel be recognized as a legitimate entity by their neighbours.

The first 20 years of occupation did not pass without diplomatic effort. There were always political figures in the Israeli and Arab camps who believed that a diplomatic resolution to the conflict could be reached. But time and again such efforts were frustrated by the principal actors in both camps. Israel remained implacably opposed to an international conference to resolve the conflict preferring at best to negotiate separately with the Arabs. The PLO, for its part, never really abandoned the gun for the olive branch and continued to reject peace negotiations led, for example, by the Jordanians on their behalf.

The wider effects of the conflict also continued to have an impact on the Middle East region. In 1973 Israel and the Arab states went to war again and an Arab oil embargo crippled the international economy. In 1979 the Israelis and Egyptians achieved peace and Israeli settlements were dismantled in the Sinai. In 1978 and again in 1982 Israel invaded Lebanon in order to mount a military challenge against the PLO. Israel subsequently became embroiled in a bitter civil war in Lebanon (1975–90) and only finally withdrew from south Lebanon in 2000.

Further reading

An unorthodox but perhaps interesting book to commence further reading with is the comic book by Joe Sacco which gives an immensely detailed pictorial portrayal of Palestinian life under Israeli occupation (New York: Jonathan Cape, 2003). Shehadeh (Harmondsworth: Penguin, 2003) describes how the occupation controls Palestinian lives. More conventional texts that give further insights into some of the issues that have been covered in this chapter include the works by Metzger (London: Zed Books, 1984), Haas (New York: Owl Books, 2000) and

Amiry (London: Granta Books, 2005). On the controversial topic of the Israeli settlers and the settlement process try Gorenberg (New York: Henry Holt and Co., 2006), Shahak and Mezvinsky (London: Zed Books, 2004) and Friedman (New York: Random House, 1992), which give a variety of perspectives with respect to the extreme ends of the movement as well as government policy by the Israeli state on the issue. Tal and Kett's book (Westport, CT: Greenwood Press, 2000) examines such issues within the remit of the national security debate. On the PLO and Yasser Arafat there are a number of competing texts and interpretations available to read. These include Rubin and Rubin (Oxford: Oxford University Press, 2005), Aburish (London: Bloomsbury, 1999) and Gowers and Walker (London: Virgin Books, 2005). The latter two books are biographies of Yasser Arafat and give some insight on his authoritarian tendencies within Fatah and the PLO.

Aburish, S. (1999) *Arafat: From defender to dictator*, London: Bloomsbury.

Amiry, S. (2005) *Sharon and my mother-in-law*, London: Granta Books.

Friedman, Robert (1992) *Zealots for Zion: Inside Israel's West Bank settlement movement*, New York: Random House.

Gorenberg, G. (2006) *The accidental empire: Israel and the birth of the settlements, 1967–1977*, New York: Henry Holt and Co.

Gowers, A. and Walker, T. (2005) *Arafat: The biography*, London: Virgin Books.

Haas, A. (2000) *Drinking the sea at Gaza: Days and nights in a land under siege*, New York: Owl Books.

Metzger, J. (1984) *This land is our land: West Bank under occupation*, London: Zed Books.

Rubin, B. and Rubin, J.C. (2005) *Yasir Arafat: A political biography*, Oxford: Oxford University Press.

Sacco, J. (2003) *Palestine*, New York: Jonathan Cape.

Shahak, I. and Mezvinsky, N. (2004) *Jewish fundamentalism in Israel*, London: Zed Books.

Shehadeh, R. (2003) *Strangers in the house: Coming of age in occupied Palestine*, Harmondsworth: Penguin.

Tal, I. and Kett, M. (2000) *National security: The Israeli experience*, Westport, CT: Greenwood Press.

7 The war of the stones and guns

Chapter outline

- Insurrection   143
- Palestinian political goals   145
- An Arab 'shaking off'?   147
- Israel responds   148
- The strategy for change   150
- Consolidation and political progress   152
- Actions speak louder than words: getting to the second Intifada   153
- The al-Aqsa armed Intifada   154
- Operation Defensive Shield: unequivocal victory?   157
- Further reading   160

> Fucker, I thought to myself. So irritated by a stare!
>
> I wonder what your reaction would have been if you had lived under occupation for as many years as I had, or if your shopping rights, like all your other rights, were violated day and night, or if the olive trees in your grandfather's orchard had been uprooted, or if your village had been bulldozed, or if your house had been demolished, or if your sister could not reach her school, or if your brother had been given three life sentences, or if your mother had given birth at a checkpoint, or if you had stood in line for days in the hot August summers waiting for your work permits, or if you could not reach your beloved ones in Arab East Jerusalem?
>
> A stare and you lose your mind.
>
> (Amiry, 2005: 68–69)

The outbreak of the Palestinian uprising on 9 December 1987 both challenged and changed perceptions internally and externally of the Israeli–Palestinian conflict. The term that the Palestinians applied to this event was Intifada – meaning to shake-off – in this case primarily the Israeli occupation. The occupation was rocked to its foundations, the prospects for a peaceful resolution to the conflict increased and the ways in which the world viewed and understood the conflict changed. While Israel had once enjoyed an enduring status as a David against the Goliath of Arab hostility during the first Intifada, Palestinians with their slingshots and stones thrown against the armour of Israel's military forces inverted the analogy.

The political strategies adopted and pursued by the Palestinians and the Israelis during this period had an effect on their internal polities and created new pressures and a demand for responses. Palestinian political strategies during this period included the pursuit of mass-based civil disobedience as a means of resisting the occupation. The organization of the body politic within the Palestinian territories also led to new forms of more communal politics, creating opportunities for some groups that had previously played a limited or marginal role. Palestinian civil society was revitalized and empowered as political energies were harnessed to the project of popular resistance against the occupation.

Palestinians were perceived differently as a result of the media glare on Israel's action and, perhaps for the first time in their history, the Western perception of them was as victims rather than terrorists. This led to a political momentum that some argue culminated in the 1991 Madrid peace talks and the 1993 Oslo Accords. Aspects of the conflict also changed. On both sides of the divide the voice of the religious right, the fundamentalists and conservatives emerged amidst the cacophony of chaos that the Intifada induced. In both Israel and the Palestinian territories this led to the emergence of new political groups, new coalitions, new leaders and new political horizons and opportunities for leaders, political parties and factions.

The stones were increasingly replaced by the olive branch throughout the 1990s. The 1991 peace conference in Madrid and subsequent peace talks, the increased role and energies of the international community, the election in Israel of Yitzhak Rabin in 1992 and the discussions that culminated in the Oslo Accords being signed in 1993 all appeared to herald the beginning of the end of the conflict. In return for the PLO recognizing the state of Israel the Palestinians would enjoy a form of self-government through the creation of the ruling Palestinian Authority (PA). The return in 1994 of PLO Chairman Yasser Arafat first to Gaza and then to the West Bank and the establishment of the PA in the West Bank and Gaza Strip was greeted by Palestinians and many Israelis with immense optimism. But because Oslo was not a peace deal but the framework for final status negotiation on issues such as settlements, borders, refugees and Jerusalem things began to unravel throughout the middle to late 1990s.

The advent of proto-state politics post-1993 in the form of the PA, its institutions and structures with the Palestinian Legislative Council and the elections of 1996 will be addressed particularly in respect of wider debates about state-building, sovereignty, civil society, corruption and authoritarianism. Both Israeli and Palestinian spoilers and rejectionists and their impact on the peace process will be analysed. Israeli withdrawal and Palestinian autonomy will be reviewed. The Hebron massacre and the killing of Yitzhak Rabin will be presented in terms of the difficulties associated with moving societies from militarization and violence to normalization and peace. The settlements factor, the politics of precariousness, stalemate and suicide bombings will also be considered. The beginning of the dissolution of the Oslo process – the impact of the Netanyahu government elected in Israel in 1996, the Wye Agreement of 1998, the peace negotiations at Camp David in 2000, and Taba in early 2001 – will also be examined in this chapter.

Insurrection

In some ways, 9 December 1987 was a very ordinary winter's day in Israel and the Palestinian territories. The weather was inclement and the ordinary business of the day was conducted with haste as everyone sought to avoid the stormy elements. Despite the rain and freezing temperatures thousands of men and women from the crowded confines of the camps and cities of the Gaza Strip had streamed out of their homes and travelled to Israel for a day of labouring for low wages. If the spirit of revolt was in the air it was only because it was coerced out of a group of people whose frustrations and anger had boiled over after a group of workers had perished in a road crash caused by an Israeli driver. Amidst the personal anguish and hurt, palpable among the mourners who crowded to the cemetery and buried their dead, there emerged a powerful impulse of rebellion directed against the Israeli occupiers; against their soldiers, their settlers, their infrastructure of control, and the myriad constraints – political, economic, physical, cultural, legal – that Palestinians chafed under. In the events that followed the whole of the Palestinian territories, including East Jerusalem, were engulfed in a rebellion against Israeli occupation.

The ferocity of the revolt, in word and deed, took the Israeli government and its people, the Palestinian Diaspora, including the PLO, as well as international opinion completely by surprise. No one had predicted the uprising and in the initial stages of the revolt the Israelis appeared momentarily powerless to put an end to this mass-based assault on their system of rule in the West Bank and Gaza Strip. Nationalist or Islamist sentiment, despite the claims of Palestinian groups such as Hamas, was not at the root of the revolt. Occupation and its consequences for the hundreds of thousands of Palestinians enduring poverty and miserable living conditions was the true motive for the explosion of violence that erupted.

Indeed in the first weeks of the uprising, as demonstrations, marches, spontaneous protests, strikes, and sit-ins organized by the Palestinians spread like wildfire and the Israelis responded with the wildfire of their assault guns and weaponry, a distinct state of denial permeated the military and political establishment in Tel Aviv. The press was ordered by Israel's military censor to strike out any reference in the Arabic or English language media to an 'uprising' or 'Intifada'. The red-line of the censor's pen, however, was only able to contain the situation for so long and was eventually overwhelmed by the massed ranks of the world's press who descended en masse to cover the story of the uprising and label it as an Intifada.

Within a matter of weeks the Palestinians had quickly organized themselves and their political programme. The aim of the revolt was self-determination and the establishment of an independent Palestinian state. The leaders of the revolt harnessed the energies of the young and the old, the professional and the unskilled working classes and day labourers, men and women. They all shouldered the responsibility of the uprising together as each faction of the PLO organized a series of committees and teams to marshal the uprising. On the fringes of political society there also emerged a new Islamist group, called Hamas. Hamas also sought to bring a sense of discipline, focus and order to the mass-based uprising that seemed to grip every camp community, village, town and city across the West Bank and Gaza Strip. Hamas, along with its smaller Islamist counterpart, Islamic Jihad, would later emerge as one of the most important signs of change within the Palestinian community of the West Bank, Jerusalem and Gaza (Milton-Edwards, 1999). Their religious vision would, moreover, impact on the emergence of their counterparts among Israel's Arab population as well.

The PLO, its political leadership in exile in Tunis and its army, the PLA, dispersed across the Arab world, also had to try and get up to speed as quickly as possible with events on the ground and attempt to pull the reins of leadership back into their hands. This was an effort that, in terms of leadership, met with mixed results and once again altered the dynamic of the Palestinian polity (the inside and the outside) forever. Instead of leading the 'war of Palestinian independence' as Shlaim refers to it, the PLO were outflanked by the energies of thousands of young people and children who took to the streets in the Gaza Strip and West Bank in revolt (Shlaim, 2000: 451). PLO chairman Yasser Arafat and his stalwart cadres had to acknowledge that a new generation of Palestinians had arisen and they were the ones providing the impetus and vision and drive on the ground. Just as Arafat and his supporters had disrupted the old structures of the PLO in the 1960s and ushered in a new more revolutionary approach to resistance, so the younger generation of the 1980s had grown impatient at the old guard of leadership who they perceived as having failed in the task of winning them independence and divesting them of Israel's occupation. The guerrilla war led by the PLO had ended with the debacle of the exodus from Lebanon in 1982 and years of bitter infighting that in some respects had paralysed the movement in terms of the wider liberation struggle (Sayigh, 1997).

Amidst the general debris of burning tyres, rocks, barricades of old shopping trolleys, bins and crates scattered across the West Bank and Gaza Strip the national service and reservist soldiers of the IDF struggled to find the means to quell the uprising. All their actions, particularly in the early stages of the Intifada, seemed to inflame the rebellion rather than crush it. The disproportionate use of force – live ammunition and breaking bones – immortalized in the news bulletins of thousands of TV stations from across the globe only served to embolden the Palestinians. The Palestinians fought back with rocks and burning tyres, swinging rats on string at the soldiers of one of the most sophisticated armies in the world. Israel imposed curfews, conducted mass arrests, they forced shops open and forced shops closed. Soldiers were ordered to break the limbs of Palestinian demonstrators; they shot thousands of canisters of tear gas, thousands of rounds of rubber bullets and live ammunition, sent in tanks and other armoured vehicles, arranged for the deportation of the Palestinian leadership, and confiscated property. They raided homes, and also demolished them, and declared Palestinian areas closed military zones. They put thousands of Palestinians in jail and sought to crush the uprising through running networks of spies, collaborators, counter-insurgency tactics, information operations and propaganda.

As the early months of the Intifada passed and Palestinian energies remained undiminished a sense of disquiet grew within the ranks of the IDF. Soldiers questioned the validity of being a sophisticated fighting force sent to quell demonstrations organized and peopled by hundreds of unarmed women, small school children or the fashionable middle-class ladies of the notable Palestinian families. Fur coats and fire bombs appeared to be the order of the day. The IDF understood the power of the David and Goliath metaphor and they hated the fact that the Palestinians were turning it on its head. They complained to their commanders, they berated the political establishment and once again the intimate relationship between the military and the political elite in Israel was exposed. Within the first year of the uprising it was becoming clear that the Palestinian revolt would not be crushed through the exercise of sheer military force. The actions of the Palestinians had challenged the legitimacy of the occupier and placed it under the focus of the world's media. It was starting to look like a public relations and military disaster as international censure was heaped upon the Israeli government. Would political opinion in Israel change?

Palestinian political goals

The deaths of the Palestinian workers in the car accident in December 1987 precipitated an unprecedented outbreak of civil rebellion. But the rebellion was not just a means of bloodletting for the sake of bloodletting and anyway in the first months of the Intifada the majority of casualties were civilian bodies that littered the Palestinian side of the barricade. In its more political sense the rebellion was against the occupation itself and the conditions that this structure of control established for ordinary Palestinians was the real reason why Palestinians engaged en masse in this uprising. Hence the goal of the uprising was to end the occupation and achieve independence and statehood. This was soon articulated in a set of demands that the local leadership of the uprising – called the United National Leadership of the Uprising (UNLU) – in coordination with the PLO, set out in January 1988. The demands enshrined the role of the PLO as the representative organization and voice in any future negotiations on behalf of the Palestinian people. To this day the PLO remains the party that will engage in any future negotiations with Israel.

Palestinians believed that they and their cause had virtually been abandoned by the rest of the Arab world, the United Nations and the international community. They had to countenance the fact that none of these parties could bring a political solution to their predicament. Within weeks of the outbreak of events, however, local activists, political leaders of the various factions of the PLO and the Islamic movement, professional people and others had begun to systematically articulate their political demands and goals. In order to stop the rebellion

descending into internecine conflict the factions of the PLO through the organization of the UNLU projected a force for unity. The UNLU was responsible for
articulating the national vision of the Palestinians of the West Bank and Gaza Strip
as well as liaising with the PLO leadership in Tunis over the wider strategy of the
national goal of the Palestinian people in seeking to achieve independence. In
essence the demands were clear: end the occupation and grant independence.
They were initially framed in the political discourse of nationalism and the
Palestinian national movement but they came also to reflect the Islamist dimension and additionally challenges from within Palestinian society to the ways in
which power had been previously represented as patriarchal, class-based and
exclusive. The Islamists, principally Hamas, articulated the same end goal but
differed from the PLO in the nature and territorial demands of statehood and the
means to achieve this goal.

These political demands were given expression in a number of ways. First, they
were articulated widely to and among the Palestinians themselves. This was the
stated goal of the uprising, the motive for discipline among the ranks and unity.
These goals and the methods to achieve them were expressed through the clandes-
tine circulation of leaflet communiqués (*bayanaat*) printed from illegal presses and
distributed at night by the unarmed foot soldiers of the uprising. The communiqués were smuggled by whatever means to avoid Israeli confiscation and distributed everywhere. Sometimes the streets were littered with them, at others they
were limited in number and passed from hand to hand. Second, the political goals
were articulated to the wider world and this process was facilitated by the presence
of the world's press and the headline-grabbing nature of the rebellion. In this way
the demand for the legitimate right to self-determination came across in the
human interest stories reported from the Palestinian territories. They were powerfully symbolized by the pictures of unarmed women and children facing the
heavily armed soldiers of the IDF. Hence the Palestinians were once again cata-
pulted into international consciousness and this time they were portrayed as
victims not terrorists. Third, the political goals of the Intifada were formalized and
presented in diplomatic circles by the PLO as the sole representative and legitimate organization of the Palestinian people. In November 1988, the Palestine
National Council was convened and a unilateral declaration of independence for
the state of Palestine was declared. That night, despite the Israeli-imposed blanket
curfews, the ban on international telephone calls and the censorship and closure of
the Palestinian press all imposed on the Palestinians by the Israeli authorities, the
cheers and roars of delight at news of the declaration could be heard across the
cities, towns and villages of the occupied territories. Small boys broke the curfew
and ran into the streets waving homemade Palestinian flags and setting off fire-
crackers. The rumour that the announcement was coming had started a few days
earlier and everyone expected the Israeli clampdown. But by this point people had
gathered in each others homes straining to hear the news broadcasts that would
bring them one step closer to statehood. Although a chimera in so many ways the
announcement of the declaration of independence was seen as an indication of
progress in throwing off the hated occupation.

An Arab 'shaking off'?

Beyond the basic political demands of the uprising the political dimensions of the Intifada were deeply felt across the Middle East and beyond. For the Palestinian people the political dimensions of the Intifada threw up aspects of internal political competition for the leadership of the Palestinian people between the PLO and its constituent factions and the Palestinian Islamists in the guise of the newly formed Hamas movement (Milton-Edwards, 1999). Within the ranks of the PLO the endurance of the Intifada through the years 1987 to the signing of the Oslo Accords in 1993 threw up political challenges not just in terms of personalities and leadership but in the capacity of a guerrilla organization to make the transition from resistance to state-building. In many respects the Intifada also threw light on the powerful autocratic tendencies that had developed in much of the senior leadership of the PLO, and the Fatah faction in particular, which proved problematic during the negotiation of power and politics between the Palestinians locally and the rest of the international community. The PLO dilemma was partly explained by the fact that it operated as an organization for the whole of the Palestinian Diaspora including the Palestinian refugee populations of Jordan, Syria and Lebanon.

The Arab regimes thus responded to the Palestinian uprising in a number of ways; this depended on whether or not they were host states to the Palestinian refugees, to what extent the Palestinian issue had been championed by its political leadership and the huge symbolic importance that the Palestinian issue garnered in what is often referred to as the 'Arab street'. Since the inception of the state of Israel the Arab states of the region had championed the Palestinian cause. Some of these states were also embroiled in conflict with Israel because they had sought to support the Palestinians through war. Egypt, Jordan and Syria were considered front-line states. Other states such as Iraq, Saudi Arabia, Yemen, Tunisia and Libya, to name a few, had also supported Palestinian rights and the struggle for statehood.

For states like Jordan, which had annexed the Palestinian West Bank in 1952, the uprising presented a major challenge to their influence and aspirations with respect to the area and especially the status of Jerusalem and the Haram al-Sharif compound. Hashemite legitimacy in Jordan and the West Bank drew on its historic custodianship of the compound. When the Intifada broke out Jordan's King Hussein understood that he had to take a careful approach in handling the changes that the Palestinians were instituting. In some respects, though by no means all, the Intifada was also a Palestinian indication of wishing to distance itself from its ties to Jordan. In the kingdom itself, moreover, nearly 50 per cent of citizens were by that point Palestinian in origin. The King gave public support to the Intifada but in private he recognized that Palestinian backing for the King in favour of the PLO led by his old rival Yasser Arafat was waning. In July 1988 the King appeared on state-run television declaring that Jordan was ceding legal and administrative rights to the West Bank with the exception of al-Aqsa in Jerusalem. The implicit acknowledgement that the Palestinians and the PLO would now take the lead in determining the future of the people was understood by everyone who heard and read the King's speech. The declaration put an end to Hashemite aspirations regarding the West Bank and as such Jordan terminated its financial obligations, reconstituted its parliament and electoral boundaries to take account of the decision. For Palestinians in the West Bank who for many years had cultivated important and powerful relations with the Hashemite regime in Amman the news came as a double-edged sword. On the one hand they were compelled to accede to a dependent relationship that had brought stability and profit of many kinds. On the other hand they were powerless to resist the popular sentiment of the young in their own burgeoning societies who wanted real control over their lives free from interference from Israel or the Arab states.

In other Arab capitals there was a new assessment of what the Intifada meant in terms not only of Arab campaigns to support the Palestinian cause through institutions such as the Arab League or the Organization of Islamic Conference but also in terms of the dynamic bilateral relationship between the leaders of these regimes and that of the PLO. The Arab League, for example, immediately recognized the statehood declaration of 1988, maintained its boycott of Israel, including an economic boycott, and its member states ran fundraising campaigns and relief efforts throughout the uprising. In 2002 at an Arab League summit in Beirut a Saudi plan for a comprehensive peace settlement between Israel, the Palestinians and the rest of the Arab world was adopted.

With respect to the region, what also unfolded in the months and years following the outbreak of the Intifada was a rehabilitation of the PLO and its chairman, Yasser Arafat, in a number of Arab capitals. Arab states offered aid and assistance to the Palestinians waging the Intifada and the coffers of the PLO swelled with such assistance. Arafat was certainly astute enough to capitalize on the rising tide of Arab support. In 1990, though, he squandered this support when he swung his weight behind Iraq's President Saddam Hussein following his invasion and occupation of the petro-wealthy Gulf state of Kuwait. The Kuwaiti authorities retaliated by expelling hundreds of thousands of resident Palestinian expatriates and encouraged its neighbours to boycott aid and other support to the PLO. It was this boycott that, by the summer of 1991, led to the near bankruptcy of the PLO and compelled Arafat into accepting the restricted terms of participation in the American sponsored peace talks that took place in Madrid later that year. Many regimes of the Arab capitals were also careful to be seen to stage-manage their own country's response to the Palestinian uprising rather than allow their own domestic opposition groups to garner support and capitalize on the restive atmosphere that the Intifada seemed to spark in terms of the whole region. The efforts of regime intelligence agencies (*mukhabarat*) were doubled in order to ensure that neither Palestinian exiles nor their supporters jeopardized the host regime or its relationship with the PLO.

Israel responds

For Israel the Intifada had profound consequences for its political establishment and the ongoing national discourse on territoriality and the state. The Israeli government was completely wrong-footed by the outbreak of the uprising and once it emerged from a state of denial it then had to come to terms with the glaring fact that the status quo long secured by Israel in the West Bank, Gaza Strip and East Jerusalem through occupation and annexation post-1967 had been shattered.

Less than a month after the uprising had broken out the Israeli political establishment decided to use its military forces to break the rebellion. The then defence minister, Yitzhak Rabin, was still compelled to admit, however, that the IDF had lost control of law and order on the Palestinian streets. Rabin ordered his soldiers to literally beat the Palestinians into submission. But this strategy backfired when it was graphically publicized and an outcry ensued both at home and abroad. The iron fist was not working. Nevertheless the Israeli government organized a wide-ranging crackdown against the Palestinians and worked to demoralize and divide and rule them again. One strategy was to create a sense of siege: fuel supplies to the West Bank and Gaza were suspended, telephone lines were cut, and detention without trial (administrative detention) orders were accelerated. The Israeli authorities hoped that a siege might quickly break the will of the Palestinians.

In the initial stages of the Intifada there was general support for the government within Israel but this began to wane as the Intifada entered its second and third year and Israel's reputation abroad was progressively tarnished. The Israeli left and pro-peace bloc grew in popularity and their activities were increasingly applauded within their own society as well as among opinion-formers in Europe and the USA. Groups such as Peace Now began to organize rallies and demonstrations and marches and campaigns of solidarity. Peace Now had been founded back in 1978 but during the Intifada they stepped up their activities and ran campaigns to halt Israeli settlements, recognize the PLO and work towards a 'land for peace' deal that would mean statehood for Palestinians and Israelis side by side. The movement gained important momentum in terms of shifting Israeli public opinion, and the 1993 Oslo Accords were considered to be a milestone in their activities. Some Israeli soldiers even refused to serve in the occupied territories. They joined an Israeli group called *Yesh Gvul* (Courage to Refuse) and were sentenced by the Israeli state to jail terms for their refusal. Such groups and movements began to call on their government to end the occupation and make peace with the Palestinians. But such actions also served as a reminder of the polarization of the Israeli polity during the first Intifada as well. It was only a matter of time before those engaged on the right of the Israeli spectrum began to campaign around issues of maintaining Israel's claims to the Palestinian territories. This was reflected in the general election of 1988 where the right-leaning Likud and left-leaning Labour parties tied for power and were compelled into a unity government, which later collapsed in 1990. The Intifada had a definite impact on the Israeli electorate and the issue of peace with the Palestinians would come to figure strongly in future electoral deliberations in Israel's democratic structure.

As the Intifada wore on the sense that Israel was experiencing or feeling the effects of Palestinian rejection of the occupation was manifest in a number of ways.

The withdrawal of cheap Palestinian day labour from the Israeli market had an important but negative impact on Israel's economy. Palestinian campaigns to boycott Israeli-produced goods, refusal to pay Israeli-imposed taxes and permits also meant that a widespread belief grew that Palestinians themselves were no longer subsidizing the occupation and that the Israeli treasury would have new demands made upon it. Palestinians argued that without any form of representation they would withhold taxes to Israel. They believed that Israel itself should shoulder the burden of financing the deployment of extra Israeli troops and armaments to the West Bank and Gaza Strip. They contended that this would lead to internal Israeli pressure on the government as the real or full cost of the occupation was made apparent to all ordinary Israelis. Were they right?

The strategy for change

It is clear that the Intifada was something unprecedented not only in terms of the spontaneity of the initial revolt but for other reasons too. One dimension of difference that resulted in political gains for the Palestinians was the extent to which the uprising epitomized the changing capacity of the Palestinians in respect of political mobilization. The grassroots nature of the action and the campaigns that followed simply had not been in evidence anywhere in the Middle East before. Throughout the 1980s Palestinians had become involved in grassroots activism in their refugee camps, their villages and their neighbourhoods. The people that spearheaded the movement were the occupation generation that had been born since 1967 and grown up under the strictures of the Israeli occupation. Many of these young people had achieved levels of education and professional qualifications that their elders could only have dreamed about. These young people used their opportunities to engage in activist organization in the schools, universities, community organizations, trade and professional associations, as well as the political factions that made up the polity. People joined the committees to serve their people and constantly ran the risk of arrest from the Israeli authorities. Where they differed, once again, from their elders was that the emerging leadership eschewed the inherited confines of the patriarchal structures inherent in the notable classes and traditional pro-Jordanian leadership (especially in the West Bank). These activists and their committees were the backbone of the uprising when it broke out.

Within weeks popular committees were formed – often in factional alliances – to mobilize the thousands of Palestinians who were ready to volunteer their time, their skills, their resources as individuals and communities to support the cause. Committees were organized across the West Bank and Gaza Strip to offer immediate first aid and assistance to the hundreds and subsequently thousands of Palestinians who were injured in clashes with Israeli soldiers and settlers. As schools and universities were closed hundreds volunteered to run 'classrooms' in any 'community space' available even if that meant teaching seminars in the back of station-wagons on the side of the road. Seeds and tools were donated to agricultural committees and land turned over for the production of crops that could sustain people as they experienced the effects of prolonged curfews, lack of wages, the boycott of Israeli-produced goods and extended commercial strikes. What was most notable about such work was the ability of the Palestinians to sustain it over prolonged periods of time and despite the pressures inherent in the Israeli crackdowns, prohibition, arrest and detention of the leadership of such groups.

The leadership of the UNLU also capitalized on what notions of civil disobedience, direct action, and passive resistance meant. At first, when some Palestinian intellectuals had suggested following 'Gandhi's route' to throwing off the shackles of occupation, the traditional leadership of the PLO ridiculed their advocates. Yet civil disobedience campaigns came to characterize the early and more successful stages of the uprising. Actions and activities took place in an unprecedented fashion. In the spring of 1988, following a direct call from the leadership of the UNLU, hundreds of Palestinian policemen who had served in the West Bank and Gaza Strip in Israel's ranks resigned en masse from their jobs. They quit their job of policing the Palestinians on behalf of Israel. Many Israelis speculated that such an action would lead to an outbreak of Palestinian law-breaking and looting in their own society. But instead society regulated itself and crime rates remained low. Such actions did not make life easy but they did appear to inspire people with a sense of virtue, communal solidarity and hope that such action could translate into political gains that the inevitable Israeli retribution was somehow easier to bear. The palpable sense of communal solidarity did not only make things easier to organize and bear but was empowering. This journal entry from 1988 highlights this point:

> I was on my way home from work and going through the old city. At Damascus Gate the soldiers had two young guys in their hands. But a crowd had gathered and they were asking the soldiers to let them go. I was pulled into the throng. It wasn't threatening but in the gloom of the dusk and without superior back-up the soldiers were starting to feel the pressure and were shouting at everyone, swinging their guns at us and pulling the young guys closer to them. Then . . . as if realizing the futility of it all they released the guys, a kick and a few curses on their mothers to help them on their way and that was it. I knew that Israel's power had been diminished.
>
> (Milton-Edwards, 1988, unpublished journal entry)

Popular resistance through civil disobedience was turning society on its head. In posh predominantly Christian towns such as Beit Sahour the residents hit the headlines when they organized a mass-based tax boycott at the same time as they systematically initiated and ran a self-reliance campaign. Almost echoing the classic Ealing Comedy 'Passport to Pimlico' the residents of Beit Sahour ended up contained in their own mini-republic as the Israeli authorities laid siege to the town and tried to break the will of the defiant residents. In the succeeding battle the Israelis eventually managed to break the campaign but not before the residents had refused to pay taxes, ceremoniously ripped up and burnt their Israeli-issued identity cards at the local town hall, tilled their own fields and received visiting diplomatic delegations that came to offer support and recognition to the townspeople.

One additional dimension to such campaigns was the emergence of Palestinian women from the shadows into the political spotlight. As thousands and thousands of men were arrested it was Palestinian women who assumed the mantle of responsibility – not just at home but in the arena of the uprising and its political demands too. Palestinian women assumed some leadership positions within the nationalist camp in ways which hitherto had seemed impossible. There were costs as well; patriarchal forces across the political spectrum were only willing to cede so much power to the women and by and large they eventually succeeded in keeping them away from the front line.

Consolidation and political progress

As the Palestinian uprising entered its third year it began to develop in different ways. While it was true that the community had been mobilized in a resistance campaign against the occupation and that communal solidarity was supporting people in a variety of ways the overall impact of the Intifada on Israel had become rather routine and cyclical in pattern. The uprising had made Israel face up to the problem of its own making on its own doorstep too. But the overall problem was that neither side was able to muster a decisive victory in terms either of achieving an end to occupation and thus statehood or in suppressing the rebellion and returning to the status quo ante. In sum, both sides had reached a form of 'hurting stalemate' (Zartman, 2001). What was needed was some kind of political breakthrough, a form of negotiation, external intervention or change. The Intifada had changed the Palestinian political landscape; it was more factionalized, tending towards internecine conflict and propelled by new forms of populism that spelled as much trouble for the leadership of the PLO as it did for the Israelis. Islamic fundamentalists in the Islamic Jihad and Hamas movement now appealed to the masses with their calls for jihad against the 'Zionist' entity until the liberation of the whole of Palestine 'from the sea to the river'. Intifada shock forces such as the Black Panthers and Red Eagles, associated with factions such as Fatah and the PFLP, were using their firepower against their own as much as the occupation forces. By 1990, as the Intifada entered its third year, the consolidation of the uprising must have made both sides baulk in terms of the coming year. It would be events outside of Israel and the Palestinian territories as much as those inside it, however, that would alter the course of events and establish opportunities for historic peacemaking between Israel and the Palestinians.

As we discuss in the following chapter of this book, the Iraqi invasion of Kuwait, the PLO's support for Saddam Hussein, US embroilment in the conflict, the threats to Israel and the economic imperatives behind sustaining both a costly resistance and occupation all played their part in pushing Palestinians and Israelis to the Madrid conference in late 1991. Back home in Tel Aviv, Jerusalem, Jabalia camp, Nablus and Gaza City, however, not everyone saw the potential for peace in the inception of the Middle East Peace Process. In this respect it is important to remember, therefore, that the Intifada and Israel's routine counter-offensives carried on. This is understandable given how little effort was devoted in the official peace negotiations to substantive confidence- or trust-building measures between the Israelis and Palestinians. This is not to say that there were not changes on the ground but rather that they were often fleeting and flimsy. In large part the major features of the uprising and Israel's response to it were maintained.

From 1991 to 1993, when the Oslo Accords were signed by Yasser Arafat and Yitzhak Rabin, the Israeli war of attrition and Palestinian violence would intensify, abate and intensify again. Palestinian attacks on Israeli targets began to increase. The Islamic groups kidnapped and killed Israeli soldiers and police personnel. The Israeli government responded by deporting hundreds and arresting thousands of others. Hamas capitalized on obstacles encountered by Palestinian nationalists in the peace talks with Israel to denounce the process and attack local Palestinian representatives to the talks as traitors. In 1992 the election of a new Israeli government, headed by Yitzhak Rabin, prepared to make or listen to peace overtures with the PLO, signalled progress which in turn led to the now famous Oslo Accords. By the summer of 1993, when the deal of the century was made public and both the Palestinians and the Israelis prepared for a new era of peace-building, the uprising was declared defunct and at an end by the leadership of the PLO.

What had the Intifada achieved? Had it played a major part in bringing the Palestinians and Israelis closer to peace, to enabling the Palestinians to get closer to their goal of independence and statehood? Had the Intifada altered the nature of Palestinian society through populism and emancipation? Tamari describes both the gain and limitations of the Intifada in terms of 'eroding bases of Israeli colonial rule until the PLO [could] establish state power in the occupied territories,' and warned of the 'inevitable retreat' if such gains were not also translated into the development within Palestinian society of alternative bases of power (Tamari, 1990: 8).

Actions speak louder than words: getting to the second Intifada

With the formal ending of the Intifada in the summer of 1993 and the inauguration of the PA led by the PLO it appeared to all intents and purposes that Israel would allow the Palestinians to start to enjoy autonomy over their own affairs and shake off the institutional structures of occupation. The commencement of Israeli withdrawals and the closing of Israeli civil administration offices in some fields of Palestinian public life such as education and health augured well for such steps. In time, although Israel retained its principal power as an occupier, it was hoped that the final status negotiation would put an end to this situation. In reality the steps taken between 1993 and September 2000 when the second (and armed) Intifada broke out were utilized and interpreted by both sides as bad instead of good omens for peace.

Despite the millions and millions of dollars poured into peace-building projects and the efforts of peace groups on both sides to engage in the construction of trust between the two peoples, the Palestinians perceived Israeli actions as ultimately betraying a desire never to relinquish the West Bank, Gaza Strip and East

Jerusalem. The much-vaunted Israeli redeployments were constantly delayed or simply never materialized. The curfews and restrictions, arrest campaigns and allegations of human rights abuses and torture continued to surface. The Israeli failure to adhere to the Oslo and subsequent agreements was explained away by the leadership of the PLO and the PA as a small price to pay if it meant that the Palestinians were in a position to close a deal in final status negotiations. The Israeli government, in 1997, commenced illegal settlement construction in the Bethlehem district of Jebel Abu Ghneim. The move, approved by the right-wing government led by anti-peacenik Bibi Netanyahu, was seen as a deliberate attempt to undermine the Oslo process and stymie hopes for negotiation on final status issues, which of course included the contentious settlements. As Hammami and Tamari contend, the 'PA preside[d] over a "peace process" which after seven years, left Palestinians penned into disconnected fragments of territory encircled by ever larger settlements' (Hammami and Tamari, 2000: 5).

For Israelis the same type of perceptions about the Palestinian will to seek peace with their neighbour also permeated society. From 1994 onwards the Palestinian opposition groups of Hamas and Islamic Jihad had launched a series of suicide bomb attacks that had not only succeeded in immobilizing the peace process but pushed Israeli public opinion closer to the right-wing and its anti-Palestinian agenda. Instead of enjoying the fruits of peace many Israelis concluded that their own society was experiencing more not less violence under the Oslo era. Their prime minister, Yithak Rabin, had been assassinated by a peace-hating Jew. Their daily lives were substantially altered by the fear that Hamas or Islamic Jihad 'mujahideen' would explode themselves on a bus, in a shopping centre or a pavement café. On both sides despair quickly replaced hope.

Aware of the diplomatic impasse between Israel and the Palestinians as well as the fact that the deadline set in the Oslo Accords for final status negotiations had come and gone, the chief external actor, the US government, sought to give peace the kind of push that had worked so well in other places such as Northern Ireland. The election of a Labour government led by Ehud Barak in early 2000 was also read as sign of an Israeli swing back to the peace option. The convening of the peace talks at Camp David in the summer of 2000 is discussed and analysed in subsequent chapters of this book. Suffice to say at this stage that the deal was not brokered, the diplomatic impasse resumed and after a highly provocative visit to the Muslim holy site of the Haram al-Sharif by opposition leader, Ariel Sharon, the Palestinians responded with the opening salvo of a second Intifada.

The al-Aqsa armed Intifada

The visit by Sharon to the Haram al-Sharif was seen as deliberately provocative by Palestinian protesters who took to the streets the day after the visit. Confrontations between the protesters and Israeli forces resulted in four Palestinians being killed and hundreds of others injured. It was later concluded by the Mitchell Commission charged with investigating the outbreak of the Intifada that:

what began as a series of confrontations between Palestinian demonstrators and Israeli security forces, which resulted in the Government of Israel's initial restrictions on the movement of people and goods in the West Bank and Gaza Strip (closures), has since evolved into a wider array of violent actions and responses.

(Mitchell Report, 2001)

If the first Intifada had been symbolized by Palestinian stone-throwers the al-Aqsa Intifada was symbolized by 'adult, male, armed and partially uniformed' Palestinian armed forces engaged in a 'resistance' against their Israeli counterparts. Inevitably, civilians on both sides of the divide were drawn into this new dimension of the conflict. The vortex of violence between 2000 and 2005 resulted in an estimated 3,800 Palestinians and 1,000 Israelis dead. It was also estimated that as many as 53,000 Palestinians and 7,000 Israelis were injured in that time as well.

A series of what we might call key political variables can be identified in relation to the outbreak of the al-Aqsa armed Intifada. These include:

- loss of momentum in peace negotiations
- areas of failure in confidence-building measures
- extant experience of occupation
- failure of peace dividend to materialize
- multi-track/people-to-people initiatives sacrificed to primary track security and political dialogue
- weakness in institution/state-building efforts
- poor mechanisms of accountability by donors
- path-dependency which inhibited dialogue about alternatives
- creation of new stakeholders for non-democratic purposes
- overly-focused on security rather than society transformation.

These variables had to be taken into consideration within what is commonly identified as a very complex environment. There was the inevitable historical dialectic at the heart of the conflict and its enduring impact on the state of relations between the Palestinians and Israelis. Historical experience and myth clearly weighed heavily on all involved in the conflict. There was evidence of a complex cultural environment shaped by dissonance and disbelief in the ability of the 'other culture' to change and accommodate in terms of transforming society from conflict to peace. The religious environment had remained largely averse to ecumenical overtures and instead there was the generation of much religious hostility within the opposing Israeli and Palestinian discourses. In terms of a more stable economic environment emerging as a result of the Oslo process, Palestinians began to be convinced of the limits of such dividends and horrified at the extent to which their own political leadership was defrauding them of some of the financial benefits of peace in order to line their own pockets. The proliferation of arms on the Palestinian side, combined with the failure by Israel to reduce its own armed and militarized means of conducting a relationship with the Palestinians, made for a permissive armed environment that drew in civilian elements. Increasingly violence became the replacement for political leverage on either side. By this I mean that violence – Palestinian violence against Israelis and Israeli violence against Palestinians – took the place of politics, of dialogue, of negotiation, of compromise, of the prospect that a relationship based on peace and stability could be generated between the two parties. The nature of the violence also altered the political environment. The civilian rather than armed/military death toll grew on both sides but once again with the Palestinians suffering a disproportionate amount of the violence. This argument is illustrated in the events surrounding the Israeli 'Operation Defensive Shield' launched in the spring of 2002. In March 2002 Palestinian suicide attacks had resulted in the deaths of 135 Israeli civilians, including 28 who were killed at a Passover meal in an Israeli hotel. Israeli military experts concluded that they needed to re-establish a deterrent capacity against the Palestinian suicide bombers. They could do this by invading the Palestinian territories and re-establishing their power there. In April 2002 the Israelis re-occupied the West Bank and laid siege to Yasser Arafat's headquarters in Ramallah and to other Palestinian towns, villages and refugee camps.

The phenomenon of the Palestinian suicide bomber seemed to define the death of politics during the armed Intifada. The Palestinian suicide bombers targeted Israeli civilians and military and their attacks were mostly launched over the 'Green Line' within Israel proper. Although Hamas and Islamic Jihad were initially responsible for the suicide bombing campaigns, as the Intifada entered its eighteenth month other groups linked to the nationalist factions of the PLO also engaged in such tactics. By September 2004 it was estimated that some 130 suicide attacks had been launched; at least 500 Israelis had been killed. Those carrying out the suicide missions often left a chilling last will and testament on video in which they declared their hatred of Israel and the desire to liberate Palestine through what they referred to as their own martyrdom. There is no doubt that as a 'tactic', in what some called an asymmetric war between Israel and the Palestinians, the suicide missions had a huge impact in Israel, creating a climate of fear and propelling public opinion against the Palestinians. Palestinian discourse reflected a growing national obsession with martyrdom and the suicide bombers as the tools of Palestine's liberation and resistance against Israel. Across the Palestinian territories a popular iconography of the suicide bomber grew.

Israel responded to the new Intifada with a series of measures that were designed to close off and coerce Palestinians within their own centres of population. An iron fist of fearsome military measures such as targeted assassinations of Palestinian leaders – political and armed – was designed to convey Israel's seriousness in crushing the new rebellion. The government approved a series of military operations against Palestinians in cities and towns throughout the West Bank and Gaza Strip. Air strikes targeting the PA became common. Since 2000 the basic services provided by the PA for the West Bank and Gaza – including all-important security provision in the terms of civil police and national forces – has been destroyed by Israel. In addition, important infrastructure, such as bridges, electricity and water supplies have also been subject to Israeli military wrath. Along the way hundreds of Palestinian civilians were caught up in the 'collateral damage' of such operations. Cities, towns and villages have been sealed off and subject again to Israeli military authority. Hundreds have been rounded up and arrested. In order to break the Intifada Israel once again imposed 'security' measures such as curfews and house demolitions. One of the most significant operations was conducted in 2002 during one such Israeli campaign, codenamed 'Operation Defensive Shield'.

Operation Defensive Shield: unequivocal victory?

During March and April 2002, some 18 months into the al-Aqsa Intifada, the Israeli government ordered its armed forces to launch a new military campaign codenamed Operation Defensive Shield (ODS) against the Palestinians in order to break the Intifada. ODS was to be the largest IDF operation in the West Bank since the Israelis had occupied the territory in the war of 1967. The objective of ODS, as communicated by the Israeli government, was to undertake measures that would dismantle the 'terrorist infrastructure', create deterrent effects against future Palestinian suicide attacks and further isolate the Palestinian President, Yasser Arafat, by virtually besieging him in his Ramallah headquarters (known as the Muqata). Israel's chief military officer declared, 'the only solution is to achieve an unequivocal victory over the Palestinians' (Catignani, 2005: 254). Prime Minister Ariel Sharon announced that the purpose of ODS was to:

> enter cities and villages which have become havens for terrorists; to catch and arrest terrorists and, primarily, their dispatchers and those who finance and support them; to confiscate weapons intended to be used against Israeli citizens; to expose and destroy terrorist facilities and explosives, laboratories, weapons production factories and secret installations. The orders are clear: target and paralyze anyone who takes up weapons and tries to oppose our troops, resists them or endanger them – and to avoid harming the civilian population.
>
> (Sharon, 2002)

The implicit objective was to smash the Palestinians ability to hurt Israel and to dismantle much of the infrastructure of the PA; this included raiding and destroying facilities in the Ministry of Health, media and communications, and the Ministry of Education. The usual military measures and tactics were employed. The most significant event to occur during the campaign took place in the northern West Bank town of Jenin in its refugee camp.

Jenin refugee camp was targeted during ODS in the belief that it was a centre of Palestinian terrorist operations against Israel. The IDF were determined to eliminate the capacity of militant groups within the camp. The 'battle of Jenin' as it became known, lasted some ten days as the IDF encountered heavy resistance from Palestinian fighters. Israeli destruction of the camp, including the bulldozing of homes, destruction of emergency vehicles like ambulances and the number of well-publicized civilian deaths, was condemned by international bodies such as the United Nations and the Red Cross as disproportionate. The IDF suffered what many considered to be a high casualty rate too. By the end of the operation over 150 buildings within the camp had been destroyed, nearly 60 Palestinians had been killed, and organizations such as Human Rights Watch were accusing the IDF of war crimes and civilian massacre.

Once the dust had literally settled there was a sense that Israel's actions in the camp had lost them the moral high ground and was seen as a strategic setback in terms of terminating the uprising. Israeli motives became obscured:

> The thought was as unshakable as the stench wafting from the ruins. Was this really about counterterrorism? Was it revenge? Or was it an episode – the nastiest so far – in a long war by Ariel Sharon, the staunch opponent of the Oslo accords, to establish Israel's presence in the West Bank as permanent, and force the Palestinians into final submission?
>
> (Huggler and Reeves, 2002)

Palestinians were claiming the events as a symbolic victory and across the Arab world thousands rallied in support of Jenin.

Operation Defensive Shield came to an end in April 2002 and although aspects of Palestinian militancy did diminish in the immediate wake of the operation the overall Israeli objective of ending the al-Aqsa Intifada was not achieved. Bloodied but unbowed, besieged but defiant, the Palestinians and their leadership vowed to continue in their attacks against Israel. The emasculation of the PA and its President also led to the growing empowerment and popularity of Hamas as its members and supporters filled the social and welfare gap left by the Israeli destruction of the PA. Suicide missions did not diminish either. The unequivocal victory eventually proved elusive and the Israelis and Palestinians resumed a variety of forms of low intensity warfare with each other.

The political dimension of the al-Aqsa Intifada is assumed to have lain in the desire by PA President, Yasser Arafat, and his supporters to use Palestinian violence as a lever for Israeli concessions within peace negotiations. The Israelis complained that Arafat was providing financial succour to the armed militants that sprung up from the factions of the PLO (including the Tanzim). Others contend, however, that it was misleading to suggest that Arafat had that kind of authority over the militants – particularly those opponents within Hamas whom he had battled with in the late 1990s on Israel's behalf. In reality such support or direction was limited but it did not stop Israel and its international supporters from declaring Arafat persona non grata with respect to the peace process. All diplomatic bets were off when the USA appeared to agree with Israel in terms of severing official contacts with Arafat. With his credibility and legitimacy within the international community diminished Arafat became an isolated figure and, while he still commanded much popular support among his people, this did not stop his opponents in Hamas from pointing to his weaknesses and failures with respect to the peace promises he had made his people.

Hamas were able to capitalize on a popular sentiment that reflected deep pressures at work in Palestinian society. In the seven years between the signing of the Oslo Accords and the outbreak of the al-Aqsa Intifada, Palestinians lost faith in the peace process and experienced a decline rather than an increase in their incomes. Ajluni notes that by 2000, when the Intifada broke out:

> per capita income levels . . . were estimated to be about 10 percent below their pre-Oslo level [and] despite considerable external assistance living standards were lower than before the process began. Aggravating the political situation were continuing Israeli policies of land and water confiscation, settlement expansion, movement restrictions, and numerous violations of important elements of signed agreements with the PA.
>
> (Ajluni, 2003: 66)

As mentioned previously in this chapter the rate of settlement expansion did not appear to have diminished either. Throughout 2002–04 the Palestinians were pressured to end their Intifada and accede to external demands. Sometimes the leadership of the PA appeared to play the game – Arafat divested of some executive power, unilateral but short-lived ceasefires – but they also came to believe that irrespective of such concessions Israel would not bend. In 2003 the 'performance-based' Road Map to a permanent two-state solution was issued by the international community but it was unclear if they had managed to get either side to sign up to the confidence-building measures that were required to get the two sides back to the negotiating table. The bunker mentality apparent in both camps allowed little room for talk of peace. Israeli Prime Minister, Ariel Sharon, did nothing to diminish this perception when he continued to make clear that any peace deal while Arafat remained in power would be a non-starter for Israel. Hence, when Yasser Arafat died in November 2004 and his replacement Mahmoud Abbas (Abu Mazen) was popularly elected to the post of President in January 2005 there was a hope that the peace negotiations might re-open again. Abu Mazen had long called for an end to the armed Intifada seeing it as more damaging to the Palestinians than the Israelis. He had maintained that Palestinians could only achieve statehood through negotiation, with a US broker, at the table with Israel. Thus it was no surprise that the new President announced a formal end to the al-Aqsa Intifada in early 2005.

Such steps, however, were not enough to create enough confidence between the Palestinians and Israel to resume negotiations on the basis of a final resolution of the conflict. Though it was true that the al-Aqsa Intifada was formally at an end there was no evidence that either side had abandoned the enmity against the other or the political objectives of contested occupation and resistance for liberation. In the 18 years that had passed since the outbreak of the first Intifada and the end of the second the dynamics of conflict had changed, hopes for peace had risen and then expired, a generation of Israelis and Palestinians had grown into a fatal atavistic embrace of the other. Political means to resolving the conflict were in abeyance as the struggle for power between Israel and the Palestinians continued.

Two societies on a war-footing against the other had also laid the foundations internally for a raft of problems that each now struggles with in terms of a domestic profile to the conflict. If rebellion against occupation had appeared to bring the Palestinians one step closer to peace in 1987 the armed uprising in 2000 had allowed Israel to go some way in reclaiming the argument that they were surrounded by a nation of terrorists baying for Israeli blood. Building new foundations for peace would never be simple again.

Further reading

There is a vast array of books on the Palestinian Intifada and the course of the conflict from 1987 to 2005. Some of them are written from a particular perspective – Israeli or Palestinian – as a means of explaining to external audiences their cause over the other. There are also journalistic accounts and personal memoirs from many of the participants involved in the Israeli–Palestinian arena during this period. Assessment and analysis of the first Intifada might usefully begin with McDowall (London: I.B. Tauris, 1989), Beinin and Lockman (London: I.B. Tauris, 1990) and the book by Schiff and Ya'ari (New York: Simon and Schuster, 1990) if you can get hold of it. These could be read in conjunction with personal narratives such as those written by Grossman (New York: Farrar, Straus and Giroux, 2003) in *Death as a way of life*, detailing both Palestinian and Israeli perspectives, or the book by Amiry (London: Granta Books, 2005). Books that take into account the effects of the second Intifada and its impact on the Israeli–Palestinian conflict that are worth delving into include Haas (New York: Owl Books, 2000), Usher (London: Pluto, 1999), Pearlman (New York: Thunders Mouth Press, 2005) and Pratt (Glasgow: Sunday Herald Books, 2006). Beinin and Stein (Stanford, CA: Stanford University Press, 2006) provide an analytical framework for study in their work examining the 1993–2005 period.

Amiry, S. (2005) *Sharon and my mother-in-law*, London: Granta Books.

Beinin, J. and Lockman, Z. (eds) (1990) *Intifada: Palestinian uprising against Israeli occupation*, London: I.B. Tauris.

Beinin, J. and Stein, R.L. (2006) *The struggle for sovereignty: Palestine and Israel 1993–2005*, Stanford, CA: Stanford University Press.

Grossman, D. (2003) *Death as a way of life: Israel ten years after Oslo*. Translated by Haim Watzman, New York: Farrar, Straus and Giroux.

Haas, A. (2000) *Drinking the sea at Gaza: Days and nights in a land under siege*, New York: Owl Books.

McDowall, D. (1989) *Palestine and Israel: The uprising and beyond*, London: I.B. Tauris.

Pearlman, W. (2005) *Occupied voices: Stories of everyday life from the second Intifada*, New York: Thunders Mouth Press.

Pratt, D. (2006) *Intifada: The long day of rage*, Glasgow: Sunday Herald Books.

Schiff, Z. and Ya'ari, E. (1985) *Israel's Lebanon war*, New York: Simon and Schuster.

Usher, G. (1999) *Dispatches from Palestine: The rise and fall of the Oslo peace process*, London: Pluto.

8 A global concern

Chapter outline

- Date with destiny: the USA and the conflict   165
- A regional concern   172
- The international arena   176
- A European approach   178
- A concert of actors?   179
- Further reading   180

One unique dimension of the Israeli–Palestinian conflict has been its 'international character'. This chapter will pull out a series of debates and discussion about the role of regional and other international actors in the conflict and the various effects this has had in both exacerbating the conflict and contributing to its resolution. Various 'circles of interaction' will be revealed with respect to regional actors such as various Arab states and organizations, including the Arab League, plus radical versus conservative regimes and their role in the conflict. In this chapter we will also examine the 'Muslim dimension' of the conflict, as well as the response and symbolism of the conflict for the worldwide Jewish Diaspora and Christianity. This is important because these vital constituencies of support, in turn, have lobbied, supported and played a part in shaping the conflict. Additionally, international actors such the USA, the former Soviet Union, Britain and France will be scrutinized for their involvement and foreign policy motivations. Finally the role of international and regional organizations such as the United Nations, the Organization of Islamic Conference and the European Union will be debated with respect to historical turns in the international order as well as the specific issues that determine the nature and character of this conflict.

The Israeli–Palestinian conflict is perhaps one of the most deeply studied and most frequently addressed in the modern age. Barely a week goes past when the latest twists and turns of events in Israel and the occupied Palestinian territories are not addressed in the news pages of the European, North American, Asian and African press. Thus, since the European 'rediscovery' of Palestine, it has always been so. For a variety of reasons events in Jerusalem matter more than in Johannesburg or Jeddah to foreign policy-makers, news gatherers and diplomats. Of course one reason why the role of external actors matters so much to the history of the conflict – its momentum and dynamic in terms of crisis as well as peace-making – is the role that these very same actors have played in terms of the inception, consolidation and functioning of the conflict and its principal actors to the present day.

It is as if the conflict is the atomic nucleus of a chain reaction that is felt not just across the Middle East, North Africa and West Asia but by the rest of the globe as well. Jerusalem, in particular, is the symbol of three of the major monotheistic faiths of the world and thus motivates its adherents to an attachment, an interest, an ambition, a spiritual commitment or commandment to care about what happens and play a part in shaping or determining its present and future. Of course it may be argued that in a secular age and global world system of nation states that such views are irrelevant to world politics. In the case of the Israeli–Palestinian conflict, however, the influence of such religious thinking has been apparent in the policies of states and the opinions of state actors such as prime ministers, presidents and other global personalities. Indeed it has been argued, for example, that '[t]oday the most prominent feature of Christian Zionism in America is its political application. We are told regularly from our pulpits that we have a spiritual obligation to "bless Israel"' (Burge, 2005: 57). Much the same could be said about the oration of the imams in mosques across the globe: that they seek to remind Muslims of the religious obligation to remember Jerusalem and its blessed state in their prayers. Moreover many contemporary Islamist organizations and manifestations of Muslim political discourse have proffered a perspective on events in Palestine and the fate of its Muslim population. It is stated that extreme elements of Islam claim Palestine as 'the property of Islam' and that its occupation by Israel compels Muslims to undertake a jihad for its liberation.

For the Diaspora community of Judaism, Jerusalem also holds a special resonance. Ever since King David conquered the city Jerusalem has been considered sacred by believing Jews. Jews in the Diaspora direct their prayers towards Jerusalem and for hundreds of years prayed for a return to their Zion. In 2006, however, this debate about Jewish identity and the Diaspora was detonated into a furore as the result of the explosive comments of Israel novelist A.B. Yehoshua. Yehoshua in an address to celebrate the centenary of the American Jewish Committee was accused of inferring that Judaism only had a true meaning and chance of survival in Israel and not outside it. He maintained that:

> As long as it is clear to all of us that Israeli Jewish identity deals, for better or worse, with the full spectrum of the reality and that Diaspora Jewry deals only with parts of it, then at least the difference between whole and part is acknowledged. But the moment that Jews insist that involvement in the study and interpretation of texts, or in the organized activity of Jewish institutions, are equal to the totality of the social and political and economic reality that we in

Israel are contending with – not only does the moral significance of the historic Jewish grappling with a total reality lose its validity, there is also the easy and convenient option of a constant flow from the whole to the partial.

(Yehoshua, 2006)

For Jews in the Diaspora Yehoshua's comments sparked a fierce debate about Israel, identity and the spiritual resonance of places such as Jerusalem. Moreover, it is important to remember that the ideological thrust of modern Zionism in the twenty-first century and the state of Israel centres on Israel as the heart of Judaism and the 'right of return' and citizenship in the Jewish state for every Jew world-wide. Such ideological givens sustained the Jewish communities of the former Soviet Union, and movements such as the Jewish 'Birthright' movement which have brought 100,000 young Jewish people on trips to Israel. In these ways and many others the international dimension of the Israeli–Palestinian conflict is apparent and pertinent both to its evolving dynamic and hopefully its eventual resolution.

From the perspective of traditional international relations theory, the orbits of superpower rivalry, the Cold War, economic and strategic thinking, the arms race, the balance of power, and clash of civilizations, axis of evil, and the rise of funda-mentalism all find expression in the Israeli–Palestinian conflict. The orbit of regional and inter-regional relations, global power structures and the major ideo-logical battles of the twentieth and twenty-first century are reflected in and epito-mized by the conflict. The linkages between and among international actors in the Israeli–Palestinian arena also indicates a multiplicity of international actions that play their part in constricting or unfettering local actors as they seek to determine the nature and outcome of the conflict.

Others see Palestine, and Israel, and Jerusalem in particular, as a spiritual repository of the faith and its adherents. The labelling of the conflict as religious – Israeli Jew versus Palestinian Muslim or Christian – has a powerful pull on all sorts of actors in the international community. It is not only statesmen and policy-makers that determine legitimacy for their case in the religious aspects of the conflict but religious organizations themselves, and their figure heads serve as important voices in supporting one side or the other, exacerbating conflict or promoting peace. In 2000 Pope John Paul II, the leader of over 1 billion Catholics worldwide, made a pilgrimage to the Holy Land. During his pilgrimage he also visited a Palestinian refugee camp and the Holocaust Museum of Yad Vashem. Opinion at the time was divided on the political import of this religious journey and the Pope's choice of destinations. Yet, as one commentator observed:

The visit of the pope is political in the sense that a head of state can do nothing that doesn't have political implications. If what he does is read with goodwill, then you get one interpretation. Exactly the same gesture is read with bad will, you get a totally negative interpretation. And that is the risk he's taking, in going into the lion's den.

(Murphy-O'Connor, 2000)

Throughout the first half of the twentieth century the future of Palestine was largely determined by external actors such as Great Britain, and international bodies such as the League of Nations. Following the end of the Second World War and the termination of the British Mandate in Palestine other external or international actors replaced Britain. These actors included the USA and the newly formed United Nations, and have been joined by the European Union, Russia, and the Arab League and Muslim states of the globe. World Zionist movements and Christian faith missions have also been in evidence. Christian Zionists, for example, have engaged in mixing faith with a political agenda of support for Israel that extends to financial assistance for Jewish immigration to Israel and settlement activities in the Palestinian territories (Lampman, 2004). All of these actors, and perhaps the USA in particular, have gone some way in determining their national or spiritual interests through the prism of the Israeli–Palestinian arena.

For the neighbouring Arab states of Egypt, Jordan and Syria, support for the Palestinian cause has been expressed through debates about security, strategic and economic interest, minimizing the influence of external parties such as the former Soviet Union and the USA. Egyptian, Syrian and Jordanian support for the Palestinians and against Israel has also been defined in terms of national interest as part of the wider discourse that sustained such Arab regimes in the 1960s and 1970s. Solidarity for the Palestinians in seeking to achieve their rights proved and remains (to a certain extent) a potent call across the Arab world and there is little evidence of Arab leaders not seeking to realize this or capitalize on it in terms of their own legitimacy and definition of individual national interest. The Arab or Middle Eastern state that can claim the prize of Palestinian independence will enhance its legitimacy immeasurably. Such considerations begin to explain the regional rivalry between states such as Saudi Arabia and Iran in supporting different political strands within the Palestinian polity against Israel. Both parties see their ability to influence the Palestinians as evidence of their strategic reach within the region and against each other.

In the case of the USA, national interest in the sphere of foreign policy making has become entwined and closely allied to Israel and defined as a 'special relationship' (Milton-Edwards, 2006). Since the mid-1940s, irrespective of political hue, successive American administrations have expressed almost unwavering support for Israel. This support has not been merely diplomatic but includes a history of significant military assistance and economic support through loans, sales, aid and investment. There is also a general consensus that, despite the best will of other international actors, such as the European Union or the United Nations, American diplomatic leverage is the key to past, present and future resolution efforts and the willingness of Israel to accede to the demands of the rest of the international community. The former Soviet Union also played its part for nearly five decades in seeking to influence the conflict as part of its Cold War rivalry with the USA and its ideological commitment to the Third World, resistance movements and support for the export of communism. While it is true that such considerations may appear quite antiquated in the twenty-first century they remain a key element to the understanding of the role of international actors in this conflict. The Soviet Union sought to excise US and Western influence from the region, and their support for the Palestinian nationalist movement and its revolutionary cadres was certainly important in terms of the competencies of the Palestinian Diaspora and its struggle for recognition as a people and its fight against Israel. In the wake of the break-up of the Soviet Union in 1989, the end of the Cold War and the emergence of the USA as the dominant global superpower, the effects and influence of the former Soviet states have gone into decline. Russia under the leadership of Vladimir Putin, however, began to reinsert itself into the Israeli–Palestinian arena and is a key member of the international Quartet for the Middle East Peace Process (MEPP).

The United Nations is also an important player in this arena. UN resolutions (even though they have often been 'vetoed' by the USA) have sought to remind Israel of its obligations as an occupying power, to censure it for its violations of international law vis-à-vis its treatment of the Palestinian population, and to advocate a just resolution to the conflict. Israel has baulked at UN criticism and accused the General Assembly and other forums of the UN as being open to Arab manipulation and bias against them. As an Anti-Defamation League report opines, 'the United Nations has long been a forum for political attacks against Israel' (ADL, 2006). The Arab League and the Organization of Islamic Conference (OIC) have both regularly sought to support the Palestinian cause, protect the rights of Muslims globally in terms of access to Muslim holy places and promote a just resolution of the Israeli–Palestinian conflict. In Beirut in 2002 the Arab League determined a formula for recognizing Israel in return for Israeli withdrawal to the 1967 borders and (among other things) recognition of UN Resolutions 242 and 338. The Arab League remained pivotal in determining the legitimacy of the Hamas government that was elected by the Palestinians in January 2006.

The role of the European Union has become increasingly important in the twenty-first century. Proposals initiated or led by the European Union have also proved decisive at certain stages of the conflict, particularly in areas of aid and conflict mediation and resolution. Despite the challenges of presenting a common line among so many disparate member states, the European Union has played a part in shaping the dynamics of this conflict. It would be fair to say, however, that the parameters of European involvement in the conflict have been based on diplomacy, development and economy, as Europe looks to its south-eastern Mediterranean border.

Date with destiny: America and the conflict

There was very little doubt, in the wake of the Second World War, that the USA would not lift the mantle of international leadership that Great Britain and France had been forced to abandon. Under this mantle the issue of Palestine and its future loomed large. The USA had already been significant supporters of the Zionist project for the establishment not merely of a Jewish homeland but a Jewish state in

Palestine, and had been pivotal in influencing the vote of approval for the UN Partition Plan in Resolution 181 in November 1947.

Although Eisenhower cautioned against unwarranted influence in the realm of foreign affairs, it was under his administration that US national interests and foreign policy were outlined with respect to the Israeli–Palestinian issue. Although American national interest was defined in terms of the wider Middle East, to include such issues as unhindered access to the supply of oil and heading off the Soviet sphere of influence in the region, the emergence of a special relationship with Israel quickly became a defining feature of such policy. This special relationship was queried in the following way by Walt and Mearsheimer:

> Why has the US been willing to set aside its own security and that of many of its allies in order to advance the interests of another state? One might assume that the bond between the two countries was based on shared strategic interests or compelling moral imperatives, but neither explanation can account for the remarkable level of material and diplomatic support that the US provides [Israel].
>
> (Mearsheimer and Walt, 2006)

The connection between Israel and the USA is rooted in the historic fallout of the Holocaust and American re-positioning in the wake of the end of the Second World War, as well as the outbreak of the Cold War. While the roots of this relationship are based in historic events there are other dimensions and levels to this bilateral relationship that explain why so many are convinced that a blind spot has developed vis-à-vis the American view of Israel and its treatment of the Palestinian issue. US policy as regards the Israeli–Palestinian conflict is shaped directly out of this core relationship, but has to be successfully married with US foreign policy positions on democracy promotion, the free flow of oil (and thus support for the Arab supporters of the Palestinian cause), and anti-colonialism (in the past). Conflict management and conflict resolution has assumed an important function in terms of US policy in the Israeli–Palestinian dispute, because failure to engage would have left space for other actors (such as the former Soviet Union or the European Union) to exploit. Hence the USA has promoted itself as an 'honest broker' between the two sides to the dispute.

The USA, however, is irrevocably shackled in the task of being legitimately accepted as an honest broker because of the nature of the special relationship with Israel and the extent to which the domestic organization of the pro-Israel lobby is perceived as unduly influencing policy towards Israel's end.

It is argued that US economic support to Israel has assisted it in enjoying a military asymmetry of power against the Palestinians that has never been duly recognized as such in subsequent American-brokered peace talks. Yet while it is true that America has consistently supported the Palestinians with humanitarian aid and development monies, this pales in significance compared with its financial support to Israel. Since the 1970s Israel has enjoyed more economic and military aid, loans and assistance from the US than any other country in the world. It has been claimed that, 'the total cost to the US of its backing of Israel in its drawn-out, violent dispute with the Palestinians . . . adds up to more than twice the cost of the Vietnam War' (Francis, 2002). Israel's US aid amounts to about $500 per person on an annual basis. This can be compared with the annual GDP per capita for the average Palestinian, which is a mere $1,100, and with reports in 2006 that while the Israeli economy was on the upswing, 'per-capita income – a measure of the standard of living – is 17 times higher in Israel than among its neighbors from the West Bank and Gaza Strip' (Mitnick, 2006). In this case it has been surmised that American money has bought Israeli might over the occupied Palestinian people. Such support has been vital in the past to Israeli resistance or support for a negotiated solution to the conflict. Yet, there has only been one occasion when America has chosen to use the issue of its funding to Israel to act as a lever in persuading the Israeli government to go to the negotiating table with the Arabs (the Palestinian were denied direct negotiating status at this point).

Diplomatic leverage against Israel then is a rarely employed aspect of the American side of the 'special relationship' even in terms of pushing for a negotiated solution to the Israeli–Palestinian conflict. At the United Nations, for example, the USA has, since 1982, vetoed an unrivalled 32 UN Security Council resolutions critical of Israel's abuse of human rights and activities against Palestinians, the United Nations and international civilians in the occupied territories. When the USA has brokered peace talks, dialogue and negotiation, even their own officials have acknowledged that they have been biased and one-sided actors:

> For far too long, many American officials involved in Arab–Israeli peace-making . . . have acted as Israel's attorney, catering and coordinating with the Israelis at the expense of successful peace negotiations. If the United States wants to be an honest and effective broker . . . surely it can have only one client: the pursuit of a solution that meets the needs and requirements of both sides.
>
> (Miller, 2006)

In part this lack of diplomatic leverage and almost unqualified support for Israeli positions vis-à-vis the Palestinian side is also explained by looking at the American position on the Palestinians themselves. Until relatively recently the perception of the Palestinians in the minds of successive American administrations and in American culture more generally was one of ignorance. As one author comments:

> In line with the principle that what is out of sight is out of mind, the Palestinians rarely entered US policy considerations throughout the 1950s and 1960s . . . After their dispersal in 1948, the name *Palestine* disappeared from the world's political register, primarily because for Israel and even some Arab states the name was inconvenient. . . . As far as the United States was concerned, the Palestinians did not exist politically . . . and, as a result, an

entire generation of policy makers came of age not knowing, and not thinking it necessary to learn, the *Palestinians* story.

(emphasis in original, Christison, 2001: 95)

In the 1970s and early 1980s the major impact that Palestinians had on American consciousness, including that of policy-makers, was through terrorist actions that grabbed the headlines from across the globe. Palestinians were thus framed as terrorists and Israelis and Jews as the victims of their brutal assaults, hijackings, attacks and violence. This was encapsulated in the Palestinian hijacking of the Achille Lauro cruise ship in October 1985. The hijackers, determined to demonstrate the seriousness of their demand that Israel release 50 Palestinian prisoners, shot dead a wheelchair-bound elderly American Jewish passenger called Leon Klinghoffer and threw his body overboard. As nothing more than a bunch of crazed terrorists, the Palestinians were thus denied legitimacy from the USA.

Palestinian rights, even those recognized in the forum of the United Nations, were largely ignored by successive US administrations in preference to supporting Israel as a beleaguered friend surrounded by hostile Arab states. The outbreak of the first Palestinian uprising in 1987 and the impact that news reports had on popular opinion in the West did, however, result in a shift of perception. Palestinians were recognized, for the first time, as victims of Israeli violence, and the brutal facts of life lived under military occupation and their national aspirations were starting to be acknowledged. It was not until 1988 that the USA broke its taboo on the Palestinians by recognizing the PLO. The relationship with the Palestinians and the US government was never going to blossom in concordance in the way it did with Israel.

But while it was true that the Palestinian issue was already in crisis before the events of 11 September 2001, the perpetration of the atrocity in the USA only served to confirm ascendant hardline right-wing opinion in America vis-à-vis the threat to national security and global stability posed by what they believed to be an alliance of terrorism that included the Palestinian element. Palestinian political violence became increasingly conflated with the threat posed by al-Qaeda: 'Palestinian strategy makes no sense except in the context of alignment with al-Qaeda . . . the goals of the Palestinians and those of al-Qaeda have converged' (STRATFOR, 2002). From this point on America reverted to the default option of agreeing with Israel that there was no 'partner for peace' on the Palestinian side. The initial concern of the US administration, as it sought a response that would meet the demands of a devastated people and a sense of national insecurity, was to ensure that the all too apparent crisis between Israel and the Palestinians did not undermine US efforts to keep Arab states such as Saudi Arabia on board, as it prepared to launch a war on terrorism and the Taliban-run (and Saudi-recognized) Afghan entity in particular.

Henceforth the actual military aspect of the war on terrorism had, in many ways, little to do with the contest for power played out between the Palestinians and Israelis on a daily basis. Instead it had much more to do with an Israeli determination to equate al-Qaeda terrorism and the American response to it to

Palestinian terrorism and the Israel and American-supported response to that. This was highlighted in a speech by former Israeli Prime Minister, Bibi Netanyahu, to an American audience in early 2002 when he declared:

> the imperative of defeating terror everywhere is being ignored when the main engine of Palestinian terror is allowed to remain intact. I'm concerned that the State of Israel, that has for decades bravely manned the front lines against terror, is being pressed to back down just when it is on the verge of uprooting Palestinian terror.
>
> (Netanyahu, 2002)

Palestinians – Islamists included – had disavowed Bin Laden's attack on America but such statements were treated with scepticism in Israel and among America's ascendant neo-conservative class. Although Bin Laden's bombers were not icons in the Palestinian camps and such terror was not perceived as 'representative' of the Palestinian struggle and demands, al-Qaeda's method of suicide terrorism against civilians established a form of guilt by association with Palestinian violence against Israeli targets. The Hamas leadership expressed fears in private that attempts to associate their struggle with those of al-Qaeda could prove disastrous. For many Israelis, however, there were important echoes and similarities in the experience of terror and they believed that the same motives were at work. In the USA too, for many Americans any incipient sympathy for the Palestinian issue that had built up since the outbreak of the first Intifada in 1987 was abolished when their media screened and re-screened the now infamous 'Palestinian celebrations' of the 9/11 bombings. Subsequent official Palestinian disavowal of the attacks, including Yasser Arafat donating blood for the American victims of 9/11, was an image largely lost in the coverage of the aftermath, and of course the earlier images made it easier for the Bush administration to pursue its policy with respect to the War on Terror. Ariel Sharon had also warned the USA in no uncertain terms of the consequences of appearing to go soft on any Arab opinion in his remarks in October 2001 when, in a speech he made in the wake of the killing of three Israelis in northern Israel, he declared:

> I call on the Western democracies, and primarily the leader of the Free World, the United States, do not repeat the dreadful mistake of 1938 when Europe sacrificed Czechoslovakia. Do not try to appease the Arabs at our expense . . . Israel will not be Czechoslovakia. Israel will fight terrorism.
>
> (Sharon, 2001)

The implications of the 9/11 attack for Palestinians would be important in terms of new weight given to Israeli statements on the nature and motive of Palestinian attacks against them as well as international legitimacy and support for the Palestinian cause more generally.

First by boycotting Palestinian President, Yasser Arafat, then by dragging their heels when Abu Mazen became Prime Minister and President and then boycotting the Hamas government elected to the PA in January 2006, the Bush administration appears to have complied with Israel's stance.

Hence, historically speaking, there is little evidence of US intervention in the conflict – either in terms of management or resolution – where there was an attempt by policy-makers and politicians to legitimate those Palestinian groups or individuals that represented the case for Palestinian rights. It was not until the late 1980s that the US government entered into any kind of dialogue with the PLO (officially the sole legitimate representative of the Palestinian people) and of course it was not until the conclusion of the secret negotiations that led to the Oslo Accords in 1993 that the USA recognized the Palestinians as having the right to represent themselves in formal peace negotiations with Israel. Instead of granting the Palestinians recognition and thus legitimacy, the USA had preferred to pursue strategies pertaining to the Israeli–Palestinian conflict that involved sovereign states and not stateless people. Until relatively recently the American default option in terms of a solution to the Israeli–Palestinian conflict was to draw Arab states such as Jordan, Egypt or Syria into the equation. It was envisaged that these states would solve the Palestinian problem – providing mechanisms for the absorption of the Palestinian refugees (thus obviating the need to pressure Israel to recognize their 'right of return'), to pacify the PLO and its armed elements and eventually normalize relations and recognize Israel. If only American will had been the sole factor in resolving the conflict it would have been settled through the Arab states solution.

The default option left Israel in a strong position in terms of American policy towards the wider Middle East. The special relationship survived the 1967 war, and the illegal annexation by Israel of East Jerusalem and its occupation of Arab territories including the West Bank, Gaza Strip, Sinai and Golan Heights. In the wake of the 1973 war the USA again focused on mediating between Israel and the Arab states as US Secretary of State Henry Kissinger's 'shuttle diplomacy' culminated in the Sinai II Accord between Egypt and Israel. The revolution of 1979 meant the loss of Iran as the other special ally of the USA and strengthened Israeli leverage over America. Under the Carter administration peace talks between Egypt and Israel culminated in the historic peace treaty between the two states in March 1979. The peace treaty was the first to be signed between Israel and an Arab state and had been brought to fruition as a result of American mediation during the Camp David peace talks. During the negotiations Israel, supported by the USA, deflected Egyptian attempts to incorporate a direct recognition of the Palestinian right to self-determination and independence. The Egyptian President, Anwar Sadat, much to the ire of the rest of the Arab world, was only able to secure an agreement within the text of the treaty to call for Palestinian autonomy with final status negotiations to be held at a later date. Autonomy would only pertain to the Palestinian inhabitants of the West Bank and Gaza Strip and it allowed the Israeli government to continue building settlements and avoid dealing (once again) with the rights of the Palestinian refugees. Even Palestinian autonomy was avoided as Israel embarked on its campaign against the PLO with its invasions of Lebanon in 1978 and 1982 and its subsequent occupation of the country.

The Israeli invasion and occupation of Lebanon in 1982 inevitably drew in the Americans. For the Americans the involvement would cost them dearly and result in hitherto unknown tensions in their relationship with Israel. American public opinion was firmly against US involvement and after a bomb attack on American targets in October 1983 that left 241 dead it was only a matter of time before the Americans reached a decision to halt their involvement in Lebanon alongside their Israeli allies. As has already been noted in this chapter, the outbreak of the first Palestinian Intifada in 1987 served to temporarily jolt American public opinion to the extent that the government in Washington had to take diplomatic steps to intervene. It appeared that the impetus to find a solution to the conflict had, at last, been truly discovered. This impetus was strengthened in the wake of the Iraqi occupation of Kuwait and the war that followed it in 1990–91 when President Bush (Senior) recognized that the stability of the Middle East (and thus the New World Order) pivoted on the resolution of the Israeli–Palestinian conflict. It is also important to acknowledge that it was at this point that some private qualms were expressed within the Bush administration regarding the strategic value of having Israel as such an important ally in the Middle East. It had started to look that such an unequivocally supportive relationship might be inimical to American national interests in the region.

This relationship is, in many respects, unlike any other diplomatic relationship that the USA has conducted with a foreign ally. It is a relationship that both sides admit is 'special'. Successive administrations of the US government have been loyal allies of Israel. One way of interpreting this support is to reflect on the extent to which Israel's interests are seen as part of, or a reflection of, American foreign policy interests in the Middle East.

The USA–Israel relationship has been subject to a process of institutionalization and close links that are reflected in more than one area of the American system of governance and more broadly in American society at large where sympathies for Israel and the Zionist cause remain widespread. Institutionally the extent to which Israel and issues associated with it forms a crucial element of American foreign policy in the Middle East is reflected in the office of the President, the State Department, the Pentagon, Congress and Senate. This is due in no small measure to the presence and influence of an important pro-Israel lobby in the USA, the mobilization in the past of the Jewish vote in national elections, sympathies in the highly influential Christian fundamentalist, evangelical and Christian Zionist movements and their current impact on neo-conservative discourse in the USA. It is argued in respect of the influence of the pro-Israel lobby that, 'if the pro-Israeli lobby were to sponsor a resolution on Capitol Hill calling for the abolition of the Ten Commandments, both Houses of Congress would adopt it overwhelmingly' (Avnery, 2005). The US Congress has been predisposed to the arguments of the well-organized pro-Israel lobby. The main lobby group is the American Israel Public Affairs Committee (AIPAC) and it targets Congress and other parts of the American political system directly in an attempt to influence legislation and policy in support for Israel. In other words it seeks to ensure that American foreign policy is supportive of Israel – particularly as a 'lone democracy' in the Middle East. AIPAC seeks to put in force Israeli policy in America rather than the other way round. Given the depth of the relationship between Israel and the USA, many have examined and questioned it in terms of American interests and their policy agenda in terms of the wider Middle East. The natural sympathies that the USA shares with Israel are understandable but dependence rather than mutuality is an issue that has featured in critiques of this relationship. America is now understood as an actor in the region in relation to Israel first and other states second. This in turn has shaped Arab attitudes towards the USA and their policies in the region. Such actors complain that 'every issue in the region has to go firstly through the door of Israel before it can be discussed with the United States of America and we simply don't feel this way about everything' (Moussawi, 2005).

In sum, a combination of factors, including the debt America feels that it owes Israel, the impact of the pro-Israel lobby, as well as material interests in terms of relations between these two states, continue to account for American foreign policy with regard to Israel. As President Bush asserted early in his administration:

> Israel is a small country that has lived under threat throughout its existence. At the first meeting of my National Security Council, I told them a top foreign policy priority is the safety and security of Israel. My Administration will be steadfast in supporting Israel against terrorism and violence and in seeking the peace for which all Israelis pray.
>
> (Bush, 2001)

Thus, the role of the USA remains pivotal either to the endurance or resolution of the Israeli–Palestinian conflict.

A regional concern

Accounts of the regional actors and their part in and influence on the Israeli–Palestinian conflict often start by relating the number of wars and military engagements that have centred on this issue. Such accounts include the war of 1948 between Israel and the Arab states of Jordan, Syria, Lebanon, Saudi Arabia, Egypt and Iraq (supported by other Arab allies), the 1956 Suez War when Israel sided with the British and French in an attack on the Egyptian-controlled Suez Canal. Accounts continue with the 1967 Six-Day War in which Egypt, Jordan and Syria were fighting against Israel and which resulted in defeat for the Arabs and the loss of territories such as the West Bank, Gaza Strip, Arab East Jerusalem, the Golan Height and the Sinai. They also include the war of 1973 (Yom Kippur or Ramadan War) in which Egypt and Syria launched attacks on Israel in an attempt to win back the territories lost in 1967 and focus on the use of the Arab oil boycott to create pressure for a resolution. Further accounts have included the 1978 and 1982 Israeli invasions of Lebanon and the subsequent occupation of southern Lebanon by Israel until 2000. They also take into account the more recent war in Lebanon in the summer of 2006. Taken in sum then, the region has been subject to at least four major wars that have involved Israel and the Arabs over the

Palestinian question and other conflicts that have made linkage to the resolution of the Israeli–Palestinian issue. The Israeli–Palestinian conflict has been a cause of regional instability; militarization and the arms race that has witnessed Israel acquire a nuclear capacity with little complaint from the outside world. It is worth remembering, however, despite the huge human and economic cost of these wars and the impact that solidarity with the Palestinian people has had on Arab and Muslim consciousness in the region, none of these conflagrations has resulted in the settlement of the Israeli–Palestinian issue according to internationally recognized resolutions such as those passed by the United Nations. As a means of reaching a desired outcome to the Israeli–Palestinian conflict, even war has failed to deliver a decisive and definitive victory for either side.

Yet, Arab states, Israel and armed Palestinian groups have persisted in employing the threat of arms or actual arms as a means of resolving the conflict. Unfortunately such wars have succeeded in deepening enmity and bringing in further combatant elements, and victims (including the worrying trend of civilian targets) into the conflict. Not one single peace treaty has emerged as a direct result of the hostilities waged and armistices signed between Israel and its Arab neighbours. The peace treaties concluded by Egypt in 1982 and Jordan in 1994 with Israel have brought official enmity to an end but no single party to these treaties has ever described subsequent inter-state relations as a warm peace that has brought the resolution of the Israeli–Palestinian conflict one step closer.

The Israeli–Palestinian conflict has become a regional concern for a number of reasons. As such it has, as previously mentioned, engaged certain state actors in direct confrontation with Israel and led to war. For other state actors, confrontation between them and Israel has taken place in other ways: economic boycott, propaganda campaigns, lobbying of influential international actors such as the USA, and solidarity campaigns with the Palestinian people. Regional organizations composed of Arab and other states, such as the Arab League or the Organization of Petroleum Exporting Countries (OPEC), have also become embroiled in the conflict either in terms of its perpetuation or resolution. Other non-state actors within the region such as religious organizations, including the Middle East Council of Churches and Islamic movements including the Muslim Brotherhood (*al-Ikhwan al-Muslimeen*), have concerned themselves with the Israeli–Palestinian conflict and the countless proposals for its resolution. Such elements have played a part in mobilizing opinion across the region in support of efforts to find a peaceful resolution to the conflict or in promoting a route to resolution that offers a powerful alternative discourse. Even if the governments and peoples of the West have chosen to marginalize and ignore such groups as the Muslim Brotherhood, within the region their growing local followings and postures of the Israeli–Palestinian conflict have been influential. While it is a truism of conventional international relations approaches to conflict resolution that only states have the legitimacy to enter into peace negotiations and reach resolution, the impact that civil society, non-state actors and regional organizations and associations has had on this conflict is difficult to ignore.

Let us, for one moment, focus on these regional organizations – one a collection of state actors, namely the Arab League, the other of non-state actors, namely the Muslim Brotherhood. The Arab League or League of Arab states was founded in 1945. It has as many as 22 member states: Algeria, Bahrain, Comoros, Djibouti, Egypt, Iraq, Jordan, Kuwait, Lebanon, Libya, Mauritania, Morocco, Oman, Palestine, Qatar, Saudi Arabia, Somalia, Sudan, Syria, Tunisia, United Arab Emirates and Yemen. In 1976 the PLO was accorded membership of the Arab League. The current Secretary General is the former Egyptian Foreign Minister, Amr Moussa. Throughout the history of the Arab League the Palestinian issue has acted as a spur to both Arab unity and divisiveness. In 1951 the Arab League organization worked in support of an official boycott of Israel, leading to the black-listing of thousands of companies. The boycott is supposed to work on three levels: first, a direct ban on the import of Israeli produced goods and services across the Arab world, second, a prohibition on doing business with Israeli companies, and third, a ban on dealings with companies that are on the blacklist. For many years the ban had an effective impact on the import of certain goods and services within the region – including Coca Cola, which for years was banned from the Arab market because it chose to defy the blacklist and sell its products in Israel. It was only in the 1990s, some decades after Pepsi had acquired dominance, that Coca Cola was able to get its products into the Arab market. Today there is a consensus that the Arab boycott is largely ineffective and pays nothing more than lip service to the original cause it was supposed to support.

Another way in which the Arab League has sought to influence and involve itself in the Israeli–Palestinian conflict is the role it played in establishing the PLO in 1964. The initiative to create the PLO was taken at the first Arab Summit in 1964 by Egyptian President, Gamal Abdel Nasser. The PLO, as a non-state actor, would be supported by the Arab League and would create a series of institutions that would support the Palestinian people in the struggle for their rights. Not every member state supported the initiative (Jordan objected) and nor was there consensus in the Palestinian community that the Palestinian issue should be decoupled from principal Arab support in this way. Despite the fact that by 1968 the leadership of the PLO – through the primary institution of the Palestine National Council (PNC) – had been taken over by Fatah and the Egyptian grip thus weakened, in 1974 at the Rabat Summit of the Arab League the organization officially recognized the PLO as the 'sole legitimate representative of the Palestinian people', thus stifling Jordanian and American attempts to cut them from the resolution of conflict loop.

Throughout the 1960s, 1970s and early 1980s the Palestinian issue remained at the top of the Arab League agenda, and it was only in November 1987 at the Arab League Summit in Jordan that the issue failed to make it onto the agenda (much to the ire of PLO Chairman, Yasser Arafat). Yet by 1988 the Arab League endorsed the PLO's declaration of statehood and plan for a negotiated settlement to the conflict with Israel.

In 2002, in perhaps the most important Arab League decision pertaining to the Israeli–Palestinian conflict, a Saudi initiative that offered recognition to Israel in return for Israeli compliance with UN Resolutions 242 and 338 including a full withdrawal from the territories it occupied in 1967 was ratified. This was the first fully endorsed 'pan-Arab' peace initiative and it appeared to address sensitive Palestinian issues such as the 'right of return' for refugees as well as Israel's primary concern with its security. As the Saudi Foreign Minister, Prince Saud al-Faisal, remarked:

> this is the way toward security . . . Israel can't keep the land [it occupies] and want security at the same time. It has to withdraw and give the Palestinians their rights. If Israel does that, the Arab states will put an end to the state of war. That will give Israel its security.
>
> (CNN, 2002)

Although the Arab League peace initiative failed to win either Israeli or US support:

> achievements of th[e] summit make it the most significant in the Arab League's 57-year history. For the first time since 1948, Arab states collectively offered to normalize their relations with Israel in return for Israel's complete withdrawal from the territories it occupied during the 1967 War.
>
> (Jouejati, 2002)

In respect of divisiveness it is fair to say that in looking at any of the activities and initiatives of the Arab League as outlined above – whether it be the establishment of the PLO, the boycott of Israel or the 2002 peace initiative – there has been strife among and between the member states. Often deep-seated animosity has emerged as Arab states have competed with each other to 'champion' the Palestinian issue or steer it according to their own interests. They have also variously sought to control and manipulate Palestinian organizations such as the PLO and its constituent factions. This has often made it impossible for a regional organization like the Arab League to have the diplomatic clout it might have enjoyed (if there was unity) in addressing this issue. This in turn has meant that Israel and its supporters, particularly the USA, do not really have to take the Arab League seriously.

In January 2006 following the Hamas victory in the Palestinian polls many commentators highlighted that this in turn was a tremendous result for the regional ambitions of the Islamist movement the Muslim Brotherhood. Hamas was established as an offshoot of the Muslim Brotherhood in 1988 and the Muslim Brotherhood is one of the largest and most important Islamist organizations in the Middle East region. As one author has highlighted: 'This is the movement, which, in one form or another, has been the most prominent fundamentalist current in Sunni Islam' (Zubaida, 1993: 47). Almost since its establishment in Egypt in 1928 the Muslim Brotherhood has addressed itself to Palestine, the Zionist project and the subsequent conflict that has unfolded there. Hassan al-Banna, the founder of the movement, recognized that events in Palestine were symbolic of what he believed to be the impact of Western colonialism and the decline of Islam. He advocated a return to Islam as a means not only to liberating individual Muslim souls but to Islamizing society and releasing it from the domination of outside influences and powers. In 1948 during the first Arab–Israeli war the Muslim Brotherhood organized armed forces to join the battle against Israel.

In the wake of the establishment of the state of Israel and its occupation of Palestinian territories the symbolic attachment for and to Palestine and the Palestinian issue has grown in importance to the movement of the Muslim Brotherhood. The Muslim Brotherhood and its members across the region have supported and funded their Palestinian counterparts and maintained a bellicose position against Israel. The Muslim Brotherhood organization refuses to recognize Israel, thus endorsing the view of their Islamist counterparts in the Palestinian territories. Moreover, Muslim Brotherhood leaders have, in the past, called for Muslims to engage in a jihad in order to end the Israeli presence in Palestine. This historic enmity towards Israel and support for the Palestinians has contributed to the ways in which the conflict is further engendered within Islamist circles.

In this way, we have seen that regional responses and involvement to the Israeli–Palestinian conflict have derived not just from the tensions between states such as Israel and the Arab states but through the interactions and activities of both supranational organizations such as the Arab League and non-state actors such as the Muslim Brotherhood. Such organizations, along with myriad others in the region, including solidarity committees, people-to-people initiatives, religious activities and encounters, all meld into an influence on the dynamic of the conflict as it waxes, wanes and changes over the decades of its endurance.

The international arena

> All the world's a stage,
> And all the men and women merely players:
> They have their exits and their entrances
> (William Shakespeare, *As You Like It*, Act II Scene vii)

For many of the reasons that I identified at the beginning of this chapter the energies of various actors in the international arena have been absorbed over the decades by the Israeli–Palestinian conflict. It is no exaggeration to say that there must be hundreds of books written by international diplomats, international solidarity activists, peaceniks, realists, and statesmen and women, who have recounted in detail the ways in which the conflict has impacted on their corner of the international arena. Moreover, it is the case that, as with the regional dimension to the conflict, there are myriad state, non-state, and supranational actors that one way or another are embroiled in the conflict. One of the most significant supranational organizations to address itself to the various dimensions of the Israeli–Palestinian conflict is the United Nations. Historically non-state actors such as the World Zionist Organization or the Organization of Islamic Conference have also addressed and supported divergent protagonists. Newer non-state actors that impact on the dynamic of the conflict through a range of educational, political, cultural and economic activities include such diverse groups as the International Solidarity Movement (ISM) and the Birthright Israel organization.

As detailed in Chapter 3 it was the United Nations, newly formed in 1945, that through the resolution on partition in 1947 played its part in unilaterally determining the fate of the Palestinian people and in the establishment of the state of Israel in Palestine. From that point the United Nations has been obligated to also seek a just resolution to the conflict, including asserting the 'right of return' for Palestinian refugees and a call on Israel to withdraw from the territories it occupied in the war of 1967. In dealing with the issue of the Palestinian refugees the United Nations established the United Nations Relief and Works Agency for Palestine Refugees in the Near East (UNRWA) in 1949 as a relief and later development agency providing education, healthcare, social services, emergency rations and other assistance to more than 4.3 million Palestinian refugees living in camps in the West Bank, Gaza Strip, Jordan, Syria and Lebanon. The United Nations has also deployed its peacekeepers and truce monitors in those territories pertaining to the conflict, such as the Golan Heights and southern Lebanon, as well as dispatching mediators or officials from the Office of the Special Coordinator for the Middle East Peace Process as well as Special Envoys. There have also been hundreds of General Assembly and Security Council resolutions proposed and many of them have been passed. In 2005 as many as 23 resolutions pertaining to the conflict were proposed by the UN General Assembly. The resolutions addressed issues such as the Palestinian right to self-determination, Israeli practices in the occupied Golan Heights, illegal Israeli settlement-building, Israeli respect for human rights, Israeli respect for the Fourth Geneva Convention, refugee assistance issues, the Palestine question, Quartet efforts, sovereignty over natural resources and nuclear weapon free zones in the Middle East. Some of the most important resolutions of the United Nations pertaining to the conflict, its endurance, its victims and its resolutions are shown in Table 8.1.

Table 8.1 Important United Nations resolutions

1947	181	Partition of Palestine
1967	242	Security Council resolution calling for the withdrawal of Israeli troops from occupied territories, a 'just settlement of the refugee problem' and the need to recognize 'the sovereignty, territorial integrity and political independence of every state in the area and their right to live in peace within secure and recognized boundaries.
1973	338	Following Yom Kippur/Ramadan War reaffirmed UN resolution 242 and called for immediate implementation.
1975	3379	Resolution declaring Zionism a form of racism (repealed in 1991).
1978	425	Call to Israel to end military occupation in, and attacks on, Lebanon.
2000	1322	Issued in the wake of the outbreak of the second Intifada, reaffirmed that a 'just and lasting solution' to the conflict must be based on resolutions 242 and 338.

Much controversy divides critics and supporters over the role and extent to which the United Nations should play a greater or lesser part in resolving the conflict between Israel and the Palestinians. Some of these debates are part of the wider discourse of the effectiveness of the United Nations and the ways in which the institution is dominated by certain state actors, such as the USA, or 'clubbable' nations who are subsequently accused of ganging up on individual nations such as Israel. The following excerpts from pro-Israeli and pro-Palestinian commentaries that have addressed these issues give a flavour of the tone and demeanour of such debates:

Excerpt 1: Whorehouse along the East River

When one considers that the majority of UN member states are Arab nations (22) or Islamic nations (52) or dictatorial, anti-democratic nations or nations in desperate need of Arab oil or nations desperate for business investment opportunities within Arab countries or countries fearful of discontent among their growing Arab/Muslim populations (namely ALL of Europe!), it's no wonder why so many anti-Israel General Assembly resolutions get introduced AND passed!

(www.masada2000.org/UN.html)

Excerpt 2: Double standards – double vision

[T]he International Community has taught Israel that it is above the law . . . [T]he United Nations – especially the Security Council – [is] responsible for belittling the human tragedy of the Palestinian people under the occupation, to the extent of missing all the opportunities to punish Israel for the same crimes other parties have been condemned and punished for.

(www.amin.org/eng/hichem_karoui/2003/apr25.html)

Clearly frustrations are expressed from both sides of the divide regarding the actions of the United Nations. But even given the well-acknowledged tensions between key external players within and between the United Nations over the Israeli–Palestinian issue they have failed to let one side or the other achieve a decisive solution to the conflict in this forum.

A European approach

It is fair to say that in the twenty-first century the member states of the European Union have the opportunity to dominate aspects of global affairs and international politics. The economic clout of the European Union alone singles it out as a significant competitor on the global stage. In terms of the Israeli–Palestinian conflict it is important to first remember the extent to which the European Union remains key to both Israel and the Palestinians. For Israel, Europe's clout comes not in the form of an opportunity to perform in the annual Euro-pop fest of the Eurovision

Song Contest (though it should be noted that Israeli transsexual Dana International won the contest in 1998) but in the fact that Europe is its biggest trading partner. Palestinians recognize the importance of the European Union in terms of its aid to them because it remains the most significant donor. Sometimes in concert with the USA and sometimes in ill-disguised diplomatic competition with it, the European Union claims credentials to be the truer 'honest broker' in terms of efforts to support the Palestinians and Israelis to find a fair resolution to their enmity.

The European Union has called on Israel to withdraw from the territories it occupied in the 1967 war, and recognized the right of self-determination for the Palestinian people. In the Venice Declaration of 1980 the member states of the European Union recognized Israel's right to exist within its own borders but called for efforts to promote independence and statehood for the Palestinian people. By the 1990s with the emergence of the USA as sole superpower, however, the European Union found it more difficult to flex its muscles with equity in the resolution arena pertaining to the Palestinians and Israelis. The EU member states were further shackled by increasing membership, making it difficult to achieve a unified position from within. It also has to be accepted as a fact of life that the strengthening of the Anglo-American relationship often worked against other European Union ambitions vis-à-vis the Palestinians and Israel. Hence European conflict management and resolution efforts in the Israeli–Palestinian arena can and have been in competition or conflict with the American government. The European Union becomes an assertive actor most often in policy arenas where the USA is constrained to act: we can see the influences and frustrations at work between them in issues such as the Palestinian security sector or leverage over Israel in terms of persuading them away from a unilateral path to one that gives preference to negotiations to resolve the conflict. The key point is that the European Union finds it increasingly difficult to pursue its own path in terms of its policy inclination when it meets the bulwark of the US government on this issue.

A concert of actors?

Working to come to agreement on issues of justice and internationally recognized rights seems to offer the best hope, but it must be contextualized within the global positioning of Western states in the wake of 9/11 on terrorism and conflict – particularly as it impacts on the Middle East and the Israeli–Palestinian conflict. This positioning was reflected in the unified front presented by the European Union, the USA, Russia and the United Nations (the Quartet) in the wake of the election of Hamas to government in January 2006. The Quartet made the following three demands on the Hamas government:

*   renounce violence
*   recognize Israel
*   abide by previously reached agreements including the 2003 Road Map for a two-state solution to the conflict.

Moreover the European Union and the USA, along with the government of Israel, announced the suspension of aid to the Hamas-dominated PA unless it acceded to the earlier conditions. By April 2006 the European Union had announced a halt to their funding of the PA in the West Bank and Gaza Strip. By 2007 the Hamas government had taken control of the Gaza Strip from its rivals in Fatah and the international community continued to boycott them. They did, however, resume support for the Palestinian President, Mahmoud Abbas, and the 'emergency' government based in Ramallah that he had pulled together in the wake of the Hamas takeover in Gaza. With this new government in Ramallah President Abbas pursued peace negotiations with Israel and was actively encouraged by the USA and other international actors in the hope that in the final year of the Bush administration Israeli–Palestinian peace negotiations might result in a two-state solution.

In conclusion, although the conflict between the Palestinians and Israelis has an intimacy that often makes it incomprehensible to outsiders, it has occurred within an international context that simply cannot be ignored. Never has the adage of no man being an island been more apposite than in the case of the Israeli–Palestinian conflict and external actors. The conflict has spawned regional and international conflicts, wars and atavistic tensions that have appeared to divide cultures and people across the globe. The conflict has affected the international economy in respect of the modern dependence on oil and propelled a burgeoning arms race that has led to the Middle East region being one of the most militarized, brutalized and dehumanized in the world. The international community, therefore, sees itself as having little choice but to involve itself in the conflict. How it involves itself in the conflict, how it presents its intentions and how its actions are interpreted remains as unfathomable in determining a formula for peace today as it did in the early decades of the twentieth century when international actors determined the course of unfolding political events.

Further reading

There is a lot of material to consider when looking at the role of international state and non-state actors and their impact on the Israeli–Palestinian conflict. On American foreign policy and the conflict consider the following texts: Aruri (Cambridge, MA: South End Press, 2003), Ross (New York: Farrar, Straus and Giroux, 2004), Swisher (New York: Nation Books, 2004). The accounts by Ross and Swisher have elements of 'insider' stories in terms of examining the personalities involved in key external interventions from the US perspective in the conflict. Bregman's book *How the Holy Land defeated America* gives a highly detailed account of more recent attempts at peace negotiations (Harmondsworth: Penguin Books, 2005). The study by Mearsheimer and Walt (London: Allen Lane, 2007) has become a deeply controversial book on US policy and its special relationship with Israel, having drawn the ire of critics both on the left and the right of the political divide.

Books by Quandt (Washington, DC: Brookings Institute, 2001), Freedman (Gainesville, FL: University Press of Florida, 1998), Rabinovich (Princeton, NJ:

Princeton University Press, 2004) and Brynen (Herndon, VA: USIP Press, 2000) present dimensions of the region viewed through the lens of the Israeli–Palestinian conflict. Studies that reflect on the role that international and regional actors have, could or should play in the resolution of the conflict are included in books such as former US President Jimmy Carter's tome on Palestine (New York: Simon and Schuster, 2007). The book, however, has been critically received in Israel.

Soetendorp (Houndsmills: Palgrave Macmillan, 2007) and Shamir and Maddy-Weitzman (Brighton: Sussex Academic Press, 2005) provide analyses of international actors and their impact on Israeli–Palestinian relations, including attempts at peacemaking. The theme of peacemaking and its international dimension or comparison is also apparent in Adam and Moodley's text of 2005 (Philadelphia, PA: Temple University Press). Cordesman (Washington, DC: Praeger, 2005) and Keating *et al.* (London: RIIA, 2005) look at specific dimensions of aid, diplomacy and the impact of the changing international environment.

Adam, H. and Moodley, K. (2005) *Seeking Mandela: Peacemaking between Palestinians and Israelis*, Philadelphia, PA: Temple University Press.

Aruri, Nasser. H. (2003) *Dishonest broker: The US role in Israel and Palestine*, Cambridge, MA: South End Press.

Bregman, A. (2005) *Elusive peace: How the Holy Land defeated America*, Harmondsworth: Penguin Books.

Brynen, R. (2000) *A very political economy: Peacebuilding and foreign aid in the West Bank and Gaza*, Herndon, VA: USIP Press.

Carter, J. (2007) *Palestine: Peace not apartheid*, New York: Simon and Schuster.

Cordesman, A. (2005) *The Israeli–Palestinian war: Escalating to nowhere*, Washington, DC: Praeger.

Freedman, R.O. (1998) *The Middle East and the peace process: The impact of the Oslo Accords*, Gainesville, FL: University Press of Florida.

Keating, M., Le More, A. and Lowe, R. (2005) *Aid, diplomacy, and the facts on the ground: The Palestinian experience of disconnection*, London: RIIA.

Mearsheimer, J. and Walt, S. (2007) *The Israel lobby and US foreign policy*, London: Allen Lane.

Quandt, W. (2001) *Peace process, American diplomacy and the Arab–Israeli peace process since 1967*, Washington, DC: Brookings Institute.

Rabinovich, I. (2004) *Waging peace: Israel and the Arabs 1948–2003*, Princeton, NJ: Princeton University Press.

Ross, Dennis (2004) *The missing peace. The inside story of the fight for Middle East peace*, New York: Farrar, Straus and Giroux.

Shamir, S. and Maddy-Weitzman, B. (eds) (2005) *The Camp David Summit – What went wrong?* Brighton: Sussex Academic Press.

Soetendorp, B. (2007) *The dynamics of Israeli–Palestinian relations: Theory, history and cases*, Houndsmills: Palgrave Macmillan.

Swisher, Clayton (2004) *The truth about Camp David. The untold story about the collapse of the Middle East peace process*, New York: Nation Books.

9 Moving from zero

Chapter outline

- The broken path to peace: resolving or managing the conflict   187
- Making it to Madrid   188
- Oslo and all that   190
- Opposition to Oslo   193
- Camp David and the second Intifada   195
- The second Intifada and death of peace   197
- Disengaging for peace?   200
- The rocky road to peace   202
- Annapolis or bust   202
- Further reading   204

The final chapter of this book will examine dimensions of conflict resolution and transition from conflict that have been proposed, attempted, succeeded at and failed in the context of the Israeli–Palestinian dynamic. It will examine the legacy of the Sharon and Hamas governments and their impact on the dynamics of the conflict. Hence the themes covered will include: transfer, annexations, disengagement, one-state versus two-state solutions, and how to end conflict. Issues of state recognition, legitimacy, strategies for negotiation, asymmetry and reciprocity will be debated. Ceasefires, 'periods of calm' and military and civilian evacuations from territory will be assessed for their contribution in creating or maintaining the 'resolution momentum'. In this chapter the economic dimension (particularly in terms of wider discourses of global capital and international and regional competitiveness) will be examined in the context of both societies as well as future integration ambitions.

As earlier chapters in this book have highlighted, peacemaking or conflict resolution between Israel and the Palestinians has been a task of monumental proportions. Attempts at peacemaking or resolution of the conflict through negotiation have, moreover, foundered time and time again and appear each time to plunge both sides into an ever deeper pool of enmity. No matter how often the spiritual exhortations of others are uttered, no matter how many times kings, prime ministers and presidents announce a new initiative or propose a solution, peace in the Holy Land appears elusive. There have been periods in the conflict when peace appears to have been in the grasp of Israelis and Palestinians. In more recent decades great hopes were raised across the globe that the time had come for peace to be visited upon the peoples of the benighted lands at the centre of conflict in the contemporary Middle East. Yet somehow and someway the logic of peace over war appeared to confound the constituent elements to the Israeli–Palestinian conflict.

By 2008 the situation for Palestinians in the West Bank, East Jerusalem and Gaza Strip was worse than it had ever been. The first and second uprisings, the virtual imprisonment of their President (until his death), who was also effectively declared persona non grata by the international community, the Israeli military blockade, combined with the cumulative effect of a society suffocating from forty years of military occupation, had brought the Palestinian people to their knees. Their situation was compounded by a looming humanitarian crisis as the international community cut aid in response to the accession of the Islamist Hamas government through the Palestinian ballot box. A defeated Fatah and a victorious Hamas also embarked on armed internecine clashes that had brought the people to the brink of civil war. Ceasefires and understandings to share power among themselves often foundered as a result of mutual mistrust and the interference of outside parties determined to instead push the Palestinians to the point of an internal confrontation where Hamas would be militarily defeated.

In Israel, the Prime Minister, Ehud Olmert, was proposing to move unilaterally to solve the conflict with the Palestinians, security concerns remained paramount as Palestinian Qassam rockets 'rained' on Israeli territory over the 1948 Green Line and the Israeli settlers prepared for a showdown with their Prime Minister over his plan for limited withdrawals from the West Bank. Israeli security was being bought at a cost to domestic budgets in education, health and welfare. The international community refused to endorse an Israeli unilateral move to impose a solution to the conflict, called for a negotiated settlement and made demands of the Hamas government that made it impossible for such talks to take place. There appeared to be no alternative to the state of paralysis that had gripped all parties to the conflict and little prospect of peace. The question that hung on everyone's lips was: Where do we go from here? The waiting game had commenced and conflict intensification rather than peace appeared to be the only game in town.

Over the decades there have been countless schemes for the resolution of the conflict. Such approaches have included the transfer idea of moving either the Palestinian population or the Israeli population. Some Zionists have called for the transfer of the 'Arabs' from the land which they believe should be exclusively Jewish as promised in covenant from God. As Israeli historian Benny Morris notes:

> The idea of transfer is as old as modern Zionism and has accompanied its evolution and praxis during the past century. And driving it was an iron logic:

> There could be no viable Jewish state in all or part of Palestine unless there was a mass displacement of Arab inhabitants, who opposed its emergence and would constitute an active or potential fifth column in its midst.
>
> (Morris, 2002)

For some Palestinian Islamists an anti-Semitic imperative drives their calls for the 'Jews to be kicked into the sea' and out of a land which they consider to have been endowed to them for perpetuity. The extent to which such goals have been or are presently achievable is a matter of supposition but what is apparent is that such hostile positions epitomize the strength of feeling against the other in this particular arena of conflict.

At the alternative end of the resolution spectrum lie a series of options and proposals that both Palestinians and Israeli promote that can best be described as 'negotiated and peaceful' solutions. These solutions range from the presently internationally endorsed two-state solution to a one-state proposal for the two peoples together. As one observer remarked: 'The true alternative facing the Middle East in coming years will be between an ethnically cleansed Greater Israel and a single, integrated, bi[-]national state of Jews and Arabs, Israelis and Palestinians' (Judt, 2003). One way of making sense of these various options and proposals for resolutions to the conflict, their true meaning, feasibility and import is to find a frame of analysis to assist us in our interpretation.

It would be fair to argue that most other internal and externally suggested proposals for resolving the conflict fall somewhere between the genocide/mass transfer (McGarry and O'Leary, 1993) and the negotiated binational solutions (Judt, 2003). In other words there are lots of solutions to the conflict proposed by all sorts of parties to and involved with the conflict, including constituent Palestinian and Israeli elements, and regional elements from the Arab League to the Muslim Brotherhood and al-Qaeda. International actors have also played their part in coming up with proposals for peace but the problem is not the lack of proposals but getting the parties to the conflict to a mutually agreed solution! Of course the type of proposal on the table has mattered to those charged with finding ways to resolve the conflict and obviously the more 'acceptable' the proposal the greater the chance of it succeeding in terms of any subsequent negotiations. In the early 1990s the most significant steps towards a negotiated outcome to the conflict unfolded.

For the first time in the history of the conflict Palestinians and Israelis sat at the same negotiating table, plans were agreed and the slow march to peace accelerated to such an extent that many believed that finally an end to the conflict was in sight. With the important input of outside actors as facilitators, mediators and supporters of negotiated outcomes, the opening years of the 1990s gave rise to the Madrid Peace Conference, the Oslo Accords (1993), the Cairo Agreement (1994), the Interim Agreement (Oslo II) in 1995, Wye Agreement (1998) and final status talks at Camp David, Sharm el-Sheikh and Taba in 2000–01. These were followed by the recommendations for peace in 2000 known as the Clinton

Parameters, the Mitchell Commission in 2001, the 2003 Road Map document and the Geneva Accord of 2003. By 2005 and 2006 Israel began to consider a more unilateral approach to final status. In 2005 the government of Israeli Prime Minister Ariel Sharon initiated a form of disengagement from the Gaza Strip including the evacuation of all its settlers and redeployment of the IDF. In 2006 Sharon's successor Ehud Olmert announced the Israeli 'convergence' plan, which was widely interpreted as an Israeli attempt to unilaterally impose final borders on the Palestinians. In 2006 the Palestinians elected the Hamas movement to the majority of seats in the Palestinian legislature. The position of the leadership of Hamas and the Hamas government with respect to peace was to reject the Road Map, refuse to recognize Israel and to maintain the right to organize a resistance against the Israeli occupation. By 2007 the American administration and other international actors were embroiled in attempts to revive a peace process that had little by way of 'buy-in' from either the Israelis or the Palestinians.

Often it has appeared as if some sort of final peace deal to exchange land for peace, to create mutual recognition, with two states, and with Israeli withdrawal from occupied territories and prosperity for both peoples could be realized. The failure to achieve such goals and the regression into conflict has been variously blamed by one side or the other on the opposing side. Surprisingly there is, however, a degree of unity between the two peoples on the issue of peace. Opinion polls from both sides of the divide reflect an aspiration for a peaceful settlement of the conflict and for both nations to live in peace rather than conflict, but they differ on the method and nature of a peace settlement between them.

For successive Israeli governments and the Israeli people that elected them there has emerged a wavering support for a withdrawal option for peace with the Palestinians. Withdrawal from territories that Israel occupied in the war of 1967, however, has been seen as an important lynchpin to the resolution of the conflict not just with the Palestinians but other Arab actors such as Syria as well. Israel's occupation of the West Bank and Gaza Strip and its annexation of East Jerusalem, combined with the establishment and consolidation of illegal settlements, the infrastructure to support them and, since 2002 the building of a separation wall in the West Bank, are seen as key obstacles to peace between the two peoples. These 'facts on the ground' are variously interpreted as attempts by Israel to permanently annex Palestinian territory, maintain occupation and/or fracture any meaningful hope of statehood for the Palestinian people of the West Bank, East Jerusalem and the Gaza Strip and the refugee population that awaits statehood after decades in exile. In 2007 the UN Special Rapporteur for Human Rights compared Israel's occupation of the Palestinian territories to elements of the Apartheid regime that oppressed and discriminated against millions of blacks in South Africa.

Even pro-peace Palestinians appeared to be struggling to find evidence of a desire from Israel to invigorate the peace process. As PLO Executive Committee member and peace activist, Yasser Abed Rabbo, declared in 2006:

the main problem that both sides are threatened with is unilateralism . . . Israel prefers a unilateral annexation, the cantonization of the West Bank, the physical separation of the Gaza Strip and West Bank, and the division of the Palestinian people because they know that any sane Palestinian would never agree to such a 'solution' if it were presented in negotiations.

(Abed Rabbo, 2006)

Israelis believed a similar lack of conviction was evident from the Palestinian side. As one pro-peace Israeli activist remarked: 'If they really want peace [with us] why did they elect a government of blood-thirsty terrorists and suicide bombers who would have us living under an Islamic caliphate as second class beings?'.

Thus, while it may have been true to argue in the early 1990s that many Israelis had come to realize that the occupation was becoming untenable in terms of security provisions and the drain on the national economy, the idea of cannibalizing the West Bank to give Israel its strategic advantage and maintain large settlement centres of population became increasingly acceptable.

Convergence and unilateral border setting (determined solely by Israel's interests) have become ways of achieving annexation without the headache of a Palestinian population in tow. This scenario and many of the others proposed and considered by the government of Israel and its people as a 'viable' option for peace is predicated on the maintenance of Israeli control over Palestinian territory rather than a final relinquishment in return for a mutually agreed peace. This means that Israel would avoid having to give citizenship to any more Palestinians than currently reside in Israel and who are already considered, by some, a demographic threat. Israel would benefit from territory acquired through occupation and state theft of Palestinian lands (Eldar, 2006). These options, however, are unlikely to be supported by the international community. Quartet members, including the government of the USA, resisted Israeli proposals of this nature, yet struggled to convince Israel of other mutually negotiated alternatives.

Israel thus found itself tied to pursuing its own measures for security first, with little by way of support from the international community if it implied the denial of a Palestinian input into a final settlement arrangement. At the same time the Palestinian demand for statehood was weakened, in the eyes of the international community, by the failure of the Palestinians to produce a national leadership that was prepared to accept peace on the terms offered by Israel. Palestinian options have been defined by its asymmetric position vis-à-vis Israel as the weaker and more dependent party, and have been constrained by a lack of capacity in negotiations, lack of resources for peace preparations and the lack of near-unequivocal backing of a superpower such as America. Ultimately, Palestinian aspirations for statehood as a reality are dependent on an Israeli withdrawal from Palestinian territories that they occupy as well as a peace settlement with Israel that recognizes the very important trade and economic measures that are essential if a Palestinian state is to become viable.

The transition to peace thus far has only brought the Palestinians a limited and fatally flawed opportunity for autonomy from Israel; progression to statehood has been stalled time and time again. In the post-Arafat era, however, there was little hope that Palestinian options for peace were being taken any more seriously by Israel and the international community than before. This had meant that the prospects for an end to conflict diminished daily, weekly, monthly and yearly.

The international community, throughout this period, remained wedded to the notion that a two-state solution was the only way to resolve the historic conflict between Israel and the Palestinians. In as much as the conflict has endured, so too has the international formula for its resolution. The fact that more than 70 years on from the first external proposal to solve the conflict through partition and the recognition of two states – one Jewish, the other Palestinian – the conflict remains unresolved has not deterred the international community from seeing this as the peace default option. But who does the two-state solution satisfy? By the 1990s the two-state solution was the preferred method of resolution through negotiation and it was diplomatically enshrined in the Oslo Accords and the negotiations that followed on from them. The international community, moreover, promoted the two-state solution through the significant financial and other assistance it has offered to Israel and the Palestinians throughout the 1990s and into the first years of the twenty-first century. The collapse of the peace process, the crisis of governance in the Palestinian areas of autonomy, the rising toll of civilian victims on both sides of the conflict, did not appear, however, to detract from the international vision of a two-state solution to the Israeli–Palestinian conflict (Milton-Edwards, 2005). A failure to absorb the lessons learned from the various stages in the peace process was clearly apparent.

The broken path to peace: resolving or managing the conflict

Conflict resolution, conflict transformation, peace-building, peacemaking, dispute resolution, peace processes, restorative justice, conflict management, these and many other terms have been applied to describe and explain the attempt to end the state of enmity between Israel and the Palestinian people. Because this conflict has been variously described as being religious, national, ethnic, economic, colonial, racial, a zero-sum game, and so on and so forth, the means by which it is resolved and/or managed are myriad. This makes the task of providing a framework or interpretative structure to the events since the Madrid peace talks in 1991 very difficult. Explanations and theories of conflict resolution and management in the Israeli–Palestinian context also frame debate from perspectives as varied as gender, psychology, hydro-politics, societal beliefs, structuralism and the media.

What is apparent is that from the early 1990s specific peace or conflict resolution approaches were favoured over others. Ideas surrounding 'recognition' and 'negotiation' gained considerable currency and were considered to be legitimate in terms of an aspiration to end the conflict peacefully.

Making it to Madrid

> Why Madrid? Why this castle? – I tell you why
> They want to deepen the feeling of our inferiority –
> Those Moorish castles bring back memories of defeat and weakness.
>
> (Zahar, 1991)

The movement towards peace negotiations as a method for resolving the Israeli–Palestinian conflict in the early 1990s was very much an American invention. By this I mean that the energies that were needed to bring together representatives of the Israeli government and the Palestinian people were captured and marshalled by the Bush administration, as it reassessed its wider Middle East strategy in the wake of the Gulf crisis following Iraq's invasion of Kuwait. In the wake of the crisis the USA sought to re-establish stability in the region, and once again recognized that at the heart of any settlement between Israel and the Arab states was the Palestinian issue. Saddam Hussein himself had made a 'linkage' between 'occupation' in Kuwait and 'occupation' in Palestine but of course the USA interpreted things a little differently. With the break-up of the Soviet Union, and thus its decline as a superpower in the region, as well as the emergence of a 'new world order' it was believed that a historic opportunity to go for peace was now at hand. The moment also provided the Americans, the remaining superpower, with a chance to dictate the peace they envisioned rather than rely on one promoted by actual parties to the conflict.

The right-wing Likud government in Israel, led by the then Prime Minister, Yitzhak Shamir, refused, however, to enter into any direct discussion with the Palestinian leadership. His government still refused to recognize the PLO and made it clear that the most that Palestinians could ever hope to achieve under his government was a limited form of autonomy (similar to those discussed with Sadat at Camp David) in which Israel would retain ultimate control over the West Bank and Gaza Strip. It was under these unpromising preconditions, with the Jordanians providing a cover for the Palestinian negotiators, that the historic first round of Arab–Israeli peace talks were convened under the auspices of the USA and the former USSR in October/November 1991 in Madrid.

It needs to be acknowledged then that even getting the parties to the conference in Madrid and sitting around the same table had been an achievement in terms of American diplomacy. It would have been a mistake, however, to assume that the Israeli presence at the negotiating table meant that some form of ideological capitulation had taken place in the right-wing Likud camp led by Yitzhak Shamir. Shamir, however, knew that he had to concede to American pressure if its unconditional support for Israel was to continue. In early 1991 President Bush had given a public commitment to play a part in resolving the conflict based on the 'land for peace' formula and UN Resolutions 242 and 338.

Bush had threatened to withhold a $10 billion loan guarantee to the Israeli government as a means of pressuring them to the negotiating table. It began to worry Israel that America might make support conditional, thus threatening the

$77 billion in aid that it had previously enjoyed. Bush had discovered an important lever and Israel would have to respond to a stark choice: peace talks or a serious threat to US aid. Bringing Arab parties to the peace table also presented challenges. For some Arab states it was easier than others but the fact that the USA had cajoled, pressured, persuaded and created such little room for manoeuvre that Syria came to the peace talks was an achievement in and of itself. In some sense, getting a Palestinian presence at the negotiations was the hardest part of assembling the participants for the historic meeting in Madrid in October/ November 1991. Jordan was there because, after King Hussein had sided (somewhat disastrously in terms of international opinion but not domestic support) with Saddam Hussein during the Gulf crisis, he needed 'back-in' to the American orbit in the region. Syria was there because Assad considered himself a smarter politician and tactician than the Israelis and Americans. Lebanon was there as the satellite of Syria. But the Palestinian presence presented the Americans with a real problem. The PLO was considered to be the 'sole legitimate representative of the Palestinian people' but in 1991 Israel refused to recognize the PLO and had criminalized any form of contact or membership with heavy prison sentences. Internally the Palestinian leadership was in some turmoil in the wake of the 1991 war and the decision by PLO Chairman Yasser Arafat to side with Saddam Hussein. In the West Bank and Gaza Strip local leaders were somewhat estranged from the leadership in exile in Tunis and the Intifada had begun to falter as internal clashes broke out between local armed elements. The local leadership, moreover, had to contend with the accelerating pace of Israeli settlement in the West Bank, which was being promoted at the time by the Israeli Housing Minister, Ariel Sharon. The threat of Israeli annexation and talk of transfer of the Palestinians was increasingly expressed in Israeli circles and the Palestinian leadership knew any action was better than no action. The solution was to send local Palestinian representatives as part of the Jordanian delegation. Admission to the talks, then, would be by the side door and the Palestinians were warned by the Americans not to wear their identities on their sleeves.

At Madrid, once everyone had got over the shock of seeing the enemy on the other side of the table and the opening ceremonies were concluded, a series of bilateral peace talks ensued. Although the basis of the talks was the 'land for peace' formula of UN Resolutions 242 and 338, the United Nations were merely observers at the talks and the roles of the European Union and Russia were largely nominal. In other words, despite American declarations that they were there as 'facilitators' and honest brokers of the peace process, the whole shebang had an American imprint on it and they were determined to steer the event to their own agenda. America was resolute about bringing a conclusion to this conflict: they had found an amenable Palestinian partner and were able to cajole and lever Israel – but they were soon to discover – only so far.

After only a few days of 'talks' the Madrid formula began to go wrong. The chemistry was not right, the ingredients for peace were proving unpalatable and for all the parties there was a difficulty in departing from behaviours previously conditioned by hate and enmity. The absence of trust and the failure of the Americans to see this as an important element of getting the parties to the table led to the whole thing quickly unravelling. In all the razzle-dazzle and fanfare of assembling the participants in Madrid, one vital ingredient of any peace negotiations – confidence and trust-building measures – appeared to have fallen by the wayside (Lederach, 2003). As the first sessions closed amid bickering over where the next talks should be held, the Israeli government proceeded with its settlement activity and its parliament issued a statement declaring that certain territories taken and occupied by Israel in the 1967 were non-negotiable. These were hardly textbook measures designed to promote mutual trust and a belief that obstacles to peace would be removed.

Such action, on all sides, was clearly designed to up the ante and display strength to doubting domestic rather than international audiences. Ultimately the final court of opinion would always be the domestic one for both Israel and the Palestinians. A belief quickly grew that the Israeli Prime Minister had happened upon a strategy of just spinning the talks out while his government established so many 'facts on the ground', through settlement-building, infrastructure and annexation, that land for peace would become impossible (Inbar, 1996). Political leaders knew they had to play a strategic game in balancing demands for peace with domestic demands for security and resolution of the conflict that left a sense of victory and a defeated enemy. A peace among equals never really entered the equation at this or any further stages in the peace process. Faith in peace dissipated so quickly after the Madrid talks that even though subsequent rounds of bilateral negotiations were held in Washington and Moscow most people began to believe that nothing would come from the process. The process just limped on for two years as the parties to the talks bickered with each other over procedural rather than substantive issues. Few truly believed that the peace process had any meaning but most did not know that a secret Israeli–Palestinian channel had opened in Norway and that they would culminate in a mutually agreed agenda for final status talks and autonomy for the Palestinians in the interim.

Oslo and all that

There is a plethora of accounts explaining how the Israelis and Palestinians reached a series of Accords (or Declaration of Principles as they are formally known) that culminated in that historic handshake between Israeli Prime Minister Yitzhak Rabin and PLO Chairman Yasser Arafat at the White House in 1993. How then is it possible to sum up what the Accords represented: whether how the Accords were negotiated mattered, whether who played a role mattered? Why had it been possible to reach agreement in Oslo when Madrid had failed, what concessions had been made, what type of bargaining had gone on, who were the key strategic players, and did ordinary Palestinians and Israelis believe that peace between them was truly on the horizon?

A good starting point in terms of reviewing the Oslo Accords is to note that they were very much the product of secrecy and dialogue between a select few on both the Israeli and Palestinian political spectrum. Over a period of nine months a series of talks were held in Norway. A small team of Israeli negotiators led by Yair Hirshfeld and Ron Pundak briefed their political leaders in the Rabin government on progress with their PLO counterparts. The PLO negotiators led by Ahmed Queiri (Abu Ala) for their part reported back to PLO Chairman Yasser Arafat and his deputy Mahmoud Abbas (Abu Mazen). All the other players in the conflict, the representatives of other political parties, the local Palestinian leadership, the European Union, the Russians and the Americans were kept completely in the dark regarding the talks that were unfolding.

The motives for essentially a small elite emerging to handle negotiations for peace in one of the most protracted conflicts in the globe are numerous and each side often differs in interpreting these motives. For the leadership of the PLO the early part of the 1990s had been a rough ride at the hands of the Palestinian people as broadly constituted both in the occupied territories and the refugee camps of Lebanon, Jordan and Syria. Anger at the exiled leadership in Tunis had grown in the wake of setbacks and disappointments associated with the Madrid Peace Process. The PLO had failed in achieving recognition as an equal at the peace talks, and in the eyes of the world really looked like the poor dependent relative of every other political actor in the Middle East region. Popular sentiment against Yasser Arafat began to turn against him and in favour of the new kids on the block in the Islamic resistance movement of Hamas (Milton-Edwards, 1999). The PLO were partly compelled to reach agreement with Israel in order to restore its legitimacy from those who challenged them from within and the rest of the world where the claim to be the 'sole legitimate representative of the Palestinian people' had began to fall on deaf ears. In some respects this move by the PLO was highlighted by the significant opposition that arose from the Palestinian camp when the Accords themselves and the issue of the recognition of Israel were made pubic in the early summer of 1993 and through the first year of the Accords in 1994.

For the Labour Party of Israel the opportunity to marshal negotiation according to their prevailing interests at the expense of a weaker party was, perhaps, too great to resist in 1993. This is certainly one criticism that has been waged against the Rabin government of the time. Another way of looking at it is that there were those in power and with access to power on the Israeli side who truly believed that the time for occupation had come to an end and that, although negotiations since Madrid had taken place, their attention was best directed to the real representatives of the Palestinian people in the PLO. Certain elements of the Israeli political elite also believed it was better to make peace with Arafat (the devil they knew) than the militants of Hamas who were threatening to wage a jihad till all of historic Palestine was liberated.

In some respects the details of the Oslo Accords/Declaration of Principles were initially obscured by the fanfare and euphoria surrounding first the fact that the PLO and Israel had reached a point of recognition (whether mutual or not is open to debate) and second the 'historic handshake' at the signing ceremony between Yasser Arafat and Yitzhak Rabin. To seasoned participants and observers of the conflict it did appear as if the unthinkable was happening and the international media played its part in peddling the popular mantra of 'peace of the braves' as the two 'men of war' grasped the hand of peace.

After the dust had settled, however, the true import of the issue of mutual recognition between Israel and the PLO and the ambiguity of the Oslo Accords started to come to light.

The Oslo Accords established the following:

- The principle of recognition between Israel and the PLO (including refugees in the Diaspora).
- Israeli troop redeployments from Palestinian centres of population – towns and cities like Jericho, Hebron, Jenin, and Gaza City, Ramallah, Nablus, Tulkaram and Bethlehem would be IDF-free zones. This should have meant, in principle, an end to curfews, military closures, arrest raids, collective punishments, house demolitions, restrictions on the freedom of movement, and free association. The front-line face of occupation would be removed to a safe distance!
- An interim period would include the holding of elections for the newly established Palestinian National Authority/PA.
- The PLO would be allowed to form an authority of self-rule under strict terms of autonomy in certain areas of Palestinian life but Israel would retain responsibility for external security and foreign affairs. Some might have contended that these were meagre pickings in terms of self-government but after 26 years of being stifled under Israeli military occupation and rule the Palestinians could be forgiven for wanting to celebrate small measures of autonomy such as the creation of their own police and security forces.
- The Oslo Accords also outlined a series of issues over which it was agreed that final status negotiations should be held within five years. These were issues that were generally considered to be obstacles to a full 'land for peace' deal according to UN Resolutions 242 and 338 that were too difficult to negotiate at the time but that both sides recognized would be part of a final deal between the two sides. The issues were: the future status of Jerusalem (a possible capital of two states), refugees, settlements, security, and borders.

Hence, according to the timetable detailed in the Oslo Accords, by May 1999 the envisaged outcome would be a 'land for peace' deal between the Palestinians and Israel, which the Palestinians, in particular, hoped would include statehood and independence.

In the heady months following the agreement it was hoped that trust-building would lead to an implementation of the Oslo Accords that would expedite the passage of those travelling the path of peace. So many aspects of the new era enshrined in Oslo were supported by the international community and it appeared as if the peace coffers were finally open for Israel and the Palestinians to plunder at will (Bouillon, 2004). By the summer of 1994 PLO Chairman Yasser Arafat had returned from decades in exile to head up the fledgling Palestinian Authority in Gaza, but within months the momentum for peace began to slow.

Opposition to Oslo

In some respects it would be fair to say that quite a few people did not like the Oslo Accords. Although both Israeli and Palestinian public opinion was broadly in favour of the Oslo Accords when it was first announced, a form of opposition emerged right from the start and it grew and grew as the peace process became characterized by stalled implementation and antipathy to the way in which the Oslo Accords structured the next phase of Israeli–Palestinian relations. To be fair the emergence of factions or groups that oppose 'peace deals' are not unique to the Israeli–Palestinian peace process. For example, elements known as 'spoilers' or rejectionists have been known to attempt to derail peace in a number of other post-Cold War civil peace settlements (Darby, 2001).

Opposition on the Palestinian side to the Oslo Accords came from many quarters and this was somewhat surprising because it included major national figures key to the peace process in the past, such as Haider Abdel Shafi and Edward Said, as well as most of the other nationalist factions of the PLO and Hamas. Critics raised a variety of issues that they were concerned with. They asserted that the Oslo Accords, agreed to by Fatah as the majority faction of the PLO was:

> an instrument of surrender, a Palestinian Versailles. What makes it worse is that for at least the past fifteen years the PLO could have negotiated a better arrangement than this modified Allon Plan, one not requiring so many unilateral concessions to Israel.
>
> (Said, 1993)

The Palestinian Islamists, including Hamas, Islamic Jihad and Hizb Tahrir, also condemned the Oslo Accords and publicly denounced them as a non-peace and betrayal of their historic claims to the liberation of the whole of Palestine in the name of the people (Milton-Edwards, 1996). First, various elements claimed that too few people had signed up to the Oslo deal and in the absence of a national referendum on the subject the real response to the Oslo Accords would not be known. Second, they believed that the Oslo Accords and the letters of recognition that were exchanged between Israel and the Palestinians offered far too many concessions from the Palestinian side in return for far too few on the Israeli one. Third, opponents contended, moreover, that the structure of the Oslo Accords was not conducive to the implementation of the 'land for peace' formula contained in UN Resolutions 242 and 338. The asymmetric nature of the conflict – with Israel stronger than the Palestinians, was, according to the opponents, merely reflected in the Oslo Accords. They did not believe that this was a good starting point for a fair and just peace (Rabbani, 2001). Fourth, although most literature on peace agreements contends that textual ambiguity is a good thing – allowing all sides to a conflict to act, relay and sell their own interpretation of the deal to a domestic audience – Palestinian critics complained that the ambiguity was not a deliberate construction but more a question of a fudge on issues that in reality were too critical to peace not to be subject to more specific delineation.

They felt that such misgivings were justified when it appeared that no sooner than the ink had time to dry on the agreement that Israel began to tarry and welsh on the timetable and substance of implementation vis-à-vis troop withdrawals, security cooperation and liaison, and economic cooperation. As one former negotiator commented, 'Oslo was bad. Fine. But Oslo isn't even there anymore, because Israel has violated it to the point where it has become irrelevant' (Shafi, 1995). The more Israel seemed to delay and prevaricate, combined with the election by 1996 of the hardliner Bibi Netanyahu on a platform of renegotiating previously agreed interim agreements, the more the Palestinians became convinced that real peace was proving to be elusive once again. The decision by successive Israeli governments in the post-Oslo era to pursue the illegal settlement of the West Bank and Gaza Strip was also seen as at best working against the spirit of the Oslo agreement and at worst as a deliberate signal that 'land for peace' formulas would not be about relinquishing the lands illegally settled by Israel.

Hence throughout the Oslo period from 1999–2000 the settler population continued to increase, more Palestinian land was expropriated by Israel and settlement-building and expansion, including the infrastructure such as roads through Palestinian territories and water from Palestinian aquifers, continued unabated. Palestinian spoiler elements, such as Hamas, had by this point also embarked on a series of suicide bombing attacks against vulnerable Israeli civilian targets that were guaranteed to put additional pressures on the peace process.

Israeli support for the Oslo Accords was also less than equivocal and it appeared just as difficult for them to build trust with the 'other' as it was for the Palestinians. Some Israeli elements rejected the Oslo Accords outright because they could be interpreted as offering Palestinian statehood. To agree to Palestinian statehood in the West Bank and Gaza Strip was, for many Israelis, an anathema in terms of the central tenets of Zionism. Moreover, other elements in the Israeli political arena were suspicious of the Palestinian leadership and contended that it had failed to provide and maintain the kind of security guarantees from Palestinian violence that the Israelis saw as a prerequisite for any kind of negotiations.

The Israelis were simply not comfortable at all with the idea of 'negotiating under fire' or negotiating with the Palestinian Authority when they held that self same authority responsible for failing to curb or end Palestinian attacks on Israeli targets. The Israeli settler population – especially those political-religiously motivated to settle – were also fundamentally opposed to the Oslo Accords and the placing of settlements on the final status agenda. They united with the Israeli right-wing to round on the Rabin government and accused it of betrayal. These accusations grew and reverberated to the point that in 1995 an Israeli, Yigal Amir, assassinated Yitzhak Rabin at a peace rally in Tel Aviv. Rabin's son remarked a year later:

> I am not saying that the entire right wing was guilty of murder. But the right played a role in creating the atmosphere of incitement . . . But they did believe in the need to change a democratically elected government, claiming that it had acted against the people of Israel.
>
> (Frucht, 1998)

The Netanyahu era (1996–99), which included the negotiation of the Wye Agreement, seemed to reaffirm the opposition of many in Israel to the Oslo Accords. This caused a growing sense of unease about whether final status negotiations would ever take place.

Throughout this period the dynamic propelling peace between the Israelis and Palestinians often came from outside rather than internal actors (Ben Zvi, 1999; Aruri, 1999). The USA, under the Clinton administration, recognized that an opportunity for conflict resolution could be pushed through with their involvement. Though many believed this to be important in terms of keeping Israel in the game, others believed that the increasingly central role that America played was also detrimental in terms of the ultimate goal. They argued this in recognition of the asymmetric favouritism exhibited by the USA in favour of Israel. The European Union input to the process was important in terms of the funds for peace-building, nation-building and state-building processes that were considered an essential component for the conclusion of any peace process. In fact the European Union is the largest donor to the Palestinians, including the refugee community. Since the outbreak of the al-Aqsa Intifada in 2000 the European Union has given emergency support and aid for institution-building and reform.

The European Union, through membership of the Quartet for the Middle East Peace Process (MEPP), the offices of its Special Envoy to the MEPP, its Commissioner for External Relations, Common Foreign and Security Policy and agreements to promote peace through economic prosperity, also established alternative and complimentary processes for peace.

Other major aid and development institutions such as the World Bank have also funded measures designed to establish confidence-building measures, development and good governance in ways which are supposed to impact positively on the Israeli–Palestinian peace process. Development began to impact positively on both the Palestinian and Israeli economies. A 'strong Palestinian economy, delivering growth, and above all jobs', was considered 'a vital part of any beneficial political process', as it related to peacemaking (Roberts, 2006).

Camp David and the second Intifada

Despite the setbacks, tarrying, suicide bombs and closures, the middle to late 1990s delivered a series of agreements, memorandums and understandings (usually brokered by the USA) that were regarded as attempts to keep the peace process alive. The election in 1999 of former Israeli general Ehud Barak on the pro-peace Labour platform to Prime Minister raised the hearts of the liberal left and centre ground in Israel. Barak, however, wanted to pursue peace with Syria first, end Israel's occupation of Lebanon and then turn his attention to the Palestinian track (Bregman, 2005). Nevertheless there was a belief that the momentum for peace had been recovered and that with US support (Clinton's chance to go down in the history books as the peacemaking President) both sides could be pushed to reach a final peace deal. Throughout 1999 second-track negotiations between the two sides resulted in increased activities around the final status issues such as Jerusalem, security, refugees and the settlements. This was reinforced by the signing of the Sharm el-Sheikh Memorandum (SSM) by Ehud Barak and Yasser Arafat in September 1999. The SSM re-activated final status talks and timetabled their conclusion for September 2000.

When the final status negotiations were convened in Camp David in July 2000 it appeared that everyone had more to gain than to lose but, in the conflicting analysis that followed in the wake of the peace talks breaking down, it appeared that this was not the case. In the talks themselves there was progress on some issues but not the kind of progress that would have eventually led to a peace treaty. Israeli negotiators made proposals of the kind that had never been forthcoming from their side before. Negotiators did talk about final status issues – the talks were supposed to put the failures of the past behind the two parties (ignoring the obvious and deteriorating effects of the interim period and all the failures to build trust therein) and just go straight to the negotiation of a full peace treaty.

A new momentum for peace was being constructed but the failures and perils of recent attempts at peace-building were largely ignored in favour of the rush to make history. Those close to the process were keenly aware of the substantive asymmetry of capacity and skills to negotiate peace and to maintain a balance of power between the weaker Palestinians and the stronger Israelis. At pre-negotiations on Jerusalem, for example, the preparedness of the Israeli delegation and the resources at their fingertips gave them a starting advantage over their Palestinian counterparts. This pattern of negotiating behaviour would epitomize the talks at Camp David. The talks, however, broke down and the parties came away with nothing more than bitter recriminations, with the larger portion of blame placed on the Palestinians because they were unwilling to accept what Israel and its American supporters believed to be a 'most generous offer'.

Most, though by no means all, analysts of the talks agree that problems arose when it appeared that one side would have to concede more than the other. The problem was that it was the weaker party that was being asked to almost sacrifice itself on the altar of peace. The terms of the 'generous offer' included an Israeli proposal to return slightly more than 90 per cent of the West Bank to Palestinian hands, let the Palestinians have East Jerusalem as their capital, share control between them on the Haram al-Sharif (the third most holy site in Islam) and withdrawal from many (though not all) of the hundreds of illegal settlements and outposts that Israel had built in direct contravention of international law regarding occupying powers. On the issue of the 'right of return' of the Palestinian refugees who had been sitting in refugee camps since 1948 and 1967 there was an Israeli fudge. Yasser Arafat declined the terms arguing he could never sell them to the Palestinian people and in the wake of the talks the Israeli and American version of events led to a widespread belief that Arafat, therefore, was the chief villain of the piece because he was the one not willing to compromise.

Critics believed that Israel had offered reasonable terms for peace but as one of President Clinton's negotiators at the talks remarked, the real reason why the Palestinians rejected the Israeli proposal was that, 'strictly speaking there never really was an offer', and that at the end of the day Israel was not prepared to return the territories it had occupied since 1967 nor the city it had illegally annexed or allow the return of Palestinian refugees (Agha and Malley, 2001).

The failure at Camp David was not the end of the story. Some believed that amidst the recriminations and counter-recriminations there was still hope for a negotiated solution. Much of what had been discussed had never been discussed before and some sense of consensus on some issues had been achieved. The question was, however, would it be enough to get people back round the table and to what extent would external factors hinder this? The answer was that events did conspire to stymie the creation of an environment hospitable to renewed peace talks but the Palestinians and Israelis were persuaded back to talks nonetheless.

Between July and September 2000 the Israelis announced a series of measures, including more settlements, the construction of Jewish-only roads, and a refusal to withdraw their troops from Palestinian villages, which led to an increasing sense of hostility between the two sides. On 29 September that year the coup de grace by the Israelis was the decision by the Barak government to allow the right-wing Likud leader Ariel Sharon to visit the Muslim site of *Haram al-Sharif* in Jerusalem where the Dome of the Rock and al-Aqsa mosque are located. The proposed visit was deliberately provocative but, from the Israeli side, was said to be nothing more than a man exercising his democratic right to choose wherever he may go in his own country and its 'capital' city. For Palestinians the move was akin to Usama Bin Laden being allowed to visit the Western Wall. As one Palestinian official noted at the time, 'It will be the beginning of clashes between Israelis and Palestinians . . . if Sharon visits the Haram there will be a crisis and no one could control it . . . a serious crisis between Israel and the Palestinians' (Bregman, 2005, p. 125). Sharon pressed ahead with his visit and as he stood at the Haram al-Sharif declared: 'The Temple Mount [Haram al-Sharif] is in our hands and will remain in our hands' (Goldenberg, 2000). He was asserting a Jewish claim to sovereignty over a venerable Islamic site and the response to such a provocation were a series of Palestinian demonstrations in which Israeli forces killed four Palestinians and wounded over 200. The broadcast by global media of the blood-spattered holy site and pictures of the dead and wounded led to further protests, demonstrations and violence across the Palestinian territories and among Israel's Arab population. The second uprising had broken out.

The second Intifada and death of peace

A relapse to violence is not an uncommon outcome of attempts to make peace in the course of protracted and complex conflicts such as the Israeli–Palestinian one (Reychler, 2002). Many academics have examined the spiral of violence and the ebbs and flows of the expression of politics through shooting, shelling, bombing and killing in such conflicts. There are plenty of common platitudes about the path to peace never being smooth or easy and in the case of the Israeli–Palestinian conflict they seem to apply with unerring accuracy. Amidst the blood and victims, however, the international community renewed its efforts to keep the two sides looking at various options for peace and in some form of talks and negotiations. Thus between the outbreak of the second Intifada in September 2000 and the announcement in 2006 of a unilateral Israel proposal to begin to set final borders there were a variety of attempts to inch closer to peace and away from war (see Table 9.1).

Table 9.1 Israeli–Palestinian peace process 1993–2006

Date	Document	Details
September 1993	Declaration of Principles – Oslo Accords	Israel and PLO mutual recognition, Palestinian interim limited autonomy, final status issues agreed and timetable for negotiation.
April 1994	Paris Protocol	Economic accords between Israel and the Palestinians.
May 1994	Gaza Strip and Jericho Agreement	Israeli redeployment and assumption of Palestinian authority.
September 1995	Oslo II Interim Agreement	Interim agreement between Israel and the PLO on the West Bank and Gaza Strip.
January 1997	Hebron Redeployment Protocol	Agreement on Israeli redeployment in Hebron city, division of the city into areas of authority between Israel and the Palestinian Authority.
October 1998	The Wye River Memorandum	Agreement on phased Israeli redeployments, security, interim committees and economic issues, permanent status negotiations and desire to avoid unilateral actions.
September 1999	Sharm el-sheikh Memorandum	Agreement to timeline of mutual implementation of outstanding commitments signed since September 1993 and resumption of permanent status negotiations.
July 2000	Camp David Negotiations	Negotiations between Israel and the Palestinians on final status issues to conclude a peace treaty between the two sides. Broke down without agreement.
October 2000	Sharm el-Sheikh Agreement	Agreement to engage in bilateral security cooperation, Israel to curb restrictions on Palestinians, efforts by both sides to curb violence, and agreement to set a Commission to investigate the cause of violence and make recommendations.
December 2000 –January 2001	Clinton Parameters, Taba negotiations	Guidelines for final accelerated negotiations which followed between Israel and the Palestinians with US mediation in Taba, Egypt. Talks broke down with no agreement.
April 2001	Report of Sharm el-Sheikh Fact-finding Committee	Calls for immediate halt to violence from both sides, rebuild confidence and resume negotiations for peace.
June 2001	Tenet Plan	Security and Ceasefire Work Plan for security coordination and cooperation between Israel and the Palestinian Authority.

Table 9.1 (Continued)

Date	Document	Details
March 2002	Zinni Plan	Peace between Israel and the Palestinian Authority.
March 2002	Arab League Plan	Peace with Israel based on the principle of mutual recognition.
July 2002	Ayalon-Nusseibeh Statement of Principles	Two-state solution with borders based on 4 June 1967, settler evacuation from the Palestinian state, Jerusalem as capital of two states, Palestinian refugee return only to the state of Palestine, end of conflict and end of all claims.
April 2003	Performance-based Road Map to a permanent two-state solution to the Israeli–Palestinian conflict	A performance-based and goal-driven road map, with clear phases, timelines, target dates, and benchmarks aiming at progress through reciprocal steps by the two parties in the political, security, economic, humanitarian, and institution-building fields, under the auspices of the Quartet [the USA, European Union, United Nations, and Russia]. The destination is a final and comprehensive settlement of the Israel–Palestinian conflict by 2005.
October 2003	Palestinian–Israeli Geneva Accord	Two-state solution land for peace deal with borders set according to 4 June 1967. Mutual recognition and permanent status agreement, Jerusalem as capital of two states, settlements evacuated, land corridor for West Bank and Gaza Strip. Provision for refugee compensation and resettlement but not principally in Israel.

As the second Intifada waxed and waned in terms of occurrences of violence from both sides – including famous episodes such as: the Israeli killing of the 12-year-old boy, Mohammed Durra, the spates of Palestinian suicide bombings against Israeli civilian targets in cafes, buses, shopping centres and discos, Israeli-employed collective punishments and killings of Palestinian civilians, the policy of closure, the siege of Yasser Arafat's headquarters in Ramallah, the 'battle of Jenin', and the illegal construction of a wall around the Palestinian territories (Dolphin and Usher, 2006) – so too did attempts at finding routes from the spiral of violence to more peaceful and negotiated strategies. For the most part the most important initiatives to end violence through negotiated means came at the behest of outside actors as part of a strongly seated desire to keep the Oslo process alive. Such initiatives, which in common with conflicts across the globe focused on ending or managing violence in such a way as to remove or reduce civilian casualties, centred on issues to revive peace talks, support bilateral security coordination between Israel and the Palestinians and create monitoring mechanisms and audits of actions by both sides. In response to such initiatives both sides have engaged in activities which have been variously construed as having a positive or negative impact on the peace process (Milton-Edwards, 2005).

The first initiative to tackle the breakdown of the process in the wake of the outbreak of the second Intifada included the resumption of peace talks between Israel and the Palestinians and came in the dying days of the Clinton presidency in December 2000 (Clinton Parameters). Clinton was determined to try and get a final round of negotiations between the two sides before he left office in January 2001. Hence for one week in January 2001 everyone reconvened in the Egyptian resort of Taba and negotiated over the final status issues. Rumours emanating from the talks and an unofficial EU summary actually gave grounds for hope; that is until Ehud Barak decided to halt the diplomatic initiative and turn himself over to the Israeli electorate in a poll which by February 2001 saw him replaced by a new Prime Minister in the form of Ariel Sharon. Israel, under the leadership of Ariel Sharon, was steered away from any form of negotiated settlement of the conflict with the Palestinians.

Dubbed the 'Bulldozer' and regarded by many as the man responsible for war crimes in Lebanon that led to the Sabra and Shatilla massacre, Sharon disassociated himself from the Clinton Parameters and the Taba process, denounced the Palestinian leadership as failing in terms of providing a 'partner for peace', and succeeded in convincing much of global opinion in the wake of 9/11 that Arafat was Israel's Bin Laden. Amidst the change in political direction prompted by Sharon's uncompromising stand on the Palestinians others took the peace baton trying to revive hope amongst the increasingly hopeless sides to the conflict. In 2002 some heralded the decision by the members of the Arab League to endorse a Saudi initiative for peace, including recognition of Israel, as encouraging. But such decisions were almost stillborn in the wake of Sharon's re-occupation of the West Bank, the infamous 'battle of Jenin' and his siege of the Palestinian leader's headquarters in Ramallah.

Disengaging for peace?

In the absence of a 'partner for peace', Ariel Sharon was literally given a free rein to unilaterally determine his own two-state solution and impose it on the Palestinian 'non-partner'. Palestinian attempts to reduce or cease violence against Israel, such as the 2003 *hudna*, went unreciprocated by Israel (Milton-Edwards and Crooke, 2004). Hence the opportunity to create some breathing space, establish incremental trust and avoid the resort to violence, including attacks on civilians, was missed. In the wake of the announcement of a new peace initiative entitled 'A Performance-Based Road Map to a Permanent Two-State Solution to the Israeli–Palestinian Conflict' (2003) many were shocked at Sharon's announcement to carry on building the wall in the West Bank, to disengage from the Gaza Strip and a small number of settlements in the West Bank and to avoid substantive engagement with the Palestinians after they elected Mahmoud Abbas (Abu Mazen) as President of the PA in the wake of Yasser Arafat's death in November 2004.

In August 2005 Sharon pulled off his Gaza disengagement plan amidst protests from the settler community and others in Israel but with the full support and backing of the government of the USA. Some had concluded that the policy of the Bush administration in terms of the Israeli–Palestinian conflict was essentially determined by Sharon, 'the real consequence is that Prime Minister Sharon and his approach, unilateral actions, including removal of settlements and settlers, was the Bush administration's policy' (Miller, 2006). There certainly appeared to be a tendency to support Sharon in a way that would undermine earlier assurances by the administration to the government of Mahmoud Abbas. This has made it very difficult for Abbas to convince the Palestinian people that the international community is serious about a negotiated peace to the conflict.

The succession of Ehud Olmert, in the wake of an election called after Sharon fell into a coma, consolidated Israeli electoral support for the resort to a unilateral solution. Yet it appeared that Olmert's plan for unilateralism contained in the strangely termed 'convergence plan' was knocked off kilter in the summer of 2006 by the crisis that unfolded in the wake of the kidnapping of Israeli soldiers in the Gaza Strip and from across the 'Blue Line' by Hizbullah in Lebanon. The international community, moreover, had concluded that in the wake of the Hamas victory at the polls in January 2006, the Palestinians too had turned their back on some form of mutual recognition, land for peace, and negotiated settlement of the conflict. Hamas, which went on to form a government led by Ismail Haniyeh, had, since it was founded in 1988 rejected '[Peace] initiatives, and so-called peaceful solutions and international conferences . . . There is no solution for the Palestinian problem except by Jihad. Initiatives, proposals and international conferences are but a waste of time, an exercise in futility' (Hamas, 1988).

Palestinian President of the PA, Mahmoud Abbas, who had been described as one of the architects of the Oslo agreement, simply did not have enough support internally or externally to weigh-in on the side of his long-cherished principle that the conflict could only be solved through the negotiation of a two-state solution. The man of peace was surrounded on all sides by the nay-sayers and enemies of a negotiated solution.

By the summer of 2006, as the Hamas government continued to 'flout' or override their President, some believed it would only be a matter of time before the usefulness of this conduit for peace personified would disappear from the political arena. Moreover, with the absence of international recognition of the popularly elected Hamas government, after it refused a Quartet demand to renounce violence and recognize Israel, and the consequent cut of foreign aid and assistance to the Palestinian Authority, some commentators believed the Hamas government would only enjoy a short tenure and that states like the USA should assist in hastening their demise:

> Hamas's success poses such a threat to vital US interests that we should do everything possible to abort Hamas rule. We should do this as quickly and peacefully as circumstances allow. We should work both openly and clandestinely with allies and partners who share our concern.
>
> (Satloff, 2006)

The rocky road to peace

After more than a decade of peacemaking there was a consensus, despite the diplomatic rhetoric of certain actors, that if the mid-1990s had been epitomized by a hope that Palestinians and Israelis could build peace together then the present was characterized by a return to enmity and a deepening of the disconnection between the two peoples. That disconnection would be reinforced by Israeli unilateralism, which although it may have separated the people and created a partition of sorts, did nothing to achieve the kind of peace and security that would promote a generational settlement of the conflict. It was reinforced on the Palestinian side by the election of Hamas to power and its refusal to agree to Quartet demands to recognize Israel, halt violence and adhere to the terms of previously signed agreements.

Those in both camps who a decade earlier had striven to build peace through a myriad of people-to-people initiatives opined that in the present day, 'there is an unholy alliance and synchronicity of hostility by the government of Israel and Hamas against the peace camp on both sides' (Zananiri, 2006). The common ground for peace-building was now ablaze, even when people wanted to cross the barricade and engage with each other it often became impossible to get permits to meet in the same place, to get external funding for such dialogue, to truly establish a parity of esteem that would allow a grassroots momentum to build up enough steam to create pressure for change on the government of Israel or the government of the Palestinian authority. And yet, the majority of Palestinians and Israelis polled declared that they did want peace with their neighbours.

Credible attempts at peacemaking were thus hindered by developments on both sides of the Israeli–Palestinian divide. They were further undermined by a US mediator whose energies were dissipated by events elsewhere in the Middle East; namely Iraq. Nor did it seem possible to achieve peace so long as Israel, the USA and other international actors considered the presence of Hamas in any form of Palestinian government as unacceptable unless it recognized Israel. Hamas, for its part, courted international opinion hoping to open a split within the international community and thus create the momentum for their acceptance. This acceptance, it was believed, would lead to the end of sanctions against the PA. Some were led to conclude that the diplomatic horizon for the solution of the conflict was effectively obscured by the detrimental actions of both parties and ineffective American mediation.

Annapolis or bust

In 2007 the Israeli–US idea of a move to discussing the territorial, security and legal parameters of the Palestinian state was mooted. A fait accompli solution appeared to be the only way forward but once again it appeared to ignore the reality on the ground. Despite the repeated insistence of the Quartet members that the Road Map was alive and well and remained *the* only game in town it was hard to find evidence of either an Israeli or Palestinian buy-in.

Then, when it looked as if all hope might fade, the Hamas takeover of Gaza allowed the Palestinian President in Ramallah and his supporters to create a new opening for peace. Declaring the Hamas government illegitimate and freezing them from the political arena allowed the President to return to the diplomatic path that he had so long espoused. Israel announced that it would begin to release some of the Palestinian tax remittances that it had been holding from the Hamas government to the coffers of Abbas's Emergency government led by Salam Fayyad in Ramallah. The USA also came to believe that an opportunity for peace might be seized.

In the winter of 2007 the Americans thus called a summit meeting in Annapolis to devise a peace deal between Israel and the Palestinians. In the months ahead of the summit there were countless fears that the summit would fail in its principle task of conflict resolution.

The summit came in the wake of many earlier attempts to define the terms of lasting and sustainable peace between the two sides, including the Oslo Accords, the Clinton Parameters, the Taba Summit, the Arab League proposals, and international law. In large part these efforts had resulted in a sense that everyone (no matter how much it ill-behoves them) knows what a lasting peace deal requires.

There were palpable fears, however, that both sides would be persuaded to peace talks simply as an exercise in 'reinventing the wheel' with the prospect of a real peace settlement removed from the negotiations. Many also doubted that Israeli Prime Minister, Ehud Olmert, and PA President, Mahmoud Abbas, could actually reach peace terms with each other while they endured little in terms of domestic support at home. Such assessments relied on the Annapolis talks being a personal popularity contest rather than a mutually desired objective as expressed by the majority of Israelis and Palestinians in countless opinion polls. As if the political imperative for peace were not enough it was becoming apparent within Israel and the Palestinian territories that the recent descent into enmity was wreaking economic havoc on both societies. And while Israel, in comparison to the Palestinian territories, might have been inured from the worst excess of economic crisis, as a result of its wars with the Palestinians and their Arab neighbours, it was becoming apparent that the economy would not necessarily survive long-term war-footing and collapse in confidence when it came to private capital.

To be sure, the economic pressures on the Palestinians were calamitous. Many hoped that this might propel them to the peace talks and to sue for any form of peace that might in some way alleviate the pressures that had led to the breakdown of the rule of law and intense internal frictions within Palestinian society. The Palestinian business community has become desperate for peace and security to encourage capital into their society. More than 50 per cent of Palestinians in the West Bank and Gaza are aged 18 years and under, and nearly 50 per cent of Palestinians now live in poverty.

The peace 'spoilers' remain significant threats to negotiations and, if they are successful, their implementation. Spoilers exist on both sides of the conflict and include the right-wing settler groups of Israel, with their expanding projects in the West Bank and East Jerusalem, and Hamas and some rejectionist left-wing elements on the Palestinian side. Some even argue that the recent collapse of the

Palestinian nationalist camp also creates spoiler elements in a peace settlement. Yet failure, as the US government and others have acknowledged, may create unprecedented instability not just in the Israeli–Palestinian conflict but across the Middle East region and possibly the globe.

Hence national conflict over Palestine endures, with the claims of Israel and the Palestinians to the same territory remaining unresolved either as a result of a negotiated solution or a military victory. It is hard to say whether the involvement of a multiplicity of external actors in the conflict has further engendered difference or pushed the two sides closer to reconciliation. Clearly the peace formulas that have appeared to work in comparable national or ethnic conflicts such as Northern Ireland, South Africa or the former-Yugoslavia have not worked as well in the Israeli–Palestinian arena. Tailoring a solution has become almost a mission impossible.

Further reading

A wealth of accessible and readable resources exists on this period in the conflict and on the issues raised in connection with the peace process. Some of the material mentioned here will lead you to those sources that may act as a supplement to these issues. Other material will address different dimensions of the peace process, such as the political economy of peace, the role of non-governmental organizations and the enduring and yet pernicious influence of individual statesmen during this period of the conflict. There are many books, as I have noted above, that have covered this period. They include personal accounts from those at the heart of the peace negotiations, such as those by Beilin (New York: RVD Books, 2004), Ashrawi (New York: Touchstone Press, 1996) and the aforementioned books by former US President, Jimmy Carter (New York: Simon and Schuster, 2007) and the US's former special Middle East coordinator Dennis Ross (New York: Farrar, Straus and Giroux, 2004), and Miller (New York: Bantam Books, 2007).

'On-the-fringe' accounts from journalists and others on peacemaking include the BBC's Jane Corbin (Washington, DC: Atlantic Press, 1994), Bregman (Harmondsworth: Penguin Books, 2005) and Swisher (New York: Nation Books, 2004). Heribert and Moodley (London: UCL, 2005) and Jones (Manchester: Manchester University Press, 1999) provide incisive examination of peacemaking as it pertains to Israel and the Palestinians. Critiques of the process and accounts of events in the Oslo era include: Beinin and Stein (Stanford, CA: Stanford University Press, 2006), Roane and Shanin (New York: The New Press, 2002), Enderlin (New York: Other Press, 2003) and Reinhart (London: Verso, 2006). Helmick also offers a critique of US mediation efforts (London: Pluto Press, 2004) and in many senses the analysis can be contextualized by reading Enderlin's books on why peace is so difficult to bring to the region because of the failures pertaining to the Israeli–Palestinian conflict (New York: Other Press, 2003 and the 2007 sequel).

Ashrawi, H. (1996) *This side of peace: A personal account*, New York: Touchstone Press.

Beilin, Y. (2004) *The path to Geneva, the quest for a permanent agreement, 1996–2004*, New York: RDV Books.

Beinin, J. and Stein, R.L. (2006) *The struggle for sovereignty: Palestine and Israel 1993–2005*, Stanford, CA: Stanford University Press.

Bregman, A. (2005) *Elusive peace: How the Holy Land defeated America*, Harmondsworth: Penguin Books.

Carter, J. (2007) *Palestine: Peace not apartheid*, New York: Simon and Schuster.

Corbin, J. (1994) *The Norway channel: The secret talks that led to the Middle East peace accords*, Washington, DC: Atlantic Press.

Enderlin, C. (2003) *Shattered dreams. The failure of the peace process in the Middle East, 1995–2002*. Translated by Susan Fairfield. New York: Other Press.

—— (2007) *The lost years: Radical Islam, Intifada and wars in the Middle East, 2001–2006*. Translated by Susan Fairfield. New York: Other Press.

Helmick, R.G. (2004) *Negotiating outside the law: Why civil disobedience failed*, London: Pluto Press.

Heribert, A. and Moodley, K. (2005) *Seeking Mandela: Peacemaking between Israelis and Palestinians*, London: UCL.

Jones, D. (1999) *Cosmopolitan mediation? Conflict resolution and the Oslo Accords*, Manchester: Manchester University Press.

Miller, A. (2007) *The much-too promised land: America's elusive search for Arab–Israeli peace*, New York: Bantam Books.

Reinhart, T. (2006) *The Roadmap to nowhere: Israel–Palestine since 2003*, London: Verso.

Roane, C. and Shanin, J. (eds) (2002) *The other Israel: Voices of refusal and dissent*, New York: The New Press.

Ross, Dennis (2004) *The missing peace. The inside story of the fight for Middle East peace*, New York: Farrar, Straus and Giroux.

Swisher, Clayton (2004) *The truth about Camp David. The untold story about the collapse of the Middle East peace process*, New York: Nation Books.

Chronology

1516–1918   Ottoman (Turkish) Empire extends to include Palestine in its provinces.

1881–1903   Russian pogroms against Jews. First wave of Jewish immigration to Palestine known as *aliyah*.

1896–97   August: First Zionist Congress convened in Basle, Switzerland to promote the idea of a Jewish state. Publication of Theodor Herzl's *Der Judenstaat* [*The Jewish State*].

1904–28   Second and third waves of Jewish immigration to Palestine (mostly Soviet and Polish Jews) reflects the growing socialist-political form of Zionism.

1914–18   First World War. Britain makes incompatible commitments regarding future of Palestine in the Hussein–McMahon Correspondence (1915–16), Sykes–Picot Agreement (1916), and Balfour Declaration (1917).

1917   November: Balfour Declaration issued by the British government outlining a commitment to 'facilitate the establishment of a Jewish national home in Palestine' that was supposed to not forgo recognition of the rights of the existing population.

December: British General, Edmund Allenby, enters Jerusalem and accepts the surrender of the Turkish authorities, thus ending almost 1,300 years of Muslim rule in the territories of Palestine.

1919–23   US-sponsored King–Crane Commission informs Paris Peace Conference of Arab demands for independence. Newly created League of Nations gives Britain mandatory control of Palestine.

1922   Census of Palestine shows that 78 per cent of population is Muslim, 11 per cent is Jewish, 9.6 per cent is Christian.

1924–28   Fourth *aliyah* of Jews to Palestine. Rising Jewish immigration and land purchases supported by the British authorities.

1929   'Western Wall riots' between Palestinians and Zionists. Palestinians kill dozens of Jews in Hebron.

1933–35   Hitler achieves power in Germany. Germany's Nuremberg Laws make discrimination against Jews official. Fifth wave of immigration highest ever as Jews escape from Nazi power in Europe.

1936–39   The Palestinians organize a general strike which in turn leads to a revolt of some three years in duration; Palestinian agitation is against the increases in Jewish immigration and the partition proposal in the British White Paper of 1937. British proposed partition implied the division of Palestine into two states: one Palestinian Arab and the other Jewish. Arab revolt in Palestine: Britain crushes rebellion, expels or executes its leaders. Ever-increasing persecution of Jews in Germany.

1939   A new British proposal now argues for the establishment of one binational state in Palestine for Jews and Arabs; both sides reject the proposal. Jewish immigration and land purchases are subject to restriction by British order. Jews now comprise 31 per cent of Palestine's inhabitants.

1939–45   Second World War in Europe. Holocaust: Nazi's regime responsible for death of approximately 6 million Jews (the Shoah).

1942   The World Zionist Organization demands the establishment of a Jewish state in Palestine and the lifting of British-imposed immigration quotas.

1945   United Nations established. Second World War ends, leaving more than 100,000 European Jews in camps for 'displaced persons'.

1946   The Zionist Irgun group detonate a bomb in British Mandate headquarters in the King David Hotel in Jerusalem.

1947   Britain turns over the issue of Palestine and its future to the United Nations. In a vote in November 1947 the Assembly General of the United Nations adopts UN Resolution 181 proposing the partition of Palestine into two separate states (Jewish 57 per cent of Palestine) and Arab (43 per cent of Palestine) with Jerusalem subject to international authority.

1947–48   Zionist militant forces mount attacks on Palestinian villages. Some 370 villages are 'abandoned' in the wake of massacres such as that of Deir Yassin in April 1948.

1948   April: Britain ends its mandate and withdraws its officials.
May: Israel declares independence; Arab states at war with Israel.

1948–58   Large-scale Jewish immigration to Israel from Europe, North Africa and Asia.

1950   Israeli Law of Return and Absentee Property Law enacted; extensive confiscation of Arab property.

1956–57   Suez War begins; Israel supported by Britain and France.

1964   Egypt and other Arab states establish Palestine Liberation Organization (PLO).

1967   June: Six-Day War involving Israel, Egypt, Jordan and Syria; Israel occupies West Bank, Gaza Strip, Egyptian Sinai and Syrian Golan Heights, expands Jerusalem boundaries and extends Israeli law over East Jerusalem; UN Security Council Resolution 242 calls for withdrawal of Israeli troops from territories newly occupied.

1968	First settlement established in Hebron by Rabbi Moshe Levinger.
1970	September: Civil war between Palestinians and Jordanian army. At the end of the war, PLO is expelled from Jordan.
1973	October: Yom Kippur/Ramadan War with Egypt, Syria and Israel as chief combatants; UN Security Council resolution calls for cease-fire and comprehensive peace conference; oil embargo by Arab petroleum-exporting countries.
1974	Arab League declares PLO the sole legitimate representative of Palestinian people. PLO chairman Yasser Arafat addresses United Nations which grants PLO observer status in 1975.
1976	Pro-PLO candidates contest and win Palestinian municipal elections in the West Bank.
1977	Likud wins Israeli elections, Menachem Begin becomes Prime Minister. Egyptian President, Anwar Sadat, visits Jerusalem and addresses the Israeli Knesset.
1978	Israeli invasion of southern Lebanon.
1979	Israeli–Egyptian Peace Treaty signed.
1980	Israel's Basic Law on Jerusalem annexes East Jerusalem.
1982	Israeli invasion of Lebanon; PLO forced from Beirut; massacre at Sabra and Shatilla refugee camps.
1985	Israel withdraws from most of Lebanon; southern Lebanon remains occupied.
1987	Outbreak of the first Intifada against Israel by the Palestinians.
1988	Jordan announces disengagement from West Bank. PLO unilateral declaration of independence; USA recognizes the PLO.
1990	Iraq invades Kuwait; Palestinians support Saddam Hussein.
1991	Arab–Israeli Peace Conference in Madrid includes Palestinians in joint Jordanian–Palestinian delegation.
1992	Labour Party wins Israeli elections; Yitzhak Rabin becomes Prime Minister on pro-peace ticket. Hamas and Islamic Jihad deportations to south Lebanon.
1993	Declaration of Principles (Oslo Accords) signed between Israel and the PLO, interim self-government and timetable for final status negotiations.
1994	Hebron massacre; Hamas suicide bombs in Israel. Yasser Arafat establishes Palestinian Authority headquarters in Gaza. Israel and Jordan sign peace treaty.
1995	Oslo II Accords establish three types of control in the West Bank (Area A: direct Palestinian control, Area B: Palestinian civilian control and Israeli security control, Area C: Israeli control). Israeli Prime Minister, Yitzhak Rabin, is assassinated by pro-settler Israeli.
1996	Palestinians hold presidential and legislative elections. Palestinian suicide bombings in Jerusalem and Tel Aviv. Israeli 'Grapes of Wrath' operation against Lebanon. Binyamin Netanyahu elected Israeli Prime Minister.

1997	Israel begins settlement-building at Har Homa between East Jerusalem and Bethlehem.
1998	Wye River Memorandum; PLO renounces anti-Israel clauses in PLO charter.
1999	Ehud Barak elected Israeli Prime Minister. Sharm el Sheikh Memorandum.
2000	Camp David peace negotiations. Ariel Sharon visits the Haram al-Sharif in Jerusalem. Outbreak of al-Aqsa Intifada
2001	Taba negotiations.
2002	Operation Defensive Shield conducted by Israel. Palestinian suicide bombings and Israeli 'targeted killings' continue. Arab League meeting in Beirut issues plan for peace with Israel. Road Map for peace in the Middle East issued by the Quartet.
2004	President Yasser Arafat dies.
2005	Mahmoud Abbas (Abu Mazen) elected President of the Palestinian Authority. Israeli troops and settlers withdrawn from Gaza.
2006	Hamas win majority of seats in popular elections to the Palestinian Legislative Council. Hamas forms a government. Israel, the USA and the European Union announce complete boycott of the Hamas government. General elections in Israel return Ehud Olmert the leader of the right-centrist Kadima Party as Prime Minister and a national unity government is formed.
2007	March: Palestinian National Unity Government (NUG) sworn in uniting Fatah and Hamas plus independents in government.
	June: The NUG falls apart after a Hamas takeover in the Gaza Strip. From his headquarters in Ramallah Palestinian President, Mahmoud Abbas, declares the formation of an emergency government headed by Salam Fayyad.
	November: Israeli and Palestinian peace talks are held for the first time in seven years.

Bibliography

Abdallah, S.L. (1995) Palestinian women in the camps of Jordan, *Journal of Palestine Studies*, vol. 34: 3 (Summer), pp. 62–72.

Abed Rabbo, Y. (2006) Speech at meeting of IPCRI, Jerusalem, 21 June.

Abu Manneh, B. (1990) Jerusalem in the Tanzimat period: The Ottoman administration and the notables, *Die Welt des Islames*, vol. 30: 1, pp. 1–44.

Abu Mohammad, (1993) interview with author, Nussierat camp, Gaza Strip, 5 September.

Aburish, S. (1991) *Children of Bethany, the story of a Palestinian family*, London: Bloomsbury.

—— (1999) *Arafat: From defender to dictator*, London: Bloomsbury.

Abu Sief*, (1994) Interview with author, Nablus, October. (*This is a pseudonym.)

Abu Zayyad, Z. (1994) The Palestinian right of return: A realistic approach, *Palestine-Israel Journal*, 2 (Spring), pp. 74–78.

Adam, H. and Moodley, K. (2005) *Seeking Mandela: Peacemaking between Palestinians and Israelis*, Philadelphia, PA: Temple University Press.

Adwan, A. (2003) A history of displacement, Islamonline debate, 25 June. Online: www.islamonline.net/livedialogue/english/Browse.asp?hGuestID = mVxe30, accessed 20 November 2006.

Agha, H. and Malley, R. (2001) Camp David: The tragedy of errors, *New York Review of Books*, vol. 48: 13, 9 August.

Ajluni, S. (2003) Palestinian economy and the second Intifada, *Journal of Palestine Studies*, vol. 32: 3 (Spring), pp. 64–73.

Al-Mawed, H.S. (2000) The Palestinian refugees in Syria: Their past, present and future, *Expert and Advisory Services Fund–International Development Research Centre*, Magill University. Online: http://www.arts.mcgill.ca/MEPP/PRRN/al-mawed.pdf.

Amayreh, K. (2004) Balfour renewed, *Al-Ahram*, No. 686, 15–21 April.

Amiry, S. (2005) *Sharon and my mother-in-law*, London: Granta Books.

Anderson, B. (1991) *Imagined communities: Reflections on the origin and spread of nationalism*, London: Verso.

Anglo-American Committee of Inquiry (AAIC) (1946) *A survey of Palestine*, Jerusalem: Government Printer of Palestine.

Anti-Defamation League (ADL) (2006) Online: www.adl.org/international/Israel-UN-2-background.asp

Arafat, Y. (2004) Interview with author, al-Muqata Ramallah, 5 July.

Arian, A. (1989) *Politics in Israel, the second generation*, Chatham, NJ: Chatham House Publishers.

—— (1997) *The Second Republic: Politics in Israel.* Chatham, NJ: Chatham House Publishers.

Aronson, G. (1987) *Creating facts: Israel, Palestinians and the West Bank*, Washington, DC: Institute of Palestine Studies.

—— (1995) Rabin assassination places settler extremists in international spotlight, *Settlement Report*, vol. 5: 6 (November).

Aruri, Nasser H. (1999) The Wye Memorandum: Netanyahu's Oslo and unreciprocal reciprocity, *Journal of Palestine Studies*, vol. 28: 2, pp. 17–28.

—— (2003) *Dishonest broker: The US role in Israel and Palestine*, Cambridge, MA: South End Press.

—— (2007) 40 years of Israeli occupation and the prospects for peace, *Vancouver Radio*, 26 March.

Arzt, Donna E. (1997) *Refugees into citizens: Palestinians and the end of the Arab–Israeli conflict*, New York: Council on Foreign Relations.

Ashrawi, H. (1996) *This side of peace: A personal account*, New York: Touchstone Press.

Avineri, S. (1981) *The making of modern Zionism: Intellectual origins of the Jewish state*. New York: Wiedenfeld.

Avishai, B. (1985) *The tragedy of Zionism: Revolution and democracy in the land of Israel*. New York: Farrar, Straus and Giroux.

—— (2002) *Tragedy of Zionism: How its revolutionary past haunts Israeli deomocracy*, New York: Allworth Press.

Avner Yaniv (ed.) (1993) *National security and democracy in Israel*, London: Lynne Rienner.

Avnery, U. (2005) King George: The USA sinking to new depths of ugliness and brutality. Online: www.redress.btinternet.co.uk, accessed 21 May 2007.

—— (2007) 40 bad years, *Gush Shalom*. Online: http://zope.gush-shalom.org/home/en/channels/avnery/1181338783, accessed 9 June 2007.

Barari, A.H. (2004) *Israeli politics and the Middle East Peace Process 1988–2002*, London: Routledge.

Barbour, N. (1946) *Nisi Dominus, a survey of the Palestine controversy*, London: G.G. Harrap.

Barghouti, M. (2003) Foreword. In Stolhman, N. and Aladin, L. (eds) *Live from Palestine: International and Palestinian direct action against the Israeli occupation*, New York: South End Press.

Beilin, Y. (1992) *Israel: A concise political history*, New York: St Martin's Press.

—— (2004) *The path to Geneva, the quest for a permanent agreement, 1996–2004*, New York: RDV Books.

Beinin, J. (2004) No more tears: Benny Morris and the road back from liberal Zionism, *MERIP*, No. 230. Online: www.merip.org/mer/mer230/mer230.html, accessed 6 June 2007.

Beinin, J. and Lockman, Z. (eds) (1990) *Intifada: Palestinian uprising against Israeli occupation*, London: I.B. Tauris.

Beinin, J. and Stein, R.L. (2006) *The struggle for sovereignty: Palestine and Israel 1993–2005*, Stanford, CA: Stanford University Press.

Beit-Hallahmi, B. (1992) *Original sins: Reflections on the history of Zionism and Israel*, Concord, MA: Pluto Press; reprint, New York: Olive Branch Press, 1993.

Ben-Ami, S. (2006) *Scars of war, wounds of peace. The Israeli–Arab tragedy*, New York; Oxford University Press.

Ben Gurion, D. (1947) Statement to the elected assembly of Palestine Jews. Online: www.mideastweb.org/bg1947.htm, accessed 3 April 2007.

Ben-Rafael, E. and Sharot, S. (2007) *Ethnicity, religion and class in Israeli society*, Cambridge: Cambridge University Press.

Bentwich, N. and Bentwich, H. (1965) *Mandate memories 1918–1948*, London: Hogarth Press.

Ben Zvi, A. (1999) *The US and Israel: The Netanyahu era*, Tel Aviv: JCSS.

Besant, W. and Palmer, E.H. (1899) *Jerusalem – the city of Herod and Saladin*, 2nd edn, London: Chatto & Windus.

Bishara, M. (2002) *Palestine/Israel: Peace or apartheid. Occupation, terrorism and the future*, 2nd edn, London: Zed Books.

Black, E. (2004) *Banking on Baghdad*, New York: Wiley.

Bligh, A. (2003) *The Israeli Palestinians, an Arab minority in the Jewish state*, London: Taylor and Francis.

Bouillon, M. (2004) *The peace business: Money and power in the Palestine–Israel conflict*, London: I.B. Tauris.

Bowden, T. (1977) *Breakdown of public security: The case of Ireland 1919–21 and Palestine 1936–39*, London: Sage.

Bowker, R. (2003) *Palestinian refugees: Mythology, identity, and the search for peace*, Boulder, CO: Lynne Rienner.

Bowle, J. (1957) *Viscount Samuel: a biography*, London: Victor Gollancz.

Brand, B. (1998) *Palestinian in the Arab world: Institution-building and the search for state*, New York: Columbia University Press.

Bregman, A. (2005) *Elusive peace: How the Holy Land defeated America*, Harmondsworth: Penguin Books.

Brown, N.B. (2003) *Palestinian politics after the Oslo Accords: Resuming Arab Palestine*, Berkeley, CA: University of California Press.

Brynen, R. (2000) *A very political economy: Peacebuilding and foreign aid in the West Bank and Gaza*, Herndon, VA: USIP Press.

Burge, G.M. (2005) Theological and biblical assumptions of Christian Zionism. In Ateek, N., Duaybis, C. and Tobin, M. (eds) *Challenging Christian Zionism, theology, politics and the Israel–Palestine conflict*, London: Melisende.

Burston, B. (2007) Israel needs a new anthem, one that Arabs can sing, *Haaretz*, 18 March. Online: www.haaretz.com/hasen/spages/838984.html, accessed 18 March 2007.

Bush, G. (2001) Speech to the American Jewish Committee, 3 May. Online: www.jewish-virtuallibrary.org/jsource/US-Israel/presquote.html, accessed 20 May 2007.

—— (2004) Address, 14 April. Online: http://domino.un.org/UNISPAL.NSF/2ee9468747556b2d85256cf60060d2a6/4351626d2958c32885256e7700659f04!OpenDocument, accessed 9 April 2008.

Carey, R. (ed.) (2001) *The new Intifada: Resisting Israel's apartheid*, London: Verso.

Carter, J. (2007) *Palestine: Peace not apartheid*, New York: Simon and Schuster.

Catignani, S. (2005) The security imperative in counter-terrorist operations: The Israeli fight against suicidal terror, *Terrorism and Political Violence*, vol. 17: 1–2, pp. 245–64.

Chatty, D. and Hundt, G.L. (eds) (2005) *Children of Palestine: Experiencing forced migration in the Middle East*, London: Berghahn Books.

Christison, K. (2001) *Perceptions of Palestine: Their influence on US Middle East Policy*, Berkeley, CA: University of California Press.

Civic heads (n.d.) British White Paper on Palestine 1939. Online: www.civicwebs.com/cwvlib/constitutions/gb/e_palestine_brit_white_paper_1939.htm, accessed 5 April 2008.

CNN (2002) Arab summit adopts Saudi peace initiative, *CNN*, 28 March. Online: http://transcripts.cnn.com/2002/WORLD/meast/03/28/arab.league/index.html, accessed June 8 2006.

Cohen, M. (1978) *Palestine: Retreat from the Mandate: The making of British policy 1936–45*, London: Paul Elek.

—— (1979) The Moyne assassination, November 1944: A political analysis, *Middle Eastern Studies*, October, pp. 358–73.

—— (1988) *Palestine to Israel: From mandate to independence*, London: Frank Cass.

Collins, L. and Lapierre, D. (1972) *O Jerusalem! Day by day and minute by minute the historic struggle for Jerusalem and the birth of Israel*, New York: Simon and Schuster.

Colonial Office. Reports CO733/1939; CO733/398/11 1939. Public Records Office, Kew.

Cook, J. (2006) *Blood and religion: The unmasking of the Jewish and democratic state*, London: Pluto.

Corbin, J. (1994) *The Norway channel: The secret talks that led to the Middle East peace accord*, Washington, DC: Atlantic Press.

Cordesman, A. (2005) *The Israeli–Palestinian war: Escalating to nowhere*, Washington, DC: Praeger.

Crick, B. (1990) The high price of peace. In Giliomee, H. and Gagiano, J. (eds) *The elusive search for peace*, Oxford: Oxford University Press.

Dajani, R. (2006) The Gaza crisis. Online: http://ga3.org/btvshalom/notice-description. tcl?newsletter_id = 3518540#5, accessed 18 July 2006.

Darby, J. (2001) *The effects of violence on peace processes*, Washington, DC: USIP.

Darwish, M. (2000) *The Adam of two Edens*, New York: Syracuse University Press.

Dimbleby, J. and McCullin, D. (1979) *The Palestinians*, London: Quartet.

Dolphin, R. and Usher, G. (2006) *The West Bank wall: Unmaking Palestine*, London: Pluto Press.

Eldar, E. (2006) Ministry admits 'blacklist' of Palestinians who left W. Bank, *Haaretz*, 5 July.

Ellis, M. (1989) *Toward a Jewish theology of liberation: The uprising and the future*, 2nd edn, Maryknoll, NY: Orbis Books.

—— (2002) *Israel and Palestine out of the ashes: The search for Jewish identity in the twenty-first century*, London: Pluto Press.

Enderlin, C. (2003) *Shattered dreams. The failure of the peace process in the Middle East, 1995–2002*. Translated by Susan Fairfield. New York: Other Press.

—— (2007) *The lost years: Radical Islam, Intifada and wars in the Middle East, 2001–2006*. Translated by Susan Fairfield. New York: Other Press.

Evron, B. (1995) *Jewish state or Israeli nation?* Bloomington, IN: Indiana University Press.

Fanon, F. (1969) *Black skin, white masks*, New York: Grove Press.

Farsoun, S.K. with Zacharia, C.E. (1997) *Palestine and the Palestinians*, Boulder, CO: Westview Press.

Finkelstein, N.G. (2001) *The Holocaust industry: Reflections on the exploitation of Jewish suffering*, London: Verso.

—— (2003) *Image and reality of the Israel–Palestine conflict*, 2nd edn, London: Verso.

Fischbach, M.R. (2003) *Records of dispossession: Palestinian refugee property and the Arab–Israeli conflict*, New York: Columbia University Press.

Fisk, R. (1990) *Pity the nation: Lebanon at war*, Oxford: Oxford University Press.

—— (2006) *The great war for civilization: The conquest of the Middle East*, London: Vintage.

Flapan, S. (1987) *The birth of Israel: Myths and realities*, New York: Pantheon Books.

Francis, D.R. (2002) Economist tallies swelling cost of Israel to the US, *Christian Science Monitor*, 9 December. Online: www.csmonitor.com/2002/1209/p16s01-wmgn.html, accessed 6 June 2006.

Frantzman, S. (2007) Ethnic cleansing in Palestine? *Jerusalem Post*, 17 August.

Freedman, R.O. (1998) *The Middle East and the peace process: The impact of the Oslo Accords*, Gainesville, FL: University Press of Florida.

Friedman, Robert (1992) *Zealots for Zion: Inside Israel's West Bank settlement movement*, New York: Random House.

Frucht, L.E. (1998) From father to son, *Jerusalem Post*. Online: http://info.jpost. com/1998/Supplements/Rabin/7.html, accessed 8 April 2007.

Garfinkle, A. (2002) *Politics and society in modern Israel: Myths and realities*, New York: M.E. Sharpe.

Gazit, S. (1995) *The Palestinian refugee problem*, Final Status Issues Study No. 2, Tel Aviv: Jaffee Centre for Strategic Studies.

Gelber, Y. (2006) *Palestine 1948. War, escape and the emergence of the Palestinian refugee problem*, Brighton: Sussex Academic Press.

George, A. (2005) *Jordan, living in the crossfire*, London: Zed Books.

Gerber, H. (1986) A new look at the *Tanzimat*: The case of the province of Jerusalem. In Kushner, D. (ed.) *Palestine in the late Ottoman period*, Jerusalem: Yad Izhak Ben-Zvi.

Gerner, D. (1994) *One land, two peoples: The conflict over Palestine*, Boulder, CO: Westview Press.

Gilmour, D. (1980) *Dispossessed: The ordeal of the Palestinians 1917–80*, London: Sidgwick & Jackson.

Ginsberg, A. (1897) Online: www.zionismontheweb.org/stateproblem.htm, accessed 10 May 2006.

Gold, D. (2002) From 'occupied territories' to 'disputed territories', *Viewpoints*, No. 470, Jerusalem: JCPA.

Goldenberg, Suzanne (2000) Rioting as Sharon visits Islam holy site, *The Guardian*, 29 September. Online: www.guardian.co.uk/israel/Story/0,2763,374838,00.html

Goldschneider, C. (ed.) (1995) *Population, ethnicity, and nation-building*, Boulder CO: Westview Press.

Gorenberg, G. (2006) *The accidental empire: Israel and the birth of the settlements, 1967–1977*, New York: Henry Holt and Co.

Gowers, A. and Walker, T. (2005) *Arafat: The biography*, London: Virgin Books.

Grandahl, M. (2003) *In hope and despair: Life in the Palestinian refugee camps*, Cairo: AUC Press.

Grossman, D. (2003) *Death as a way of life: Israel ten years after Oslo*. Translated by Haim Watzman. New York: Farrar, Straus and Giroux.

Guyatt, Nicholas (1999) *The absence of peace. Understanding the Israeli Palestinian conflict*, London: Zed Books.

Haaretz, (2007) The Right of Return: Real hope or deal-breaker?, *Haaretz*, 13 June 2007.

Haas, A. (2000) *Drinking the sea at Gaza: Days and nights in a land under siege*, New York: Owl Books.

Hadawi, S. (1998) *Bitter harvest: A modern history of Palestine*, Northampton, MA: Interlink Publishing.

Haddad, S. (2000) The Palestinian predicament in Lebanon, *Middle East Quarterly*, vol. 7: 3, pp. 29–39.

Halpern, B. and Reinharz, J. (2000) *Zionism and the creation of a new society*, Oxford: Oxford University Press.

Hamas (1988) *Hamas Covenant*. Online: www.yale.edu/lawweb/avalon/mideast/hamas. htm, accessed 3 November 2006.

Hammami, R. and Tamari, S. (2000) Anatomy of another rebellion, *Middle East Report*, No. 217, Winter, pp. 2–15.

Hamzeh, M. (2003) Torching the right of return, *al-Ahram*, No. 646, 10–16 July.

Hazony, Y. (2000) *The Jewish state: The struggle for Israel's soul*, New York: Basic Books.

Helmick, R.G. (2004) *Negotiating outside the law: Why civil disobedience failed*, London: Pluto Press.

Heribert, A. and Moodley, K. (2005) *Seeking Mandela: Peacemaking between Israelis and Palestinians*, London: UCL.

Hertzberg, A. (1997) *The Zionist idea: A historical analysis and reader*, New York: Jewish Publication Society of America.

Herzl, T. (1896) *Der Judenstaat*. Online: www.jewishvirtuallibrary.org, accessed 8 May 2006.

—— (2006) *The Jewish State*, New York: Filiquarian Publishing.

Hirst, D. (2003) *The gun and the olive branch: The roots of violence in the Middle East*, 3rd edn, New York: Nation Books.

Horovitz, David (2000) *A little too close to God: The thrills and panic of a life in Israel*, New York: A. A. Knopf.

Hourani, A. (2003) *A history of the Arab people*, Cambridge, MA: Harvard University Press.

Huggler, J. and Reeves, S. (2002) What really happened in Jenin? *The Independent*, 25 April.

Hutchinson, J. (2004) Myth against myth: Nation as ethnic overlay, *Nations and Nationalism*, vol. 10: 1–2, pp. 109–23.

Inbar, E. (1996) Contours of Israel's new strategic thinking, *Political Science Quarterly*, vol. 111: 1, pp. 41–64.

Ingrams, D. (1973) *Palestine Papers 1917–1922: Seeds of conflict*, New York: George Braziller.

Jannaway, F.G. (n.d.) *Palestine and the world*, London: Sampson Low, Marston and Co., Ltd.

Jones, C. (1999) Israel's democracy at fifty: from resilience to residue? In Burnell, P. and Calvert, P. (eds) *The resilience of democracy: Persistent practice, durable idea*, London: Routledge.

Jones, C. and Murphy, E. (2002) *Israel: Challenges to identity, democracy and the state*, London: Routledge.

Jones, D. (1999) *Cosmopolitan mediation? Conflict resolution and the Oslo Accords*, Manchester: Manchester University Press.

Jouejati, M. (2002) The Arab summit: Arab unity, Israeli opportunity? *Middle East Institute*, Policy Brief. Online: www.mideasti.org/articles/doc46.html, accessed June 8 2006.

Judt, T. (2003) Israel: The alternative, *New York Review of Books*, vol. 50: 6, 23 October.

Kanaana, S. (1998) Patterns of exodus, *Our Voice*, September (via Birzeit University).

Kanafani, G. (1972) *The 1936–39 revolt in Palestine*, New York: Committee for Democratic Palestine. Online: www.newjerseysolidarity.org/resources/kanafani/kanafani4.html, accessed 22 May 2006.

Kariv, G. (2006) Online: www.glbtjews.org/article.php3?id_article = 314, accessed 23 May 2006.

Karmi, G. (2001) *In search of Fatima, a Palestinian story*, London: Verso.

Keating, M., Le More, A. and Lowe, R. (2005) *Aid, diplomacy, and the facts on the ground: The Palestinian experience of disconnection*, London: RIIA.

Kershner, I. (2007) Noted Arab citizens call on Israel to shed Jewish identity, *New York Times*, 8 February, p. 3.

Khalidi, R. (1998) *Palestinian identity: The construction of modern national consciousness*, New York: Columbia University Press.

Khalidi, W. (1987) *From haven to conquest: Readings in Zionism and the Palestine problem until 1948*, Washington, DC: Institute of Palestine Studies.

Khashan, H. (1994) *Palestinian resettlement in Lebanon: Behind the debate*, Montreal: Montreal Studies on the Contemporary Arab World.

Kimche, J. (1968) *The unromantics, the Great Powers and the Balfour Declaration*, London: Weidenfeld and Nicolson.

Kimmerling, B. (1982) Change and continuity in Zionist territorial orientations and politics, *Comparative Politics*, vol. 14: 2, pp. 191–210.

—— (1999) Religion and nationalism and democracy in Israel, *Constellations*, vol. 6: 3, pp. 339–64.

—— (2001) *The invention and the decline of Israeliness, state, society and the military*, Berkeley, CA: University of California Press.

Kimmerling, B. and Migdal, J.S. (1993) *Palestinians, the making of a people*, New York: The Free Press.

—— (2003) *The Palestinian people: A history*, Cambridge, MA: Harvard University Press.

Kook, Rabbi A. (18xx) *Orot*. Online: www.orot.com/lights.html, accessed 5 May 2006.

Kushner, Tony and Solomon, Alisa (eds) (2003) *Wrestling with Zion: Progressive Jewish–American responses to the Israeli–Palestinian conflict*, New York: Grove Publishing.

Lampman, J. (2004) Mixing prophecy and politics, *The Christian Science Monitor*, 7 July.

Laqueur, W. (2003) *A history of Zionism: From the French revolution to the establishment of the state of Israel*, New York: Schocken.

Laqueur, W. and Rubin, B. (eds) (2001) *The Israel–Arab reader: A documentary history of the Middle East conflict*, New York: Penguin Books.

Lazaroff, T. (2006) Descendants of Hebron Jews divided over city's fate, *The Jerusalem Post*, 17 May, p. 3.

Lederach, J.P. (2003) *The little book of conflict transformation*, New York: Good Books.

Lerner, H. (2004) Constitutionalism and identity: the anomaly of the Israeli case, *Constellations*, vol. 11: 2, pp. 237–58.

Levitt, M. (2004) Hamas from cradle to grave, *The Middle East Quarterly*, vol. XI: 1, (Winter). Online: www.meforum.org/article/582, accessed 21 June 2006.

Levy, A. (ed.) (2002) *Jews, Turks and Ottomans, a shared history, fifteenth through twentieth century*, Syracuse: Syracuse University Press.

Levy, G. (2003) The IDFs chorus of incitement, *Haaretz*, 23 October.

Louer, L. (2007) *To be an Arab in Israel*, New York: Columbia University Press.

Lustick, I. (1988) *For the land and the lord: Jewish fundamentalism in Israel*, New York: CFR.

—— (1993) *Unsettled states, disputed lands: Britain and Ireland, France and Algeria, Israel and the West Bank/Gaza*, Ithaca, NY: Cornell University Press.

Macalister, R.A.S. (1912) *A history of civilization in Palestine*, Cambridge: Cambridge University Press.

McDowall, D. (1989) *Palestine and Israel: The uprising and beyond*, London: I.B. Tauris.

McGarry, J. and O'Leary, B. (1993) *The politics of ethnic conflict regulation: Case studies of protracted ethnic conflict*, London: Routledge.

Maiese, M. (2003) *Dehumanization*. Online: www.beyondintractability.org/essay/dehumanization, accessed 19 July 2006.

March, W. Eugene (1994) *Israel and the politics of land: A theological case study*, Louisville, KY: Westminster/John Knox Press.

Masalha, N. (1992) *Expulsion of the Palestinians, the concept of 'transfer' in Zionist political thought, 1882–1948*, Washington, DC: Institute of Palestine Studies.

—— (2003) *The politics of denial, Israel and the Palestinian refugee problem*, London: Pluto Press.

Mattar, P. (1988) *Mufti of Jerusalem: Al-Hajj Amin al-Husayni and the Palestinian national movement*, Washington, DC: Diane Publishers and Co.

Mearsheimer, J. and Walt, S. (2006) The Israel lobby, *London Review of Books*, vol. 28: 6, March 23. Online: www.lrb.co.uk/v28/n06/print/mear01_html, accessed April 2, 2006.

—— (2007) *The Israel lobby and US foreign policy*, London: Allen Lane.

Meranda, A. (2007) Majadele refuses to sing national anthem, *YNET news*. Online: www.ynetnews.com/articles/0,7340,L-3377681,00.html, accessed March 20, 2007.

Metzger, J. (1984) *This land is our land: West Bank under occupation*, London: Zed Books.

Miller, A. (2005) Israel's lawyer, *The Washington Post*, 23 May, p. A19.

—— (2006) Quoted transcript. Online: www.cbsnews.com/stories/2006/01/06/opinion/diplomatic/main1184706.shtml, accessed 17 July 2006.

—— (2007) *The much-too promised land: America's elusive search for Arab–Israeli peace*, New York: Bantam Books.

Milton-Edwards, B. (1992) The concept of jihad and the Palestinian Islamic movement: A comparison of ideas and techniques, *British Journal of Middle Eastern Studies*, vol. 19: 1, pp. 48–53.

—— (1996) Political Islam in an environment of peace? *Third World Quarterly*, vol. 17: 2, pp. 199–225.

—— (1999) *Islamic politics in Palestine*, London: I.B. Tauris.

—— (2005) Losing peace in the Middle East: The Palestinian crisis, *International Politics*, vol. 42: 3, pp. 37–65.

—— (2006) *Contemporary politics in the Middle East*, 2nd edn, Cambridge: Polity Press.

Milton-Edwards, B. and Crooke, A. (2004) Waving not drowning. Strategic dimensions of ceasefires and Islamic movements, *Security Dialogue*, vol. 35: 3, pp. 295–310.

Milton-Edwards, B. and Hinchcliffe, P. (2007) *Jordan: A Hashemite legacy*, 3rd edn, London: Routledge.

—— (2003) *Conflicts in the Middle East since 1945*, 2nd edn, London: Routledge.

Mitchell Report (2001) Online: http://news.bbc.co.uk/1/hi/in_depth/middle_east/2001/israel_and_the_palestinians/key_documents/1632064.stm, accessed 20 May 2007.

Mitnick, J. (2006) Israel's economy leaving Palestinians far behind, *Christian Science Monitor*, 22 May.

Moratinos, M. (2002). Account of the Taba peace talks. Online: www.arts.mcgill.ca/MEPP/PRRN/papers/moratinos.html, accessed 30 November 2006.

Morris, B. (2001a) *Righteous victims: A history of the Zionist–Arab conflict, 1881–2001*, New York: Knopf.

—— (2001b) Revisiting the Palestinian exodus of 1948. In Rogan, E.L. and Shlaim, A. (eds) *The war for Palestine, rewriting the history of 1948*, Cambridge: Cambridge University Press.

—— (2002) A new exodus for the Middle East? *The Guardian*, 3 October. Online: www.guardian.co.uk/israel/comment/0,10551,803417,00.html, accessed 16 June 2006.

—— (2004) *The birth of the Palestinian refugee problem revisited*, Cambridge: Cambridge University Press.

Morse, C. (2003) *The Nazi connection to Islamic terrorism: Adolf Hitler and Haj Amin al-Husseini*, New York: iUniverse Inc.

Moussawi, Ibrahim (2005) Interview with author, Beirut, 21 March.

Murphy-O'Connor, J. (2000) Symbolism and politics: Pope's Jubilee Pilgrimage. Online: www.pbs.org/wnet/religionandethics/week330/news.html, accessed 31 May 2006.

Muslih, M. (1988) *The origins of Palestinian nationalism*, New York: Columbia University Press.

Netanyahu, B. (2002) Address to the US Senate, 22 April 2002. Online: www.jta.org.

Newman, D. (2002) From national to post-national territorial identities in Israel–Palestine, *Geojournal*, vol. 53: 3, pp. 235–46.

Nimni, E. (2003) *The challenge of post-Zionism: Alternatives to Israeli fundamentalist politics*, London: Zed Books.

Nusseibeh, S. (2003) Petition for peace. Online: www.isop.ucla.edu/article.asp?parentid = 5056, accessed 21 November 2006.

O'Brien, C.C. (1986) *The siege: The saga of Israel and Zion*, London: Weidenfeld and Nicolson.

O'Loughlin, E. (2002) Jewish settlers in Hebron claim they have history on their side, *Sydney Morning Herald*, 9 December. Online: www.smh.com.au/articles/2002/12/08/1038950271659.html, accessed 9 July 2006.

Orr, A. (1994) *Israel politics, myths and identity crises*, London: Pluto Press.

Oz, Amos (1983) *In the land of Israel*. Translated by Maurie Goldberg-Bartura. London: Hogarth Press; reprint, New York: Vintage Books, 1984.

Palumbo, M. (1987) *The Palestinian catastrophe: The 1948 expulsion of a people from their home-land*, London: Faber and Faber.

Pappe, I. (1994) *The making of the Arab–Israeli conflict, 1947–1951*, London: I.B. Tauris.

—— (2004) *A history of modern Palestine: One land, two peoples*, Cambridge: Cambridge University Press.

Patai, R. (ed.) (1960) *Theodor Herzl, the complete diaries*, New York: Herzl Press and T. Yoseloff.

Pearlman, W. (2005) *Occupied voices: Stories of everyday life from the second Intifada*, New York: Thunders Mouth Press.

Peteet, J.M. (2005) *Landscape of hope and despair: Palestinian refugee camps*, Philadelphia, PA: University of Pennsylvania Press.

Peters, J. (1984) *From time immemorial: The origins of the Arab–Jewish conflict over Palestine*, New York: Harper and Row.

Porath, Y. (1974) *The emergence of the Palestinian–Arab national movement, 1918–1929*, London: Frank Cass.

—— (1977) *The Palestine Arab National Movement: From riots to rebellion*, London: Frank Cass.

Pratt, D. (2006) *Intifada: The long day of rage*, Glasgow: Sunday Herald Books.

Prince-Gibson, E. (2006) Reflective truth, *The Jerusalem Post*, 27 July, pp. 13 and 19.

Quandt, W. (2001) *Peace process, American diplomacy and the Arab–Israeli peace process since 1967*, Washington, DC: Brookings Institute.

Rabbani, M. (2001) Rocks and rockets: Oslo's inevitable conclusion, *Journal of Palestine Studies*, vol. 30: 3, pp. 68–81.

Rabinovich, I. (2004) *Waging peace: Israel and the Arabs 1948–2003*, Princeton, NJ: Princeton University Press.

Rabinowitz, Rabbi Tzadik Hacohen. Online: www.aish.com/literacy/jewishhistory, accessed 7 March 2007.

Rajoub, J. (2007) Address to IPCRI Jerusalem, 30 May.

Ramon, H. (2002) Israel's political map: After cancellation of direct election of Prime Minister. Online: www.jcpa.org/jl/vp471.htm, accessed 7 March 2007.

Rantissi, A.A. (2002) Interview with author, Gaza City, Gaza Strip, 9 September.

Reinhart, T. (2006) *The Roadmap to nowhere: Israel–Palestine since 2003*, London: Verso.

Reinharz, J. (1993) *Chaim Weizmann: The making of a statesman*, New York: Oxford University Press.

Reychler, L. (2002) *Democratic peace-building and conflict prevention: The devil is in the transition*, Lueven: ULP.

Roane, C. and Shanin, J. (eds) (2002) *The other Israel: Voices of refusal and dissent*, New York: The New Press.

Roberts, N. (2006) International aid, diplomacy and the Palestinian reality, *For the Record*, Jerusalem Fund, No. 244, 10 February.

Rogan, E. and Shlaim, A. (eds) (2001) *The war for Palestine: Rewriting the history of 1948*, Cambridge: Cambridge University Press.

Rose, Jacqueline (2005) *The question of Zion*, Princeton, NJ: Princeton University Press.

Rose, John (2004) *The myths of Zionism*, London: Pluto Books.

Ross, Dennis (2004) *The missing peace. The inside story of the fight for Middle East peace*, New York: Farrar, Straus and Giroux.

Rothstein, R.L., Ma'oz, M. and Shikaki, K. (eds) (2002) *The Israeli–Palestinian Peace Process. Oslo and the lessons of failure. Perspectives and prospects*, Studies in Peace Politics in the Middle East, Brighton: Sussex Academic Press.

Rouhana, N. (1989) The political transformation of the Palestinians in Israel: From acquiescence to challenge, *Journal of Palestine Studies*, vol. 18: 3, pp. 38–59.

Roy, S. (2006) *Drinking the sea at Gaza: Days and nights in a land under siege*, London: Pluto.

Rozenman, E. (2007) Israel's real demographic problem, *World Zionist Organization Hagshama*. Online: www.hagshama.org.il/en/resources/view.asp?id = 2181, accessed 28 June 2007.

Rubin, B. and Rubin, J.C. (2005) *Yasir Arafat: A political biography*, Oxford: Oxford University Press.

Sacco, J. (2003) *Palestine*, New York: Jonathan Cape.

Sacher H.M. (1996) *A history of Israel: From the rise of Zionism to our time*, 2nd edn, New York: Knopf.

Said, E. (1980) *The question of Palestine*, London: Routledge and Kegan Paul.

—— (1993) The morning after, *The London Review of Books*, vol. 15: 20, 21 October.

—— (1995) *Peace and its discontents. Gaza–Jericho 1993–1995*, London: Vintage.

—— (2000) *Out of place: a memoir*, London: Granta Books.

Said, E. and Hitchens, C. (2001) *Blaming the victims: Spurious scholarship and the Palestinian question*, London: Verso.

Salam, N. (1994) Between repatriation and resettlement: Palestinian refugees in Lebanon, *Journal of Palestine Studies*, vol. 24: 1, pp. 18–27.

Salibi, K. (1998) *The modern history of Jordan*, London: I.B. Tauris.

Satloff, R. (2006) Hobbling Hamas: moving beyond the US policy of the three no's, *Weekly Standard*, 3 April.

Sayigh, R. (1984) *Palestinians from peasants to revolutionaries*, London: Zed Books.

—— (1994) *Too many enemies: Palestinian experiences in Lebanon*, London: Zed Books.

—— (2001) No work, no space, no future: Palestinian in Lebanon, *Middle East International*, 10 August.

Sayigh, Y. (1997) *Armed struggle and the search for a state: The Palestinian national movement, 1949–1993*, Oxford: Clarendon Press.

Schiff, Z. and Ya'ari, E. (1990) *Israel's Lebanon war*, New York: Simon and Schuster.

Schulz, Helena L. (2003) *The Palestinian Diaspora*, London: Routledge.

Segev, T. (1986) *1949, The first Israelis*, New York: Free Press.

—— (2000) *The seventh million: the Israelis and the Holocaust*, New York: Owl Books.

—— (2001) *One Palestine, complete: Jews and Arabs under the British*, New York: Abacus Books.

Shafi, H. (1995) Moving beyond Oslo: An interview with Haydar Abd al-Shafi, *Journal of Palestine Studies*, vol. 25: 1, pp. 76–85.

Shafir, G. (1996) *Land, labour and the origins of the Israeli–Palestinian conflict, 1882–1914*, Berkeley, CA: University of California Press.

Shafir, G. and Peled, Y. (2002) *Being Israeli: The dynamics of multiple citizenship*, Cambridge: Cambridge University Press.

Shahak, I. and Mezvinsky, N. (2004) *Jewish fundamentalism in Israel*, London: Zed Books.

Shamir, S. and Maddy-Weitzman, B. (eds) (2005) *The Camp David Summit – What went wrong?* Brighton: Sussex Academic Press.

Sharon, A. (2001) Speech. Online: http://news.bbc.co.uk/1/hi/world/middle_east/1581280.stm, accessed 8 April 2008.

—— (2002) Address to the Israeli Knesset. Online: www.palestinefacts.org/sharon_speech_8apr02.php, accessed 18 February 2007.

Sharon, A. with Chanoff, D. (2001) *Warrior, an autobiography*, New York: Simon and Schuster.

Shavit, A. (2004) Survival of the fittest, an interview with Benny Morris, *Haaretz*, 9 January. Online: www.counterpunch.org/shavit01162004.html, accessed 10 January 2007.

—— (2007) Leaving the Zionist ghetto, *Haaretz Magazine*, 8 June, pp. 8–10.

Shavit, U. and Bana, A. (2001) Everything you wanted to know about the right of return but were afraid to ask, *Haaretz*, 6 July.

Shehadeh, R. (2003) *Strangers in the house: Coming of age in occupied Palestine*, Harmondsworth: Penguin.

Shimoni, G. (1995) *The Zionist ideology*, Hanover: Brandeis University Press.

Shindler, C. (2002) *The land beyond promise: Israel, Likud, and the Zionist dream*, London: I.B. Tauris.

Shlaim, A. (1998) *Collusion across the Jordan: King Abdullah, the Zionist movement and the partition of Palestine*, Oxford: Clarendon Press.

—— (2000) *The Iron Wall, Israel and the Arab world*, London: Penguin.

—— (2002) Israel's occupation turns 35, *Middle East Report*, No. 223, Summer.

Shragai, N. (2006) PM didn't know in advance of tenders for West Bank houses, *Haaretz*, 4 September, p. 4.

Simons, C. (2003) Three years in a military compound, reminiscences of a Hebron settler. Online: www.geocities.com/capitolhill/senate/7854/hebronsettler.html, accessed 20 June 2007.

Smith, C.D. (2004) *Palestine and the Arab–Israeli conflict*, Boston, MA: Beford/St. Martins.

Smith, P.A. (1984) *Palestine and the Palestinians 1876–1983*, Beckenham: Croom Helm Ltd.

Soetendorp, B. (2007) *The dynamics of Israeli–Palestinian relations: Theory, history and cases*, Houndsmills: Palgrave Macmillan.

Sternhell, Z. (1998) *The founding myths of Israel: Nationalism, socialism, and the making of the Jewish State*. Translated by David Maisel. Princeton, NJ: Princeton University Press.

Stone, I.F. (1978) *Underground to Palestine and reflections thirty years later*, London: Hutchison of London.

STRATFOR, (2002) The Palestinian strategy, STRATFOR, 24 June.

Swisher, Clayton (2004) *The truth about Camp David. The untold story about the collapse of the Middle East peace process*, New York: Nation Books.

Sykes, C. (1973) *Crossroads to Israel, 1917–1948*, Bloomington, IN: Indiana University Press.

Taha, A. (2007) Interview with author, Jerusalem, 31 January.

Tal, I. and Kett, M. (2000) *National security: The Israeli experience*, Westport, CT: Greenwood Press.

Tamari, S. (1990) Limited rebellion and civil society, the Uprising's dilemma, *Middle East Report*, Nos 164/165, May–August, pp. 4–8.

—— (2000) Treacherous memories: Electronic return to Jaffa by Salim, *Palestine Remembered*. Online: www.palestineremembered.com/Jaffa/Jaffa/Story152.html, accessed 1 February 2007.

Tessler, M. (1994) *A history of the Arab–Israeli conflict*, Bloomington, IN: Indiana University Press.

Tessler, M. and Grant, A. (1998) Israel's Arab citizens: The continuing struggle, *AAAPS*, vol. 555: 1, pp. 97–113.

Teveth, S. (1985) *Ben-Gurion and the Palestinian Arabs*, Oxford: Oxford University Press.

Thomson, W.M. (1883) *The land and the book, central Palestine and Phoencia*, London: T. Nelson and Sons.

Tirawi, J. (2006) Interview with author, Balata camp, Nablus, West Bank, 26 October.

Toubbeh, J.I. (1998) *Day of the long night, a Palestinian refugee remembers the Nakba*, London: McFarland.

Umm Rajah, (2005) Interview with author, Ramallah, 12 July.

United Nations (1974) General Assembly Twenty-ninth Session Official Records, 13 November.

UN General Assembly Resolution (UN GAR) 194 (III) (1948). Online: http://domino. un.org/UNISPAL.nsf/59c118f065c4465b852572a500625fea/c758572b78d1cd00852 56bcf0077e51a!OpenDocument, accessed 8 April 2008.

UN High Commissioner for Refugees (UNHCR) (2006) *State of the worlds refugees*. Online: www.unhcr.org/publ/PUBL/4444d3c92f.html, accessed 2 April 2008.

UN Information System on the Question of Palestine (UNISPAL) (2004) Chronological review. Online: http://domino.un.org/UNISPAL.NSF/c25aba03f1e079db85256cf4 0073bfe6/0b46bd8b2b264c4385256f6900755a76!OpenDocument, accessed 8 April 2008.

UN Special Committee on Palestine (UNSCOP) (1947) *Report on Palestine*. Online: www. mideastweb.org/unscop1947.htm, accessed 13 April 2007.

Usher, G. (1998) The enigmas of Shas, *Middle East Report*, No. 207 (Summer), pp. 34–36.

—— (1999) *Dispatches from Palestine: The rise and fall of the Oslo peace process*, London: Pluto.

—— (2000) Uprising wipes off Green Line, *al-Ahram Weekly*, 12–18 October.

Verdery, R.N. (1971) Arab 'disturbances' and the Commissions of Inquiry. In Abu Lughod (ed.) *The transformation of Palestine*, Evanston, IL: Northwestern University Press.

Vital, D. (1975) *Zionism: The origins of Zionism*, Oxford: Clarendon Press.

—— (1982) *Zionism: The formative years*. Oxford: Clarendon Press.

Wahrman, D. (2007) Is Israel falling apart?, *History News network*. Online: http://hnn.us/ articles/35958.html, accessed 4 May 2007.

Wasserstein, B. (2001) *Divided Jerusalem, the struggle for the holy city*, London: Profile Books.

—— (2003) *Israel and Palestine, why they fight and can they stop?*, London: Profile Books.

Wauchope, A. (1935) CO75156/4/35 Israel State Archives, not published.

Weiss, E. (2006) Extreme right spark Intifada to prevent expulsions. Online: www.ynet-news.com/articles/0,7340,L-3263038,00.html, accessed 5 September 2006.

Weizman, E. (2003) Ariel Sharon and the geometry of occupation. Online: www.opende-mocracy.net/themes/article.jsp?id = 2&articleId = 1474, accessed 13 January 2007.

Wilson, S. (2006) Israeli Arabs reflect on Hamas win, *Washington Post*, 5 March, p. 17.

Yehoshua, A.B. (2006) People without a land, *Haaretz*, 12 May.

Yiftachel, O. (1999) Democracy or ethnocracy: Territory and settler politics in Israel/ Palestine. Online: www.merip.org/yift.htm, accessed 5 September 2006.

Zahar, M. (1991) Hamas founder and leader, interview with author, Gaza City.

Zananiri, E. (2006) Unpublished remarks, 'People to people: what went wrong and how to fix it', Notre Dame of Jerusalem Centre, 6 June.

Zartman, I.W. (2001) The timing of peace initiatives: Hurting stalemates and ripe moments, *The Global Review of Ethnopolitics*, vol. 1: 1, pp. 8–18.

Zubaida, S. (1993) *Islam, the people and the state*, London: I.B. Tauris.

Index

Abbas, President Mahmoud (Abu Mazen)
108, 159, 169, 180, 191, 200–1, 203
Abdullah I, King of Jordan 62–3
Abdullah II, King of Jordan 107
Abed Rabbo, Yasser 109, 185
Absentee Property Law (Israel) 91
Achille Lauro hijack 168
Adwan, Dr Atef 110–11
al-Aqsa Intifada (2000) 7, 84, 116, 154–5,
157–9, 195
al-Aqsa Martyrs Brigade (AMB) 103–4
al-Aqsa mosque 37, 91, 147, 197
al-Faisal, Prince Saud 177
al-Husseini, Hajj Amin 41–2, 44, 46, 56,
65
aliyah 12, 16, 90
al-Qaeda 168-9, 184
al-Qassam, Sheikh Izza-din 41–3
al-Rida, Rashid 21, 42
American Israel Public Affairs Committee
(AIPAC) 171–2
Amman 106, 125, 148
Annapolis talks (2007) 117, 202–3
anti-Semitism 12–16, 29, 36, 184
anti-Zionism 20, 40
Arab; alliances 120, 136; armies 123,
129; attitudes to USA 172; boycott
174; diplomacy 62–3; infighting 131;
nationalism 120, 131; oil embargo 139,
172; *see also* Palestinian Arab
Arab Higher Committee 44, 46, 55
Arab–Israeli War (1948) 5, 69–71, 119,
176
Arab–Israeli War (1973) 139, 172, 179
Arab League 3, 7, 62, 148, 161, 164–5,
173–6, 184, 200, 203
Arab Summit (1964) 132, 174
Arafat, Yasser; diplomacy 135, 169; and
Intifadas 144, 158; Israeli action against

156–8, 199; as leader 104, 106, 120,
131–4, 148, 159; and peace process 1,
153, 190–2, 196

Balfour Declaration (1917) 10, 23–6, 33–4,
52, 55, 66–7
Barak, Prime Minister Ehud 80, 88,
195–6, 200; government 84, 154, 197
Basic Laws (Israel) 81, 121
Begin, Prime Minister Menachim 85–6
Ben Gurion, David 12, 48, 54, 56, 64–5,
70, 78, 83–5
Bethlehem, occupation of 154, 192
Bin Laden, Usama 169, 197, 200
Birthright Israel movement 163, 177
Bishara, Azmi 93
Britain; ambitions in Middle East 4, 21–5,
33; colonialism of 20–1, 24, 26, 28,
36, 67; declining influence of 58–9;
diplomacy 4, 32; and France 4, 10;
legacy 51–2, 66–8; and Palestinians 24,
33–8, 40, 43–6, 49, 50; promises of 22,
25, 3; and Second World War 51–2,
56–7; withdrawal from Palestine 4–5,
59, 61, 66; and Zionists 15, 20, 22–3,
29, 34, 36–40, 49, 57, 603
British Mandate (1923–47) 4–5, 25–6,
28–9, 32–9, 42, 51–2, 55, 61, 66–8, 124,
164; administration of 37–8, 40–1, 44,
47–8, 50–1, 67; policing of 43, 46, 49;
text of 26, 35–6
Bush, President (Junior) 24, 89, 117, 172,
180; administration 169–70, 201
Bush, President (Senior) 171, 188–9

Cairo Agreement (1994) 184
Camp David talks (2000) 7, 114, 126, 143,
154, 170, 184, 188, 195–8
Carter administration 170

Christians; and West Beirut massacres 104; in Israel 70, 91, 151; under Ottoman rule 10, 11, 18; in USA 171
Clinton; administration 195–6; Parameters (2000) 184, 198, 200, 203
Cold War 58, 120, 163–6, 193
Covenant with God, Jewish 2, 77, 88, 125, 127, 183

Damascus 33–5
Deir Yassin massacre 61, 69–70
demographics 55, 58, 61–2, 65, 82, 90–1, 100, 107; warfare 5, 82
Diaspora; Jewish 12–14, 39, 57, 87, 161–3; Palestinian 73, 98, 108, 118, 143, 147, 165, 192
Dome of the Rock 37, 105, 197

East Jerusalem 109, 112–13, 117, 121–2, 124–6, 128, 131, 139, 141, 143, 149, 153–4, 170, 172, 183, 185, 196, 203
Egypt 3, 5, 56, 120, 172; and Palestinians 45, 60, 147, 164; and PLO 5, 174; and refugees 99, 103; relations with Israel 6, 78, 85–6, 106, 122, 129–30, 139, 170, 172–3; and Six-Day War (1967) 119–20
Eretz Israel 19, 62, 85–6, 89, 122, 126–7, 185
ethnic cleansing 5, 54, 64, 70–2, 139

'facts on the ground' 6, 119, 121, 125–31, 185, 190
Faisal, King of Syria 33–5
Fatah 103, 106, 132–5, 152, 174, 180, 183, 193
fedayeen (PLO) 106
final status negotiations 115, 117, 122–3, 142, 153–4, 170, 184–5, 190, 192, 194–6, 198, 200
First World War 4, 10, 21–6, 28–9, 32–3
Fourth Geneva Convention 95, 121–2, 128, 177
France 120, 172; actions 34, 35; and Algeria 25, 132; ambitions 28, 32; and Britain 4, 10, 22; declining influence of 58–9, 165; and King Faisal 35; resistance to Zionist project 34; and Syria 42
French Protectorates 4, 32–3, 35

Gay Parade (Jerusalem, 2006) 89–90
Gaza 50, 62, 192; refugees 103, 177, 204
Gaza Strip 6, 60, 85–6, 88–90, 92, 95, 101–3, 109, 112–13, 117, 121–31,

134–9, 142–4, 146, 149–56, 170, 172, 180, 183–6, 188, 194, 198–200
Geneva Accord (2004) 184, 199
Ginsberg, Asher Hersh 14–15
Golan Heights 78, 120–2, 126, 129, 170, 177
Green Line (1948) 156, 183
Gush Emmunim movement 127, 129–30
Gush Etzion movement 126, 129

Haganah 39, 43–4, 49, 68
Haifa 22, 42–5, 61, 69
Hamas 24; 43, 92, 104, 110, 117, 134, 143–4, 146–7, 152–4, 156, 158–9, 169, 191, 193–4, 202–3; government (2006) 8, 24–5, 101, 110, 112, 165, 170, 175, 179–80, 183, 185, 201–3
Haram al-Sharif 37–8, 147, 154, 196–7
Haredi/Haredim 82, 89–90; parties 87
Hashomer Hazair 39
Hebron; post-1967 settlement of 126–9; riots (1929) 7, 37–8, 142
Hebron Redeployment Protocol 198
Herzl, Theodor 13–14, 15–17, 27, 52
Histadrut (Jewish Labour Federation) 13, 19–20, 47
Hizb Tahrir 193
Hizbullah 125, 201
Hope Simpson Commission 38, 40
human rights 90, 117, 177, 185; Israeli abuse of 95, 154, 158, 167
Hussein, King of Jordan 105–6, 120, 132, 134, 147, 189
Hussein, Saddam 27, 108, 113, 148, 152, 188–9
Hussein, Sharif of Mecca 22
Hussein–McMahon Correspondence (1915) 10, 22

Interim Agreement (Oslo II) 184, 199
International Court of Justice 62, 122
Intifada, al-Aqsa (second armed, 2000) 7–8, 84, 91, 110, 114, 116, 153–9, 177, 195, 197–200
Intifada, first (1987–93) 6, 24, 123, 131, 137, 141–53, 169, 189
Iraq 4, 22, 32; under British Mandate 33, 44, 50–1; occupation of Kuwait 123, 152, 171, 188; and Palestinian refugees 107, 112; under Saddam Hussein 22, 148; support for Palestinians 147; US occupation of 123, 202
Irgun group 44–5, 60–1, 63

Islam; establishment 41–2; faith of 7, 13, 37, 42, 175–6; holy sites 37, 120–1, 196–7; oppositional 41; and Palestine 18

Islamic; groups 92, 106, 153, 184, 193; movements 145–7, 162, 173, 175

Islamic Jihad 104, 138, 144, 152, 154, 156, 193

Islamic reform movement 41

Israel 76–97, 119–21; and 1948 War 59, 70–2, 83; and al-Aqsa Intifada 156–7, 160; Arab citizens of 100, 197; and Britain 29, 52; convergence plan 127, 185, 201; deportation of Palestinians 45, 49; and Egypt 122, 129–30, 173; and European Union 178–9; and first Intifada 148–50, 152; and Gaza Strip disengagement 85, 88–9, 122, 127, 185, 200–1; and Hamas government 203; and international negotiations 113–17, 170, 203; and Jordan 122, 125, 173; and Law of Return 12, 81–2, 100, 108, 163; and Lebanon 80, 104, 134, 139; nuclear capability 173; and occupied territories 78, 95, 103, 120–39, 153, 185; settlements 125–31; and status of Arab refugees 71, 81–2, 99–102, 117; and Syria 93, 107; and terrorism 168–9; and the United Nations 165; and the USA 58, 158, 166–8, 170–2

Israel Baytanu (Israel our Home) 82, 86

Israeli Arabs 77, 85, 90–4; political parties 92–3

Israeli Defence Force (IDF) 49, 90, 125, 127, 145, 185; actions 106, 144; control 91, 149; military posts 125–6; morale 145; and settlers 130; special units 103

Jabotinsky, Ze'ev 12, 83, 85

Jaffa 11, 43–4, 62, 66, 69, 108

Jenin 192; 1935 incident 43; 'battle of' (2002) 157–8, 199–200

Jericho Agreement (1994) 198

Jerusalem 9, 11, 13, 18, 23, 37–8, 45, 60–1, 64, 66, 69, 87, 89, 120–1; Old City 37, 124–5, 142, 144, 147, 162–3, 193, 196, 199

Jewish Agency 47, 57, 62, 64, 78

Jewish National Fund (JNF) 16, 63

Jewish National Home/state 13–14, 26–7, 33–5, 48, 67–8

Jewish/Zionist nationalism 3, 10, 14–16, 27–8, 77, 130

Jewish/Zionist secularism 14–15, 27–8, 77, 79, 87, 89–90

Jews; and Holocaust 55, 58, 73; immigration to Palestine 12, 37, 38, 44, 47, 55–6, 81; under Ottoman rule 10; treatment of 12–13, 28; and Zionism 15, 27

jihad 42–3, 50, 139, 152, 162, 176, 191, 201

John Paul II, Pope 163

Jordan 3, 5, 51; and Israel 106; and Palestinians 60, 96, 107; and PLO 39, 105–6; refugees 99, 105, 107; *see also* Hussein, Transjordan

Jordan Valley 62, 125, 130

Judaism 13; and politics 90; and Zionism 15, 77–8, 87–8

Judea 86, 90, 96, 129–30

Kadima Party 82–3, 85–6, 126

Karameh 106

Katsav, President 80

kibbutz/-im 12–13, 17, 52, 83, 84, 136

King David Hotel, attack on 60, 124

Knesset 78–82, 86, 88–9, 92–3

Kook, Rabbi Abraham 14

Kuwait; occupation by Iraq 123, 148, 152, 172, 188; refugees 109, 113, 148

Labour Party (Avoda) 79–80, 84, 93–4, 191

land; Arab dispossession of 38, 40, 45, 48, 67, 100; British sale of 38, 40, 44–5, 47, 50, 55–6; Israeli expropriation of 91, 100, 116, 124, 128–30, 159; Jewish purchase of 16, 23; Jewish settlement of 12, 17, 36, 125; Ottoman sale/confiscation of 13, 16, 20; partition 62

'land for peace' deal 6, 84, 86, 88–9, 92, 130–1, 149, 185, 189–90, 192–4, 199, 201

Law of Return 12, 81–2, 100, 108, 163

League of Nations 4, 25–6, 32, 35, 164

Lebanon 3, 62, 94; Israeli action against 6, 80, 85, 93, 104, 119, 123, 126, 134, 139, 170–2; PLO activity in 39, 86, 104, 134, 145; and refugees 5, 85, 99, 101, 104–5, 107, 112–13, 115, 147, 177, 191; UN involvement 177; US involvement 171

Levinger, Rabbi Moshe 126–7, 129

Liberman, Avigdo 82–3, 112

Libya 51, 107, 147

Likud Party 80, 83, 85–6, 88–9, 126, 130, 149, 197; in government 86, 130, 188

MacDonald, Ramsey 40

Madrid peace talks (1991) 6, 113, 142,
    148, 152, 184, 187–91
Mitchell Commission (2001) 154–5, 185
moshav 12, 52, 136
Moyne, Lord, assassination of 60
Mufti of Jerusalem 37, 41–2, 50, 67;
    support for Nazis 56, 65
mukhabarat 104, 148
Muslim; activism 41–2; holy places 37,
    154, 165, 197; leadership in Palestine
    43; offices under Mandate 67; as
    unifying faith 10
Muslim Brotherhood 102, 173–5, 184
myths 155; of Israelis 69; of Palestinians
    19, 43; of Zionists 15, 17, 30, 52

Nablus 103, 152, 192
nakbah 59, 73, 99, 113
Nasser, President 120, 132, 174
National Religious Party (*Mafdal*, NRP)
    79, 87–8
nationalism 4, 9, 27, 29; Arab 19, 21, 28,
    120; Jewish/Zionist 10, 13–15, 20, 28,
    38, 77; Palestinian 10, 20–1, 28, 33, 38,
    77, 146
Nazism; and Jewry 4, 33, 44, 54–5, 57;
    and Mufti of Jerusalem 56, 65
Netanyahu, Prime Minister Benjamin 80,
    86, 154, 169, 194; government of 143,
    195

Olmert, Prime Minister Ehud 183, 185,
    201, 203; government of 126, 128
one-state solution 7, 96, 182, 184
Operation Defensive Shield (ODS) 156–8
Organization of Islamic Conference (OIC)
    7, 148, 161, 165, 176
Organization of Petroleum Exporting
    Countries (OPEC) 173; boycott 172
Oslo Accords (Declaration of Principles,
    1993) 1, 6–7, 84, 114, 122, 142–3, 153,
    170, 188, 199, 201; described 190–2;
    and Israel 154, 194–5; opposition to
    193–5; Palestinian view of 2, 107, 155,
    193–4; and PLO 131, 149
Ottoman Palestine 3, 9–12, 19–21, 28

Palestine; Arab leadership of 39–46, 48,
    63; under British rule 4–5, 25–6, 32,
    33–40, 46–8, 50–2, 55–7, 59, 60–1,
    66–8; and colonialism 18, 20, 26, 28–9;
    and First World War 10, 21–3; and
    independence 35, 146; under Israeli
    occupation 78, 95, 103, 120–39, 153,

185; and Jewish history 13; Jewish
    immigration to 12, 16, 34, 36–9, 55,
    57; as 'non-nation' 19, 24, 28; under
    Ottoman rule 3, 9–13, 20, 28; partition
    (1947–48) 5, 59, 62–3, 166; partition
    proposal (1939) 47–8, 60; religious mix
    9–11, 36; and Second World War 55–7;
    as *terra sancta* 18; and United Nations 5,
    59, 61, 166; and Zionism 13–14, 16–21,
    24–5, 27, 34, 37, 39, 55, 61, 64–5
Palestine Liberation Army 132–4, 144
Palestine Liberation Organization (PLO) 5,
    39, 58, 131–9, 152, 174, 185; corruption
    in 133; in exile 134–5, 144, 146, 189,
    191; factionalism 6, 119, 133, 144–8,
    194; and Intifadas 143–5, 156, 158; and
    Oslo Accords 1, 154, 190–3; relations
    with Israel 6, 84, 106, 142, 153–4, 171,
    188–9, 190–2, 198; relations with other
    Arab states 104–6, 134, 144, 147–8,
    174–5, 189; and 'right of return'
    109–10; status of 84; and USA 168
Palestine National Council (PNC) 133,
    146, 174
Palestinian Arab; appropriation of lands
    13; clashes with Jews 37–8, 43, 44–5, 56,
    61, 65–6; declaration of independence
    35; demand for rights 34; depopulation
    68; dispossession 68; exclusion by
    Zionists 13, 17–19; expulsion 70–2;
    identity 20–1, 27; independence 21–2;
    labour 13, 19; leadership 36, 39, 65;
    nationalism 4, 19, 21, 28; opinion
    43–4, 48, 65; political parties 41, 133;
    presence in proposed Jewish state 63–5,
    71; refugees 5, 59, 64, 66, 69, 99–117;
    relations with Jews/Zionists 3, 12, 20,
    38, 40, 49, 55, 64–5; resistance 19, 36,
    45, 69; 'right of return' 81–2, 100–1,
    107–10, 112, 114–15, 117, 131, 170,
    175, 177, 196; state, proposal for 62;
    transfer 40, 48, 64–5, 68–9, 85, 112,
    183; Zionist attitude to 16–17; Zionist
    violence against 59
Palestinian Arabs; and Balfour Declaration
    24; and British diplomacy 4, 22–5,
    32–6, 48, 61; and British Mandate 36,
    67–8; and British occupation 27, 49–51;
    and British White Paper (1939) 55–6;
    and colonialism 28; denial of 18–19,
    24; discrimination against 28–9, 41, 47;
    economy 41; and Egyptian/Jordanian
    control 60; as indigenous population 28;
    in Israel 90–4; and Israeli 'occupation'

120–39; and partition (1948) 65; rights of 21; and Turks 10, 22
Palestinian Authority (PA) 6, 103, 109, 112, 120, 142, 153, 155–60, 170, 180, 192, 194, 198–9, 201–3
Palestinian Communist Party 41, 46, 133
Palestinian Islamic Jihad (PIJ) 92
Palestinian Revolt (1936) 43–6, 48, 55
Paris Peace Conference (1919) 33–4
Passfield White Paper (1930) 40
Peace Now group 126, 149
Peel Commission (1935) 33, 47–8
Plan D (*Tochnit Dalet*) 68–9
pogroms 12–13, 16, 28, 67, 99
Popular Front for the Liberation of Palestine (PFLP) 133, 135, 138, 152

Quartet for the Middle East Peace Process 165, 177, 179, 186, 195, 199, 201–2

Rabin, Yitzhak; assassination of 95, 123, 154, 194; as Defence Minister 149; government 190, 191, 194; and Oslo Accords 1, 190–1; as Prime Minister 84, 142, 153; and settlers 123
Ramadan War (1973) 139, 172, 179
Ramallah 192; Arafat's HQ in 1, 156–7, 199–200; emergency government in 180, 203
refugee camps 1, 107–8; conditions 103, 105; infiltration 105; massacres 104, 134; recruitment in 102
Refugee Working Group 113–14
'right of return'; Jewish 81, 163; Palestinian 81–2, 98–100, 102, 107–10, 112, 114–15, 117, 131, 170, 175, 177, 196
resettlement of Palestinians 105, 107, 112, 199
Revisionist parties 86
Road Map initiative (2002) 8, 110, 159, 126, 179, 185, 199–201

Sabra camp 105; massacre 104, 134
Sadat, President Anwar 170, 188
Samaria 86, 90, 96, 129–130
Samuel, Sir Herbert 23, 35, 36
San Remo Peace Conference 33–5
Second General Syria Congress 35
Second World War 4, 5, 33, 51–2, 55–8, 60, 123, 164–6
secularism; of Israelis 90; of nation state/ Israel 27–8, 77, 79, 87–9, 94; versus faith 15–16; of 'Young Turks' 20; and Zionists 14–16, 27, 79, 87

settlement of occupied territories 85–6, 103, 122–31, 138, 154, 157–8, 170, 185, 189, 194, 196–7; illegality of 95, 122, 128, 177; Palestinian resistance to 127–8, 149; withdrawal from 139, 185, 199–201
settlement of Palestine 10, 18; British support for 23, 29, 36, 51, 67; by Israelis 85–7, 125; Palestinian resistance to 42, 44, 46; by Zionists/Jews 12–17, 19–20, 26, 36–9, 57–8
Shamir, Prime Minister Yitzhak 60, 85–6, 188
Sharm el-Sheikh Memorandum (SSM, 1999) 184, 196, 198
Sharon, Prime Minister Ariel 24, 80, 85–6, 89, 91, 96, 110, 127, 129–30, 134, 154, 157–9, 169, 185, 189, 197, 200–1; government of 88, 127
Shas Party 88–9
Shatilla camp massacre 104, 134
Sinai 78, 85–6, 121, 129–30, 139, 170, 172
Sinai II Accord 170
Six-Day War (1967) 5, 81, 83, 101–2, 119–20, 172; aftermath 78, 85, 88, 95, 103, 106, 121–2, 125–6, 128, 131–2
Soviet Union 120, 164–5; break-up of 165, 188; former 7, 81–2, 100, 161, 163–4, 166
Stern Gang 60, 63
Suez Crisis (1956) 120, 172
Sunni Muslim/Islam 11, 175
Supreme Muslim Council 37, 42, 50, 67
Sykes–Picot Agreement (1916) 10, 22
Syria 3, 22, 120; and French revolt 42; and Israel 106–7, 120, 172, 195; in peace talks 113, 170, 189; and refugees 5, 99, 107, 147, 177, 191; Soviet support for 58; support for Jordan 106; support for Palestinians 164

Taba talks (2001) 7, 114, 143, 184, 198, 200, 203
Taif Agreement (1989) 112
Tanzim 103, 158
Tel Aviv 125, 143, 152, 194
terrorism 3, 72, 135, 179; Israelis against Palestinians 104; Israeli perceptions of 157, 160, 168–9, 186; Jews against Arabs 66; Jews against British 57, 60–1; of Palestinians 131, 134, 168; Palestinians as victims 6, 142, 146; suicide 169; US perceptions of 168, 172

transfer of Arab population 16–17, 40, 48,
    64–5, 68–9, 85, 112, 183
Transjordan 4, 32, 34, 50–1
Turkish administration 10–1, 35;
    opposition to 22–3, 35
two-state solution 7–8, 62, 96, 117, 159,
    179–80, 182, 184, 187, 199–201

United Arab List 92–3
United National Leadership of the
    Uprising (UNLU) 24, 145–6, 151
United Nations (UN); important
    resolutions 177; and Israeli settlements
    122; and Palestinian refugees 5, 177;
    Partition Plan (1947) 61–2, 64, 69, 71,
    85, 100, 166; and PLO 135–6; role in
    conflict 58–9 165, 176–9
United Nations Relief and Works Agency
    (UNRWA) 101–3, 116, 131, 177
United Nations Special Committee on
    Palestine (UNSCOP, 1947) 61–3
United States; and British 24–5; and
    European Union 179; intervention by
    154, 167, 170–2, 180, 188, 195–7,
    203–4; and Iraq 123, 202; and Israel
    52, 58, 89, 126, 166–7, 171–2, 189,
    201; Jewish immigration to 15–16; and
    Palestine/PLO/PA 136, 158, 168–70,
    201; rivalry with Soviet Union 58, 120,
    164–5; at UN 165; and UN Partition
    Plan 62, 65; and Zionists 57, 63, 165

Western Wall 37–8, 197; riots (1929) 37
Weizmann, Chaim 15, 16, 19, 34, 40, 67
West Bank 1, 6, 60, 86, 88, 90, 92, 95,
    103, 106, 108–9, 112–13, 117, 120–6,
128–31, 135–6, 139, 142–4, 146–51,
    153, 155–8, 167, 170, 172, 177, 180,
    183, 185–6, 188–9, 194, 196, 198–9,
    200, 203
White Paper (Britain, 1939) 50, 55–6, 60
Wingate, Orde 49
World Zionist Organization 176; 1897
    Congress 13–14; 1942 Congress 57
Wye River Agreement (1998) 143, 184,
    195, 198

Yesh Gvul group 149
Yishuv 16–17, 58, 64, 68, 83
Yom Kippur War (1973) 139, 172, 179
Young Mens' Muslim Association(YMMA)
    41–2
'Young Turks' revolution (1908) 20

Zangwill, Israel 16
Zionism/Zionist movement 3, 5, 13–17,
    27–8, 39–40, 63, 65, 77–9, 125, 163,
    177, 194; and aliyah 12; and British
    3, 24–6, 34, 37, 51, 60, 67; Christian
    Zionists 162, 164, 171; and colonization
    of Palestine 16–19, 29; factions within
    63, 82–90; and Holocaust 57–8, 62; and
    indigenous population 16–17, 64; Jewish
    opposition to 15–16; Labour Zionism
    12–13, 82–5; Palestinian response to 46,
    48, 63, 99; redemption Zionism 12, 14,
    86; Religious Zionism 12, 27, 79, 87–8;
    Revisionist Zionism 12, 16, 34, 84,
    85–7; secularism and 14–16, 27, 79, 87;
    splits in 34, 85